Summoning Up Remembrance

When to the sessions of sweet silent thought
I summon up remembrance of things past
I sigh the lack of many a thing I sought
and with old woes now wail my dear times waste.

SHAKESPEARE

Summoning Up Remembrance

HENRY STOB

WILLIAM B. EERDMANS PUBLISHING COMPANY
GRAND RAPIDS, MICHIGAN

© 1995 Wm. B. Eerdmans Publishing Co.
255 Jefferson Ave. S.E., Grand Rapids, Michigan 49503

Printed in the United States of America

00 99 98 97 96 95   7 6 5 4 3 2 1

Library of Congress Cataloging-in-Publication Data

Stob, Henry, 1908-
Summoning up remembrance / Henry Stob.
p.   cm.
ISBN 0-8028-0832-8
1. Stob, Henry, 1908-   . 2. Theologians—United States—
Biography. 3. Christian Reformed Church—Clergy—Biography.
4. Reformed Church—United States—Clergy—Biography. I. Title.
BX6843.S76A3 1995
230'.57'092—dc20
[B]   94-40625
CIP

CONTENTS

In loving memory of
my parents
John Stob
1862-1932
and
Anna Baker Stob
1868-1957
and for Hilda, the children, and all
who have helped me on the way

1

INFANCY

(1908-1913)

I was born in Chicago, Illinois, on June 24, 1908, the tenth and last child of John and Anna (Baker) Stob. My mother was well into her forty-first year when I was born and my father was well into his forty-sixth. Before my birth, the eighth child of the family — a boy — had died at the age of two, and so I came to know two older sisters and six older brothers.

My parents were immigrants from The Netherlands. My father arrived in the United States in the company of two older brothers in 1880, when he was seventeen years old. The young men were cleared for entry at Castle Garden in The Battery, New York; Ellis Island was not yet in operation at that time. Born of peasant stock on November 10, 1862, in the Province of Groningen, Father was at an early age apprenticed to a neighboring farmer as a hired hand. He took up residence in a section of the barn where he slept on hay and was fed the simplest fare. Practically unschooled, he entered the work force after completing no more than the fourth grade. By then, however, he had acquired the ability to read and write, capacities that he employed with diligence and success throughout his life. The son of God-fearing parents, and brought up in the Reformed Secessionist Church, he was from his youth a deeply religious person who, as he advanced in years, became versed in Scripture, and acquired a considerable store of theological knowledge. Before leaving for America, he

1

Mother and Father, 1888

had made public profession of his Christian faith and was ever afterward a loyal son of his adopted American church, which he served with distinction both as deacon and elder.

My mother was born in the town of Uithuizen, in the province of Groningen, on January 3, 1868. Her parents, whom I never met because they did not join in their children's immigration, were mem-

2

The Stob Family, ca. 1910
Clockwise, from lower left: Henry, Martin, Jen, Bill, Tom,
Father, Mother, John, Neal, George, Gertrude

bers of the Reformed (state) Church of The Netherlands; but they appear to have lived on its fringes and to have provided their children with little or no religious training. It is a constant source of regret to me that I did not inquire more closely than I did into my mother's lineage and ancestry, for she was a most sensitive, attractive, and intelligent woman, and there must have been something in her background that accounted for it. Arriving in the United States at the age of sixteen with a brother and two sisters, she settled in Chicago and underwent a conversion experience while attending worship services at the Dutch Reformed Church (now the Reformed Church in America) located on Hastings Street near Ashland. Mother's piety and devotion to the Lord were ever afterward displayed in her life.

My father had joined the neighboring First Christian Reformed Church of Chicago, and though I have no record of their courtship, it is a matter of record that John Stob and Anna Baker were married on March 6, 1888. The wedding was performed by Rev. William Greve in the parsonage of the First Church, then located on 14th Street between Loomis and Throop. Apparently without benefit of honeymoon, the newly married couple established themselves on a farm several miles northwest of the church, in the vicinity of what is now Madison and Ridgeland Avenues.

Three children — all boys — were born to my parents while they resided there: William on January 14, 1889; John on June 25, 1890; and Thomas on May 13, 1892. The names chosen for these boys, as well as those chosen for the rest of us, perpetuated the names of our Stob ancestors and near kin: William (Bill) was named after his grandfather, William Stob (b. 1828), who with his wife (née Gertrude Huizenga, b. 1834) had come to the United States in May 1881. Six of the younger children accompanied them. Their firstborn, my father's sister Jennie, remained behind with her husband and did not arrive until 1882. Money for the passage of all these people was apparently provided by the three sons who had come to these shores earlier. I never met my paternal grandparents: my grandfather died in 1900, and my grandmother died in faraway Minnesota when I was barely two years old.

John, my second oldest brother, was named after my father, who himself bore the name of our earliest known ancestor, Jan Tunis (b. 1759). It was this Jan who in 1811, two years before his death, adopted the surname *Stob* after Louis Napoleon, King of The Netherlands (1806-1810), had ordered all members of the "Burger Stand" to adopt family names. Thomas (Tom) was named after my father's oldest brother (b. 1856), who himself bore the name of his grandfather, Tunis Jan (b. 1784). I assume that the male dominance reflected in this name-giving was not resented by my mother who, not caught up in the then nascent women's liberation movement, was not disposed to challenge the supposedly biblical principle of Adamic headship.

In the summer of 1893 my parents moved with their three young children to a farm near Prinsburg, Minnesota, whither the rest of the Stob family had migrated shortly before. My brother Neal (Cornelius) was born in Prinsburg on November 16, 1894; he was named after another of my father's brothers. My sister Gertrude, named after her paternal grandmother, was born on October 12, 1896. And my only other sister, named Jennie after her paternal aunt, was born on April 13, 1898. My father served a term as deacon in the church at Prinsburg, and he and a Mr. Bolt planted the trees that later shaded the churchyard there.

4

Infancy (1908-1913)

In 1899 my parents, with six children ranging in ages from one to ten, returned to Chicago, where my father established a hay and feed store on Blue Island Avenue, near 15th Street. The family lived in a spacious flat above the store, and here four more children were born. George, named after my father's brother Geert, arrived on January 25, 1900. Martin, born in 1902, was named after another of my father's brothers; but he lived only to the age of two, and his early death caused great sorrow to my parents. My mother often spoke of him in the tenderest of tones. Another son, born on July 3, 1905, was also named Martin. Because he was closest to me in age, it was with him and his peers, rather than with my older brothers, that I associated in playing the games we indulged in out-of-doors. Since my father's youngest brother was named Henry, it was natural, if not inevitable, that when his youngest son arrived he should confer on him that very name. Thus I was given the name Henry at my baptism on August 2, 1908. The sacrament was administered by Rev. Evert Breen, then pastor of the church we attended, the First Christian Reformed Church of Chicago.

*   *   *   *   *

Because the family moved from my birthplace on Blue Island Avenue before I had reached the age of three, I have no personal recollection concerning the residence, the neighborhood, or the events that took place there and then. History records, however, that Theodore Roosevelt was serving as the twenty-sixth President of the United States when I was born, that in the month of November following my birth William Howard Taft defeated William Jennings Bryan for the presidency, and that in the course of the same year Henry Ford brought out his Model-T. But of these events I was then quite unaware.

I know about family life in my infancy only from hearsay. I have been told that our flat contained four bedrooms, from which I conclude that to accommodate two parents and nine children there must have been some doubling up. Things doubtless eased a bit when my oldest brother, Bill, left the household to get married on my very first birthday; less than a year later, my brother John did the same. Because of these departures, I came to know these brothers only from some distance and tended as a youth to associate more closely with their children than with them.

It has been reported that my father's physical prowess, evidenced

5

in his easy handling of great bales of hay and heavy bags of oats, was celebrated throughout the neighborhood, and this report rings true: standing six feet tall, he had large, well-muscled arms and sturdy broad shoulders to match. My brother John is said to have been Father's equal in strength, a circumstance that sometimes tempted him to engage in unnecessary, though usually successful, fistfights with the tough Irish lads who inhabited the area.

In order to ease my mother's burdens and to assist in my upbringing, my sister Gert quit her studies after completing the sixth grade of the small Christian school she had attended up to then. At that time the school held all its classes in rooms located in the basement of the 14th Street Church. Moreover, it offered no instruction beyond the sixth grade; for further study one had to enter the public school. It was perhaps this fact, among others, that my parents considered when they decided to terminate Gert's formal education. In any case, at the age of twelve she became Mother's helper, being required, she once told me, to peel a peck of potatoes each day for family consumption, and to do other chores besides. What she especially liked to speak to me about was her role as babysitter. I became, it seems, her specific charge during my early infancy. That she rocked me to sleep, put ribbons in my hair, treated me to sweets, and gave me a daily ride in the baby buggy represents but a small part of the large debt I owe to a caring sister. Amidst all this, of course, I remained my mother's child, and she is reported to have lavished great affection on her baby, whom she called her "little Benjamin."

*   *   *   *   *

I was not destined to live long at the Blue Island Avenue address. It appears that around the turn of the century, the lure of Texas was strong among the Dutch in America. In 1894 a Dutch settlement was laid out in Alvin, Texas. In 1895 one was established in a place named Amsterdam; and in the same year the Port Arthur Land Company set aside 66,000 acres in Jefferson County for the establishment of yet another colony of Dutch farmers. By 1900, six hundred persons had settled within that county in a place called Nederland. But none of these ventures succeeded. The Alvin and Amsterdam communities disbanded after only a few years, and by 1905 the Nederland settlement counted only four Dutch families.

6

It is likely that these facts were not known to members of the Dutch community in Chicago, for around the time of my birth, in response to attractive brochures, circulars, and press advertisements issued by a land promoter named Theodore F. Koch, several families in Illinois, Michigan, Indiana, Wisconsin, and Iowa purchased prairie land in the Winnie and Hamshire districts of Jefferson County with the view of establishing yet another Dutch colony in Texas. My father and a number of his Chicago friends and acquaintances were evidently taken with the idea, for in May and June of 1909, when I was approaching my first birthday, my father purchased 174 acres of land near Winnie at $35 an acre. He was not alone in doing so. From the First Church of Chicago, to which we belonged, many others joined the venture. I later came to know their names well: Hoekstra, Ter Maat, Vander Molen, Lanenga, Hoffman, Renkema, Vander Kamp, Blauw, Teune, De Young, Dykstra, Evenhouse, etc.

So it happened that in 1910 my father sold his prosperous business and prepared his family for departure. He was, no doubt, excited about the prospect of living in what had been touted as an agricultural paradise. But he was also concerned to get his younger children out of a city that, in our neighborhood at least, was rife with crime and violence. The notorious Valley Gang, a number of whose members died in the electric chair, is said to have been headquartered in the district adjacent to ours.

On November 14, 1910, Father, Mother, and six of their children, ranging in ages from two to sixteen, entrained on the Sante Fe railroad bound for Texas. Three members of our family stayed behind. Bill and John were already married and beginning to establish families of their own. Tom, who had attended business school was, at eighteen, gainfully employed and had no interest in farming. He was therefore allowed to remain in Chicago and live with his brother Bill.

Of the train trip to Texas I have no recollection, and of my subsequent stay in Winnie I have only the faintest. But bits of information have come my way, and from these a tolerably true story can be constructed. It was not, I am told, a "farm" that my parents bought, but an expanse of untilled prairie land. On this land they first had a barn built, and the family lived there while the dwelling house was under construction. The house (of which pictures exist) was a large, two-story structure with an ample screened-in circular porch enclosing the roomy interior. It was said to be the best house in the region, and arriving visitors, including pastors occasionally sent down from Classis

7

Our Texas Home

Pella, normally stayed under its roof. We lived about a mile from the small roadside town of Winnie, which itself lay twenty-five miles south of Beaumont and fifty miles east of Houston. The Gulf of Mexico was twenty miles away.

Starting a farm is no small undertaking. Besides providing shelter for people and animals, one has to plow, fertilize, and sow the land, dig wells, lay ditches, and do a score of other things. One needs horses, wagons, plows, seed, and fertilizer for this enterprise, to say nothing of muscle and will power. Because the latter qualities existed in fair supply, Father was able, with the energetic assistance of Neal, to get part of the land broken up and readied for sowing during the winter of 1910. In the spring they planted orange and fig trees; and in the ensuing few years they grew sweet potatoes, corn, and cucumbers, as well as some peanuts and watermelon. But the promised and hoped-for plentiful harvests did not materialize, and marketing such crops as the land yielded proved more difficult than they had anticipated.

But the colonists did not immediately give up. They came together, shared their concerns, and provided each other with help where needed. Father appears to have been among the leaders in the community. Notices appearing as early as July 1911 disclose that he func-

8

tioned as the president of the Cooperative Fruit and Tree Growers Association of Winnie, Texas. He also served as "reader" at the Sunday worship services held in the little frame church that had been erected near our house on land donated by the developer.

Concerning the children, Neal spent his time on the land as Father's chief assistant. Gert, who turned fifteen in 1911, took employment as a live-in maid in nearby Winnie, but she normally spent her weekends at home with us. Jen, George, and Mart attended a one-room country school some distance from our house, and doubtless assisted with the household chores when school was out. Meanwhile, I suppose I did what three-year-olds normally do, but I cannot recall any particulars. There is, however, one event that I quite vividly remember. On March 6, 1913, my parents celebrated their twenty-fifth wedding anniversary. Approaching my fifth birthday, I recall mingling with the many well-wishers who came to the house bearing gifts and then feasting on the pies and cakes my mother had baked.

However, even as these festivities were going on, clouds of doubt and sagging hopes brooded over the colonists. The land simply did not yield its fruits. If it was not long-lasting drought that scorched the crops, it was equally long-lasting rain that rotted them. Already in 1912, some families had surrendered their mortgaged farms and returned to their place of origin. Most of the settlers fell increasingly into debt, including the Stobs. Already in February 1913 my parents made efforts at refinancing, but these desperate expedients did not succeed. Thus, in the summer and fall of 1913, having lost most of their investment and sensing that the colony had no prospect of enduring, my parents settled their Texas affairs as well as they could, and with several other families broke their ties to a once enticing and promising enterprise.

The family returned to Chicago on December 7, 1913. The Texas sojourn had lasted a scant three years. Father was now fifty years old, with no immediate prospect of employment; and I, at five and a half, had not yet been to school.

*   *   *   *   *

I do not know what forces shaped and molded me during the first five years of my existence on this earth. I must have seen, heard, smelled, tasted, and touched a great variety of things, and I know that I spoke and was spoken to, that I laughed and cried, that I acquired

9

elementary skills, and that I was loved, instructed, and disciplined. But there is such a lock upon my memory as keeps me, despite my best efforts, from bringing anything clear and concrete into consciousness. Some events occurring in the outside world during this time must have come to my attention for, as I later learned, my family's engagement with public affairs was lively and constant. I suspect, therefore, that my parents and older siblings discussed in my presence Admiral Peary's discovery of the North Pole in 1909, Roald Amundsen's expedition to the South Pole in 1911, the overthrow of the Manchu Dynasty in China by Sun Yat Sen and the establishment of the Peace Palace in The Hague during the same year, and, especially, the sinking of the *Titanic* and the election of Woodrow Wilson in 1912. But of this, too, I have no recollection. The experiences of my infancy lie beyond my powers of recall.

2

GRAMMAR SCHOOL DAYS
(1914-1922)

U pon our return to Chicago in December 1913, my parents
rented an upper flat in a building located on the southwest
corner of 14th Place and Ashland Avenue. It lay a good half mile from
my birthplace on Blue Island Avenue, roughly three miles from the
Loop, and in the very center of the Dutch community that had
gathered around church and school.

As soon as we were settled there, my brother Tom, then twenty-one
years old, unmarried, and gainfully employed, took up residence with
us. With this addition, our family consisted of Father, Mother, and
seven children ranging in age from five to twenty-one years. There
were four bedrooms to accommodate the nine of us. Father and
Mother occupied one of these, Tom and Neal another, the girls a
third, and we three younger boys the fourth. Mart and I slept together
in one bed, and George occupied an adjoining bunk.

There was a living room, usually referred to as the "front" room,
which overlooked Ashland Avenue and was accessible to outsiders
through a front door opening on a steep staircase; but members of
the family seldom used that entrance. There was a rug on the floor
(wall-to-wall carpeting was unheard of then), and some overstuffed
chairs were arranged on it; but occupancy of the room was usually
reserved for visitors. It was not the place in which the family normally
gathered.

There was a dining room, which, as I recall, was never or seldom used for dining, in part no doubt because near the center of it Father had placed a coal-burning pot-bellied stove. I was often required to sift its ashes in the interest of economy.

A corridor, flanked on one side by a bathroom and on the other by a bedroom, led from the dining room into a spacious kitchen, which was not only Mother's throne room but also a veritable family room, the headquarters of our communal existence and the scene of our liveliest interchanges. It was in the kitchen that we ate our meals, attended to prayers and Bible readings, played table games, and discussed whatever pertained to family or world affairs. It was also here that Mother did the laundry, partly upon a corrugated washboard and partly in a hand-operated machine furnished with a wringer. Father, when available, would help to churn the clothes, and I was sometimes privileged to join in. Before consigning extremely dirty clothes to the machine, Mother would soak them in an oblong copper boiler in the interest of maximum cleanliness. Dominating the room was a large cookstove in which both coal and wood were burned, and on which Mother not only cooked our meals but also heated the irons with which she pressed our clothes. From within the oven of that stove there periodically emerged the best pies and cakes in all of Cook County. Next to the stove stood the icebox, into which the itinerant iceman would insert the fifty-pound block of ice that we ordered by placing his sign at the window. Emptying the water basin that captured the melting ice soon became one of my responsibilities. At the other end of the room was a large oblong table ringed with chairs; Father sat at the head in an oaken armchair near a rack supporting the Dutch Bible, which he read aloud each time the family sat down to meals. The reading was, of course, accompanied by prayers offered both before and after eating. To foster my concentration on the reading, my father periodically asked me to repeat the last words, and at the conclusion of the opening prayer I was expected to join in with my own "Heere, zegen deze spyze, Amen" (Lord, bless this food, Amen).

The apartment was lit by gas lamps, whose mantels had to be replaced regularly. For lack of screens, flies frequently invaded our quarters, but sticky flypaper, judicially placed, or sheets of poison flypaper resting in saucers captured and killed most of them.

A window in our kitchen looked out on a smallish, uncovered wooden porch, from which wooden steps led down to a ground-floor platform from which we gained access to 14th Place. It was this exposed back stair that we habitually used to enter or leave our flat. There was a yard of sorts that stretched from the back of our house to the adjacent alley, but it was no more than twenty-five feet wide and forty feet long and it contained not a blade of grass. The yard was encumbered too by a shed in which we stored our coal and wood; but it still served boys of my age as a baseball diamond, and at the time we considered it rather spacious. A hit from one end of the yard onto the street amounted to a home run, a wallop of which one could be justly proud.

Stretched high above the yard were Mother's clotheslines, which ran on pulleys fastened to the porch at one end and to a tall pole near the shed at the other. When a frayed line broke, as sometimes happened, it required great ingenuity to restore the device to usefulness.

This account would hardly be complete if I failed to report that on the ground floor of our building was a Dutch bakery operated by the brothers La Botz. We bought sweet rolls from them, as well as delicious cream puffs. My companions and I hung around this place a good deal, and in response to our importunities, we would sometimes get a reluctantly given cookie or sweet.

*   *   *   *   *

We lived at the 14th Place address for about two years. At the end of that time, I was seven and a half and I had acquired and stored in my consciousness enough experience to give a certain shape and structure to my person and to afford me a recognizable identity and presence. I had made the pleasurable acquaintance of my classmates at school, and I had come to be accepted by most of the kids on our block. But most of all, I had been nurtured into relative maturity by a conscious and beneficent association with the members of my family.

My father's sturdy but unaffected piety, his wise counsel, his exemplary reading habits, his involvement in the affairs of church and school, his steady industriousness, and his kindly disposition affected me deeply. Reflecting on it now, I do not remember him ever raising his voice or uttering a harsh word. When I was disobedient or had done some unseemly thing, he simply called me to him, took a firm grip on my arm, and looked me in the eye. By this body language

Mother and Henry

alone he made plain to me that certain things were not done in Israel or tolerated in the Stob household.

And my mother was a gem. The house was, of course, her domain. She was vice president, treasurer, and general manager of the realm. To each of her children she assigned a place and a task, with the result that everything proceeded in an orderly fashion. She was no martinet, but with a firm hand she gently guided the family into a routine that gave our life together a certain consistency and predictability. It was known, for example, that meals were served at designated times, that we were expected to eat what was set on the table, and that no one was to waste any food: what one took on one's plate was to be eaten. She kept the house spic-and-span and would abide no unredressed clutter. We younger children were taught to wipe our feet when entering the house; we had appointed pegs on which to hang our coats and caps; and shoes and other apparel had to be neatly stored. We were to come in from play as soon as darkness fell and promptly thereafter wash the city's accumulated grime from our face and hands. Bedtime and rising time were regulated. We school children were not permitted to be underfoot when the early risers were being served breakfast before reporting for work. But she was, amidst all her managerial duties, a loving and caring mother who taught us by precept and example to be neat, decorous, and cooperative. Her lively faith in God and his providence matched that of my father, and she instilled in us a regard for the Scriptures, a respect for authority, a sense of duty, a love for neighbor, and a recognition of the absolute need for religious commitment to the Creator and Lord of all.

There are handicaps to being the youngest child in a large family. One comes to inherit clothes and toys handed down from above and to be regarded as not yet licensed to voice an opinion. Indeed, it was a rule in our house that in the presence of adult visitors a child was not to speak unless spoken to. But there are also advantages to being a minor. I grew up in the company of intelligent and articulate adults to whose conversations I was privileged to attend, whose knowledge I could draw upon, and whose concern and help I could always count on. Brothers and sisters alike served as my mentors. Tom, Neal, and George undertook to advance my education by tutoring me in reading, writing, and arithmetic, and by alerting me to the significance of events happening around us. My sisters saw to it that my hair was combed, that my teeth were brushed, that I was appropriately dressed, and that I observed the social amenities. Mart, nearest to me in age, yet my senior by three years, took pains to ensure that the several indulgences accorded to the baby of the family were kept within bounds. But what proved to be as helpful as anything else was the family gathering that took place most evenings in our large kitchen.

One must remember that the absence of internal distractions and external enticements was a feature of these early years. We had no car to lure us onto city streets and country roads. We had no radio and no television to tempt us away from reading and conversation. Dancing and attending movies (then called "nickel shows") were forbidden. The opera and the symphony existed beyond our means and doubtless beyond our level of appreciation, our musical education being limited to psalm tunes and gospel hymns. All of this left the older children with little to do outside the home except to visit friends in other homes, attend a midweek church meeting, go to an occasional ball game, or perhaps, as in the case of Tom and Neal, court the favor of some young lady. But even that last occupation was restricted in those days. At best, a young man who was "dating" saw his girlfriend only on Wednesday and Sunday evenings, and, since taverns, nightclubs, and other such worldly things were out of bounds, his time with her was normally spent in the "parlor" or on the porch swing. The minutes of private courtship lasted from the time monitoring parents retired for the night and the stroke of midnight. No proper couples continued their tryst beyond that witching hour.

Dinner was in the evening, and it was a communal affair with each member occupying his or her assigned chair as age dictated. Always attended by devotions, it was also an occasion for round-table discussion. After the girls had cleaned the table and washed the dishes, the whole company normally assembled for further talk. From this habitual activity I gained knowledge and insight not accorded to those less favorably placed than I. During 1914 much of the talk centered on the war that was brewing and then erupted in August of that year. The July assassination of Archduke Ferdinand of Austria was emblazoned in the press and generously commented on at home. The August declaration of war frightened the family and overshadowed the July announcement that the Panama Canal had been completed and would in one month permit the passage of an ocean-going vessel. Father was initially on the side of the Germans because he resented England's recent wresting of South Africa from the control of his favored Boers. Paul Kruger was in those days a hero we were taught to look up to. The older children, however, having no experience of The Netherlands, tended to side with Britain and France, though they hoped that the United States would not be drawn into the conflict. They were encouraged in this by President Wilson's August Proclamation of Neutrality.

Other issues were discussed at table with fervor and élan. A 1914 decision of the Synod of the Christian Reformed Church to allow office bearers to speak English at classical meetings became a topic of conversation, as did its purchase that year of *The Banner*. The April 1915 torpedoing of the British Cunard liner *Lusitania* by the Germans off the coast of Ireland, with a loss of 1,200 lives, modified my father's opinion of the Germans and confirmed my brothers' allegiance to the Allied cause. There was talk that year, too, about William Hale ("Big Bill") Thompson's election as mayor of Chicago, as well as Jess Willard's capture of the world's heavyweight boxing crown.

One should not suppose that ours was an academic debating society. There were no learned savants among us. Father and Mother had not gone beyond the fourth grade, and none of the children had gone beyond the eighth grade, except perhaps Tom, who had taken some

16

commercial courses after finishing grade school. But the Lord had blessed our parents with intelligence and character, and they had been able in God's good providence to fashion with their gifts a lifestyle conducive to the wholesome nurture and development of their children. Meanwhile, we were a set of ordinary people doing what seemed natural in the light of our Dutch and Reformed inheritance.

Moreover, it was not all talk that went on. We played table games too. I think there was Parcheesi, a game played with dice, no less. And then there was Rook. Card playing, like dancing and theater attendance, was forbidden by the church, but in our circles the interdiction was held to apply only to "devil cards" and gambling. Rook was considered exempt, and it was widely indulged in. Father was good at the game, and Mart later became equally adept at it. However, I took little interest in it and seldom played.

*   *   *   *   *

I am told that soon after our return from Texas, Father found temporary employment at the Badenock Grain Elevator, a wholesale establishment where he had in former years purchased his hay and feed. Within months he had reopened a retail store in these commodities at Hastings Street and Paulina. But, sensing the arrival of the automobile age, he abandoned this project and before the year 1914 had come to a close, he had established himself in a cinder-hauling business. With two wagons and a half dozen horses, he was able to realize an acceptable return on his investment.

Supplementing the income brought into the house by my father were the contributions that were made early on by some of the children. Tom was already an established bookkeeper with a steady wage. Neal, then nineteen, soon took a job with Jelke Margarine, and my sisters Gert (seventeen) and Jen (fifteen) found employment at Haywood Brothers and Wakefield, manufacturers of reed furniture, where they made pillows. George, who entered eighth grade in February of 1914, also took a job when he graduated and turned fifteen a year later. With Father profitably engaged and four or five children paying room and board, Mother was able, after setting aside funds for church and school, to defray all household expenses and also, I suspect, lay a little aside.

It was perhaps this improvement in the family's financial situation

17

Henry and Martin

that induced my parents to look around for better living quarters. When it became known that the lower apartment of the Stege house on Ashland Avenue was for rent, they decided to occupy it forthwith. I believe it was late in 1915 or early in 1916, when I was about to enter the third grade, that we moved across the street into our new residence, just a stone's throw from the 14th Place flat that we were vacating.

The Stege house was so called because it was owned and on the upper level occupied by Mr. and Mrs. Stege, proprietors and managers of the huge brewery that stood on the corner of 15th Street and Ashland, a scant half block away. The large two-story brick house was quite unlike the one we had abandoned. A wrought-iron fence stretched across the front of it and extended down one side. Two gates provided entrance onto the grounds, one at the cement walk that led to the back door, and one near the broad stone steps that led up to a roomy but unenclosed porch. The wide door opening on this porch also opened onto an interior entrance hall from which a flight of steps led to the upper apartment on one side and from which one gained access to the rooms we occupied on the other. A round garden plot filled with the season's flowers adorned the space between house and fence, and an expansive lawn flanked the house on its south side. A huge brick wall, provided with a door, stretched along the alley at the rear. The house was fitted all around with copper gutters and downspouts, a fact that would hardly be worth reporting had not wartime vandals aroused the family by trying to dismantle and sell them as scrap to dealers with access to the military authorities.

The interior matched the size and beauty of the exterior. There were four bedrooms in our apartment and, besides the large kitchen and the closet-lined, tiled bathroom, there were three spacious residential areas — a dining room, a living room, and at the very front a cozy parlor, all with polished hardwood floors that glistened along the wide borders of the twelve-foot by nine-foot rugs Mother had laid down. From the enclosed porch in the rear, steps led to the basement, where at one end was a storage room, a laundry room with three fixed tubs with faucets and drains, and a full bathroom. A hall led from this area to what apparently had once been a ballroom designed for parties and dancing. Full access to this basement was accorded us in the rental agreement. Both of my sisters held their wedding receptions in the spacious ballroom. The house was heated by a boiler, and there were hot water radiators in every room. We still relied on gas for lighting, and I continued to be assigned the task of purchasing mantels to replace those that had burned out.

The family was now well situated, with space to accommodate friends the growing children increasingly brought into the house. We still ate private meals in the large kitchen, but we served guests in the dining room. A foot-pumped organ now graced the living room, and the young adults gathered around it on Sunday afternoons to sing their favorite songs, thereafter to enjoy the evening meal of ham, cheese, eggs, and bread that Mother lavishly provided.

Life at home went on much as it did before, except, of course, for

19

the changes that advancing years and altered circumstances inevitably bring. Mart and I began to play less on the streets and more in our own yard and large basement. Mother took pleasure in the house's airy spaciousness and in the laundry facilities it afforded, but it was apparent that increased space did not lessen the tasks of cleaning and dusting. Visitors and guests from outside the family came in increasing numbers, which also kept her busy. Bill and Tillie with their young children, and John and Hattie with theirs, made frequent appearances; but in this she and Father took delight, as did we all. These visits both advanced our family life and afforded my parents ample opportunity to dote on their grandchildren.

We lived in the Stege house for about six and a half years. During that time great changes occurred. At the midterm of our stay, in 1919, Mart graduated from grammar school, and near the end of our stay there, I did the same. Chief among the changes that occurred, however, was the radical decrease in the number of those who sat around the family table. From 1916 to 1922, all the older children got married and left the house to establish their own homes. Only Mart and I were still living with our parents when, in the fall of 1922, we moved into a smaller house some six blocks away.

I shall have occasion below to report more fully about the life we lived during our stay on Ashland Avenue. I wish now to say, however, that in our first year of residence in the Stege house — the year 1916 — a number of things happened that I remember vividly. Chief among them is the marriage of my able and well-loved brother Tom to Jennie Bulthuis on May 17, 1916. His departure, though warmly endorsed and joyfully celebrated, did nevertheless impoverish those of us who stayed at home. Fortunately, he and his wife did not neglect to visit us often, and at fixed intervals he provided us with a barrel of apples from Thomas S. Smith's wholesale store on the South Water Market, where he was employed as credit manager.

What I remember with almost equal vividness is the November re-election of Woodrow Wilson to the Presidency of the United States. My father was a Republican, and he favored the candidacy of Justice Charles E. Hughes. Because of his interest in the race, we stayed up late on election day in order to read the message about the result, which was to be signaled toward midnight by a light flashed from the Wrigley Tower. A victory for Hughes was flashed that night and we went to bed satisfied; but the morning papers revealed that Wilson had won. His promise to keep us out of the war had apparently turned the tide.

General John J. ("Black Jack") Pershing's vain pursuit of Pancho Villa across the Mexican border also elicited our interest that year, but it was only when the general took command of the American troops in 1917 that the Mexican expedition took on fresh meaning. Of lesser interest, though a cause of some regret, was the movement of the Chicago Cubs from a stadium in our area to Wrigley Field on the far north side. In spite of the move, the Cubs continued to be our team, and they remain mine to this very day.

* * * * *

When we moved into the Stege house, we did not move out of the neighborhood; we stayed within it, and I was neither required to sever any of my social ties nor inclined to quit entirely the familiar streets and alleys in which I had previously roamed. It was a Dutch neighborhood we lived in, although it was not an exclusive enclave without an ethnic mix. Jews lived in numbers along 14th Street, and there was a scattering of Irish and Polish Catholics in the neighborhood; but the Dutch predominated and it was under the shelter of their culture and mores that I grew up.

To fix the geographical parameters enclosing the Dutch community is a somewhat tricky undertaking, but I dare say that our people lived in an area bounded by Throop Street on the east and Oakley or Ogden on the west. It was bounded on the south by 15th Street and on the north by 12th Street (now Roosevelt Road). Most of the Dutch, however, lived in the area that was best known to me, which, lying in the north-south axis, stretched a half mile east and west from Loomis to Wood Street.

Among our near neighbors on Ashland Avenue were the Rispens, Blauws, Huizengas, Rozendals, Kiemels, De Boers, Jacobsmas, Teunes, and others; living on 15th Street were the Ter Maats, Vander Ploegs, Dwarshuises, Tammingas, and Vander Molens. It was on 14th Place, however, that most of our acquaintances were to be found. Within the space of three blocks on that street, almost every house was occupied by a Dutch family. Other Blauws and Vander Molens lived there, as well as the Veldmans, Groenbooms, Belgraves, Browers, Konings, Mensingas, Bosmans, Vander Veldes, Stowies, Norlags,

21

Iwemas, Van Stedums, Van Byssums, Hoffmans, Dekkers, Renkemas, Lanengas, Huizers, and several others whose names I do not remember. Close by lived the Evenhouses, Ottenhoffs, Gelderlooses, Wigboldys, Wierengas, Mulders, Rozemas, Holtrops, Dryfhouts, and Venhuizens, to name but a few.

These people, most of whom had roots in the Dutch province of Groningen and who still mastered and frequently spoke the language of that region, boasted no proud ancestry and laid no claim to culture; but they espoused and generally practiced the stern morality and displayed the personal graces that the Calvinistic faith they embraced tends everywhere to engender. True to their ethnic tradition, they were also industrious and thrifty. Few of them were rich, and some would perhaps be regarded now as deprived and underprivileged, but I doubt that any of the latter thought of themselves in this way. Most lived happily within their modest means, and, though they did not despise prosperity and success, they had learned from the apostle to be content with the circumstances in which they found themselves.

The Stege house was, with its appointments, grass, and flowers, an anomaly in the neighborhood. Most houses were small and placed close together with only a narrow gangway stretched between them. There were almost no lawns, trees, or gardens, and no empty lots in which children could romp and play. Flowers sometimes appeared on window sills, but their presence did little to relieve the general bareness of the scene. The alleys were unpaved and muddy after rains. For want of adequate policing by the city's sanitary department, they were also often cluttered with refuse and debris — and consequently rat-infested. Yet, in spite of these conditions, there was among the people a pervasive spirit of friendship and neighborliness, as well as many front steps and porches from which to exercise these admirable traits.

Men and unmarried young women were, of course, the providers. The place for a married woman was in the home: matrimony led to housekeeping and the bearing and rearing of children, not to outside employment. A married woman or a widow living on the edge of poverty might indeed become a cleaning lady for the more affluent or resort to laundering other people's clothes in her own home; but she was not apt to take a job in a public workplace. In our neighborhood this outside activity was reserved for men and girls.

Although some heads of families in the community worked in shops or factories, others held office jobs, and a number ran their own small

22

businesses. Messrs. Veldman and Dryfhout owned a blacksmith shop on Fourteenth Street and Paulina, and Mr. Dekker owned another one at 14th Place and Laflin. Mr. Stowie ran a grocery store at 14th Place and Paulina, and Mr. Rispens owned one a block away, at 14th Place and Ashland; the butcher shop that he ran in conjunction with it was later taken over by Mr. Boersma. Mr. James De Boer owned a hay and feed store, which he operated with the aid of his three oldest sons at 14th Place and Loomis. Mr. Conrad Ottenhoff was an excavator who deployed heavy earth-moving equipment in his work. His brothers George and Walter dealt in real estate and insurance. The Wigboldys, Wierengas, and Evenhouses were, I believe, engaged in trucking. Mr. Van Byssum sold shoes and did shoe repair in a small shop he ran on 14th Place. Mr. Vander Velde delivered ice in summer and coal and wood in winter from his home on 14th Place and Paulina. Mr. Koning, who lived nearby, was a collector of manure, which he sold to dealers who shipped it by the carload to outlying farmers for the fertilization of their fields. Then, of course, there were the aforementioned La Botz brothers, whose Ashland Avenue bakery supplied the community with Dutch pastries.

Our dental needs were taken care of by Dr. Hartgerink, and when we got sick we could call upon the services of Dr. Van Dellen. Both had offices on Ashland Avenue near our house. I don't remember how the physician got around — he may have been among the very few who owned a car — but it was common for him to make house calls and, after ministering to the sick, to stay and chat a while. When there was a death, Mr. Leenhouts was available for embalming. He ran a funeral establishment on Ashland Avenue, just a few paces from our house, but it was more a workshop than a meeting place for mourners. The body of the deceased normally lay encoffined in the family living room; and to pay their respects and condolences, neighbors came in measured steps and muted tones to the crepe-draped house of mourning.

I can hardly omit from this account of our people a report concerning the smoking and drinking habits of its leading men. Cigarettes were unknown when I was a small boy; they were introduced, I believe, when the soldiers returned from France in 1919. In any case, they were not smoked by the elderly, who already then referred to them as "coffin nails." But pipes and cigars were everywhere in evidence. My dad usually smoked a corncob pipe, and on the rack beside the family Bible there always stood a large can of roughcut tobacco. He smoked cigars too, of course, especially on Sundays and when guests were in the house. The minister also smoked, as did the elders. The consistory invariably met, I'm told, in a smoke-filled room, though the goings-on of these stalwarts bore no resemblance to the shenanigans of the scheming politicians who were said to meet within similarly foggy confines.

They say that the Dutch and the Scots, both sons of Calvin, resorted to drink in order to withstand the wet cold blasts that blew down upon them from the turbulent North Sea. However that may be, liquor was freely — though not excessively — imbibed by a great many of our staunch burgers. It was not uncommon for elders to be served a jigger of bourbon or rye when they appeared for house visitation. Nothing so fancy as a highball existed back then; people took their drinks straight and undiluted, albeit in thimble-sized draughts. It was the custom in our circles to serve "boeren-jongens" at year's end: this was a compound concocted of whiskey and raisins, and a batch of it was prepared during the Christmas season by most Dutch matrons. People would visit each other after church on New Year's Day and be toasted with a small glass of these floating, spirit-soaked raisins. Nor did anyone object to the consumption of beer, and on hot summer days the adult members of our family drank it openly on our front porch. A good quantity of it could be fetched from the corner saloon in a tin pail for a dime, and when I was still in school, I was sometimes dispatched to perform this errand. Nobody inquired whether or not one was a minor.

The drinking, happily, was generally done with due temperance; but there would be occasional lapses, and public drunkenness was unfortunately not unknown on our Dutch streets. It was, however, strictly condemned, and any offender was bound to be visited and reprimanded by the church authorities.

It was among these people and within this neighborhood that I lived my schoolboy years. When I was in first and second grade and still living in the flat above the bakery, I seldom moved beyond that portion of 14th Place that ran from Ashland to Paulina, except of course for Sunday visits to church and daily trips through the alley to the school on 15th Street. As I grew older, I roamed widely and more freely through the neighborhood in order to absorb its sights and sounds. I liked the smell of Mr. De Boer's hay and cherished the often-granted opportunity to ride on the wagon with his sons when

24

they made a delivery of it. I delighted to see Mr. Dekker at his forge and to witness the deftness with which he fitted shoes on sometimes balky horses. The livery stable on 14th Street also interested me: I can still bring back the horsey odors emanating from it, just as I can summon to consciousness the aroma of draught beer that floated from the saloons on our corner when the doors stood open in summertime. And there still reverberates in my ears the rumblings of the El that thundered past 14th Place at Paulina.

*   *   *   *   *

What fashioned the Dutch people in our neighborhood into a community was the local church. It came into being in 1867 when several families left the Dutch Reformed denomination to make common cause with the Michigan secessionists who had left a decade earlier. The first worshipers met in a small forty- by sixty-foot frame building they had erected on Gurley Street between Miller and Sholto, and my father joined them there when he first settled in Chicago. When, around 1883, the Gurley Street structure proved to be too small to accommodate the growing congregation, it established new accommodations on 14th Street between Throop and Loomis. It was in this church building that I was baptized and in which the family worshiped until the early 1920s, when the congregation moved once again, this time into a large and handsome brick edifice on Ashland Avenue and Hastings Street that the Lutherans had put up for sale.

The church of my early years, commonly called the 14th Street Church (though incorporated as the First Christian Reformed Church of Chicago), was housed in a rather large frame building into which one entered by mounting a flight of weather-exposed wooden steps leading to the double-doored front entrance. Two small spires arose in front on opposite sides of the roof, and in the front center stood a steepled bell tower, which gave the whole an attractive appearance. The inside pews accommodated a congregation that during my time numbered somewhat over 200 families and 1,100 souls. The building contained a gallery that was normally occupied by young adults during worship services, and they were not always well behaved. Opposite it stood the centered pulpit mounted on a platform, and on the side of the pulpit were transverse benches accommodating the members of the consistory charged with monitoring the preaching.

Fourteenth Street Church

The Parsonage

Beside the church stood a three-storied, rather narrow brick dwelling that housed the janitor on the lower floor and the minister on the upper floors. During my early days, S. S. Vander Heide was the pastor. It was with him that I first took catechism lessons, and it was under his ministry that I resided until he left to take another charge sometime in 1918, when I had reached the age of ten.

I am told that before my time there had been three worship services on Sunday, but in my day these had been reduced to two, one in the morning and one in the afternoon, and these I attended regularly. Adult young people were expected, however, to be in church on Sunday evenings for singing school or for engagements in other religious activities. Boys and girls my age were exempt from attending these meetings. Midweek prayer services were not in the Dutch style and were not held, but a number of "societies" formed for Bible study did meet during the week. There was also a recitation society, in which like-minded people practiced eloquence and presented poetic readings. The latter was a kind of corollary to the so-called "Singing School,"

27

where both young and older adults learned to develop their vocal talents. However, their musical abilities were not put to use in the worship services. Nothing like a choir was permitted to complement, much less supplant, the rendition of the Psalms by the voice of the assembled congregation.

Saturdays at our house — and I suppose elsewhere as well — were set aside for Sabbath preparation. Mother began the day by scrubbing the floors and dusting the furniture in an already clean house, and assigning Mart and me to take up the throw rugs and attack them with rug beaters on the backyard clothesline. Next came Mother's inspection of the men's Sunday clothes, together with the mending and pressing they might require, whereupon Mart and I gathered up the Sunday shoes of the whole family and brought them to the back porch for polishing. We boys were free to play on Saturday afternoons, but we were expected to be in the house early enough to avoid the evening traffic that flowed in and out of the bathroom. Saturday was bath day, and every member of the family had to be given his or her allotted time in the tub. Saturday night was not a night for visiting, and neither the older children nor their properly trained peers went out on courting "dates" on Saturdays. Such out-of-house engagements were held to be deleterious in their effect on Sunday worship. Mother was not opposed to cooking on the Sabbath, and our dinners on that day were uniformly great; but to minimize Sunday labor, she usually peeled the potatoes and made other culinary preparations the evening before. Probably for similar reasons, Father, instead of shaving in the morning as was his daily custom, did so on this day just before retiring for the night. When the evening's activities subsided, we joined in chatter and conversation, but no one stayed up late. We went to bed on time in order to be rested and alert when the Sabbath dawned.

After a communal Sunday breakfast, we all dressed for church and walked in a group to the house of worship. Before we left our residence, our parents distributed peppermints all around. I was also given two pennies, one for Sunday School and one for the church "collection," which was taken up in midservice by deacons manning long poles with open-faced velvet bags at the ends for the reception of the offerings. Arriving at church, we entered as a family, and, since ushers were then unknown or regarded as an impertinence, Father and Mother took the lead in conducting us to our customary pew midway in the sanctuary. It was customary in those days for boys who had reached the age of sixteen, and had thus become licensed to discard their knickers and wear long pants, to declare their maturity and independence by abandoning the family pew and sitting in the back rows or in the gallery of the church. But Father frowned on the practice, and it was not indulged in by my brothers.

The worship services were conducted in the Dutch language. This is not remarkable: it is natural that immigrants should wish to hear the gospel preached in their native tongue and to sing the songs they learned in the land of their birth. Many of the older worshipers on 14th Street had been in America for decades, and though they spoke intelligible, if somewhat accented, English on the job and in the streets, most of them were opposed to the use of that language in the church. American religion, they believed, was Methodistic, and the Americanization of the church could only mean the dilution if not the dissolution of the Calvinistic faith. Forgetting that classic Calvinism was first articulated in French and Latin, some even held that no language was better suited to preserve and propagate it than Dutch. Whatever the reasons given, the fact is that as late as 1915, nearly sixty years after the church's founding, only seventeen of the 223 congregations in the Christian Reformed Church conducted worship services in the English language. The slow pace of Anglicizing them is no doubt regrettable on many counts; but when I consider what has contributed to my own development, I cannot much lament the community's long retention of things Dutch. I learned the rudiments of a foreign language as a child. I also came to possess the stately full-noted Dutch psalms, which on occasion I can still bring to mind, and I was insinuated into a history and into a culture of which there is reason to be justly proud.

I don't know how much benefit I derived from Rev. Vander Heide's sermons. I listened as best I could, and I believe that I grasped the elements of his discourses. But a young boy's attention span is short and the sermons were very long, so long indeed that, to retain a hold on even adult listeners, the preacher often asked for a psalm to be sung when he had arrived at the midpoint of his sermon. The congregational prayer — which omitted nothing pertaining to praise, confession, thanksgiving, intercession, and petition — was lengthy too and was commonly referred to as the "long prayer." When it was about to begin, people generally resorted to their store of peppermints; it was understood that these hard candies were to be sucked and not chewed, lest a sound disturbance be created. Hymns were not sung in church; only the Dutch psalms were used, and there were no racks with a supply of these psalters. People owned their own copies, many adorned with gold or silver clasps, and these they carried to and from church. A hand- or foot-pumped organ accompanied the singing, but when a relatively unfamiliar psalm was announced, a *voorzinger* would appear up front to lend support.

The elders marched into church as a body, with the minister at their head, and they sat together on the side benches provided for them. To express their agreement with the preached word, each shook the hand of the minister as he descended from the pulpit. I know of no case where an approving hand was not offered, but I am told that it sometimes did happen to the embarrassment of all. The communion wine was sipped from a common cup: since Jesus drank with his disciples in this way, there was strong opposition to the introduction of individual cups, although Synod did in 1918 leave the use of them to the discretion of local consistories.

Many of the modern conveniences were lacking in the church of my youth. There was no parking lot, but none was needed, since most of the people lived within walking distance of the church. There was no nursery, and crying infants sometimes proved distracting. There was no air conditioning, which meant that on hot summer days the congregation resembled a sea of waving fans. Since there was no loudspeaker, the minister had to be in good voice to be heard. Ours fortunately met the standard; but occasional guests did not, to the distress of those in the back rows. No coffee was served after the service: eating and drinking even in the basement of the church was tantamount to temple desecration.

My father was a firm believer in catechism training, but he was lukewarm toward Sunday School, since it was, in his judgment, an alien import, most likely from England. I nevertheless attended, in part because my playmates did, and he offered no objection. I don't remember much about the instruction. The teachers were no doubt devout and committed people, but they were untrained and worked under handicaps. The classes were scattered in pews around the auditorium, and the general hubbub was disturbing. English was spoken here, but we often sang Dutch hymns. One of them, "Er ruist langs de Volken een lieflijke Naam," still remains with me, and I sing it to myself on occasion. The Christmas celebration was the highlight of our Sunday School life: it was then that we all received an orange and a small bag of hard candy. But I don't believe that I ever performed in the Christmas program.

Catechism classes were held once a week after school. The instruction was conducted by the pastor — in the Dutch language. Our text was Borstius' Primer, a compendium of the Heidelberg Catechism. I still remember how it began: "Vraag: Wie was de eerste Man? Antwoord: Adam." (Question: Who was the first man? Answer: Adam.) Classes met in the sparsely equipped and dank church basement, and we had to pass through the largely Jewish settlement on 14th Street to get there. The Dutch are not normally anti-Semitic, and Hollanders and Jews did in fact peacefully coinhabit the neighborhood of my youth. But schoolboys invading an alien "turf" did sometimes get waylaid. Consequently, we tended to walk in groups and often carried sticks for use in possible combat. These we laid neatly beside our chairs when we recited Borstius' Primer. My parents required me to be prepared for class: on the evening before catechism, either Father or Mother took the book in hand and, one by one, asked the questions. Should my recitation be to any degree faulty, I was ordered into a corner, there to improve my knowledge. Only when I had learned the lesson could I go to bed.

We observed the Sabbath at our house in quiet. We attended church, ate a good meal at noon, went to church again, and for the remainder of the day arrested all of our weekly activities. We dressed in Sunday clothes, did not play outdoors, avoided team sports, threw no balls, rode no bikes, and rested. What occupied us was reading, hymn singing, and conversation, and in retrospect I know of no better way to spend the day on which the Lord arose.

* * * * *

The school I attended was only twenty years old when I entered it. It had been established in 1893 by the consistory of the 14th Street Church and was under its governance until 1902. In its earliest years it was thus a decidedly parochial institution, and it went by no other name than "the Christian School." During the first two years of its existence, classes were held in a rented store located at 685 South

31

Ebenezer School

Ashland Avenue, and thereafter, until 1906, in the basement of the church. In 1902, however, the school came under the supervision of an independent board. It then took on the character of a genuine nonparochial private school supported by a legally constituted association of parents and friends. In 1902 it was given the name Ebenezer, and three years later it was relocated in a building of its own.

I was already five and a half years old when we returned from Texas in December 1913 and thus quite ready for school; but classes at Ebenezer had already been in session for some months, and I was not allowed to matriculate until February 1914. Since there was no kindergarten, I went directly into the first grade, where our school work was done on slates. In the following year, however, the slates were abandoned and we were trained in the use of pen and ink. The inkwells inserted in the desks sometimes tempted boys to blacken the hair of the girls sitting in front of them. The student enrollment at the time was around 330. I don't know what the tuition was when I began school, but a few years earlier, parents with one child in school were charged $2.00 per month; those with two children enrolled paid $3.00. And the fees were staggered in such a way that parents with four or more children in school paid no more than $3.75 a month. Teachers' salaries were comparably low: in 1919 the average salary was $20 a week. The financial support of the school was provided almost exclusively by the members of the 14th Street congregation. People attending the nearby Dutch Reformed Church (now RCA) tended to regard the Christian school as separatistic and un-American, and almost all of them sent their children to the Clark public school located on Ashland Avenue near Hastings.

Ebenezer school was located on 15th Street between Ashland and Paulina, a half block south and another half block west of the flat we first occupied on 14th Place. I could reach it by way of two alleys in almost no time at all. The same was true when, two years later, we moved into the Stege house on the east side of Ashland Avenue between 14th Place and 15th Street.

I don't remember the process by which I was enrolled, but I do remember not being scared or intimidated by the prospect of going to school. I knew most of my classmates from church and Sunday School; moreover, my brother Mart was a formidable fourth-grader, and my brother George was in the class about to graduate. Under these circumstances there was nothing I need fear.

Of some of my teachers I have only the dimmest of recollections. I recall, however, that all of them were men, and this in retrospect strikes me as quite remarkable. Among these teachers were the Messrs. Pilon, Goeree, Bremer, Lobbes, and Van Harn, and I seem to recall that while the latter three were typical of the staff, the former two were considered distinctive in a "peculiar" sort of way, their views and habits being considered by the older folks somewhat eccentric.

Naturally, I remember our principal, Mr. Henry Kuiper, for, though I was normally a well-behaved scholar, I was occasionally sent to him for correction and nurture. This kindly man remedied my defects — and that of others — by smartly applying two rulers to the outstretched palms of any offender sent to him. I did not then, and I do not now, take this ill of him. I think corporal punishment, when exercised in moderation, is generally wholesome, although I don't recall any of my regular teachers resorting to it. They usually required us to stay after school or to write some apologetic sentence fifty or a hundred times. I may record here that my parents always took the school's side in cases of this kind, and endorsed the teacher's discipline by supplementing it with their own.

I distinctly remember Mr. Jacobsma, that lovable gray-bearded teacher who was with the school from nearly its beginning and who taught our second grade class to read, write, and tell time. He was also a near neighbor and a close friend of the family. Whether it was in his class or in the first grade escapes me now, but I remember that we learned about the letter "z" by viewing a picture of a sausage sizzling in a pan. All of us respected and admired Mr. Jacobsma. On Friday afternoons he taught us Dutch, thus supplementing the adventitious foreign language instruction I was receiving in church, catechism, and home.

Lambert Flokstra taught the seventh grade and Mr. Kooistra the eighth at Ebenezer school. I learned much from them. Mr. Kooistra excelled in mathematics, and he inspired in me a love of numbers and spaces. He later joined the high school faculty, and, when I returned to school after spending three years in the work force, I benefited once more from his tutelage. I later served on the Calvin College faculty with Dr. Flokstra, and we would sometimes reminisce about our Ebenezer days.

A grade school student does not normally concern himself with curricular affairs and I simply do not recall how the curriculum was ordered. We were, of course, taught to read, and we were made to work hard at grammar, spelling, and composition. There was also geography to learn, plus history, civics, and arithmetic — and then there was Bible. All of us had Bibles in our desk drawers, and we were required to follow in them during daily devotions in class. One of the scariest moments in my young life occurred when, in one such devotional period, I accidentally tore out part of a Bible page. On that page I read the words: "If any one takes away from the words of the book of this prophecy, God will take away his share in the tree of life" (Rev. 22:19). Accosting the teacher in some panic, I inquired about the judgment that awaited me. To my great relief, he assured me that I was in no danger of damnation. He did not even reprimand me for being careless in the handling of books. The morning Bible readings were accompanied by singing, and the hymns we sang stuck in my memory, partly because I was impressionable at the time, and partly because we also sang them repeatedly around the organ at our house.

The brick school building was erected in 1906, when my father was secretary of the school board (1904-08). A tall flagpole stood in a small flower garden in front of it, and the flag was ceremoniously hoisted every morning. The principal's office was on the basement level, as were the boiler room, toilet rooms, and some open spaces furnished with clothes racks. There were two floors above ground level, each containing four classrooms, for a total of eight. That was it. There was no teachers' lounge or faculty room. Board and faculty meetings were presumably held in one of the classrooms. There was no assembly room, no cafeteria, no gymnasium, and no library or music room for the students. Yet the whole place was a seat of learning, and no one vacated it without having come into possession of the basic elements of knowledge.

Eating lunch in school was forbidden for most of us; only a few who lived too far from school to go home during the noon recess were accorded the privilege. Instead of gym classes, we did calisthenics for five or ten minutes in the classroom aisles. In fair weather and foul, the windows were opened wide for this exercise and selected students were appointed to open them with the long notched sticks provided for the purpose.

Our gym was the schoolyard, where we played under supervision but not under instruction. It was not much of a yard by modern standards, but it suited us fine. It was about fifty feet wide on the east side of the building and ran north and south from 15th Street to the alley at the rear. It was in this space that I once broke a school record and in the process elicited from the principal a display of truly gentlemanly behavior. A game current at the time involved a device made of two tops joined at their narrow ends, where the point of one had been inserted into a small hole bored into the other. Taking in hand two thin round sticks, with 2- or 3-foot lengths of string attached to each, one tried to spin the jointed top on the string, throw it high into the air with the leverage the sticks provided, catch it on the string when it descended — and then repeat the process, counting meanwhile the times the elusive top was thrown up and caught again. I was performing this act during one recess period, and just as I was approaching a record established by another student, the school bell rang summoning us indoors. When neither I nor the rather large number of spectators heeded the call, the principal emerged frowning; but when told what was in progress, he smiled, stayed to observe, and when, having broken the existing record, I finally missed a catch, he escorted us all with due courtesy to our respective rooms.

Many different games were played in the schoolyard during recess. It was there that we played at marbles and at "Buck, buck, how many fingers up." But mostly we played ball; a home run was a hit that landed in the alley. In back of the school was a still smaller space that was usually used by the girls to jump rope or do such other things as schoolgirls do. There was no grass and no trees: the whole yard was paved with cinders, which discouraged sliding into second base. Altercations sometimes took place in the yard, and fisticuffs were not unknown. Bouts were soon broken up by the older and more responsible students, however, and by tradition a means was provided for the settlement of differences. After school, a ring (or square) was drawn on the unpaved alley behind the school, and there, with upper classmen acting as referees, the combatants were required to exhibit their fistic prowess, with or without gloves, before an attentive assembly of their peers. It is here that many of us received our first training in the fine art of boxing.

Across 15th Street to the south there was a single row of houses occupied mainly, I believe, by Polish people whose children attended a Catholic school near Ashland Avenue and 17th Street. Between that school and ours lay the Baltimore and Ohio elevated railroad tracks.

Henry with bike

This multi-tracked rail concourse ran east and west, abridging the backyards of the 15th Street houses, and was separated from them by a high concrete wall. A similar wall existed on the other side of the tracks, and these walls and tracks minimized — if they did not eliminate — schoolboy battles between the Polish Catholics and the Dutch Calvinists. Hostilities, when they occurred, took place in the Ashland Avenue viaduct, and only the very brave ventured unaccompanied through that space.

What we did after school is a very long story. Mostly we played, although when I was still quite young — in the second or third grade — engagements in rough sports and strenuous exercises were not my style, for I was rather frail and frequently sick. Like most children, I contracted measles, mumps, whooping cough, influenza, and sundry other maladies, especially rheumatic fever. I don't know how often the doctor was called, but I know that it was my mother more than anyone else who nursed me back to health from these several illnesses. Home remedies were in vogue in those days, and, when I was suffering from a cold, Mother would apply goose grease to my chest and wrap a

37

heavy woolen cloth around my upper body. This was designed to dispel the chills and fevers, and somehow it worked. I swallowed a good amount of Dr. Pieter's Zokoro in those days, as well as quantities of the evil-tasting Haarlemer Olie and unflavored castor oil. At some point during this period I had my tonsils removed, and from then on my health and strength greatly improved. In my middle years at school I was as strong and robust as any boy my age.

I lost some days at school on account of these early and recurring illnesses, but there were compensations. While recuperating in bed or in a comfortable chair, I was led to read more than I would have otherwise. Having once been introduced to books, I never abandoned the reading habit. In the ensuing years at school, I read Jane Porter's *Scottish Chiefs*, Anne Sewell's *Black Beauty*, Edward Eggleston's *The Hoosier Schoolmaster*, and Lew Wallace's *Ben Hur*, among others. And then, of course, there was Zane Grey, Curwood, Altsheller, Standish, and Horatio Alger. These I read even though my parents sometimes wondered whether such reading befited a covenant child.

Our after-school games and activities were numerous and varied. I believe that we were not permitted to use the school playground after classes were dismissed. We kids, therefore, took mainly to the street, although, as we grew older, we played our more organized games on the Clark School cinder field. It was chiefly on 14th Place between Ashland and Paulina that we rode our bikes, sped on our roller skates, pushed our homemade scooters, and in winter belly-flopped on our sleds; at times we also wrestled, boxed, engaged in tug of war, or simply ran. We played shinny, dock on the rock, and peg; we shot marbles, roasted potatoes, sailed straws along the curb after a rain, and went junking down the alleys in search of salable bottles, old rags, and pieces of metal. What we collected in our junking forays we sold for pennies to an itinerant scrap dealer we called "Sheeny Randolph."

Sometimes we went swimming in a nearby municipal pool; at other times we retreated to a friend's backyard into the clubhouse we had erected out of salvaged lumber. We often simply sat and talked — about everything. As we matured, we even debated common grace with the Veldman boys, who, being nephews of Herman Hoeksema, rejected the concept. I had learned to skate on ice, and in a juvenile race I once earned a small gold-plated medal. But mostly we played softball in summer, using well-placed manhole covers and sewer outlets for bases.

Later we formed a baseball team and joined the church league. I started out as a pitcher, but my young arm lost its dexterity when I began throwing curves prematurely. I wound up at second base, where I earned a mixed reputation as a good glove and poor bat.

It was not all play after school. Often I had to run errands for my brothers and sisters, or go to the store for items my mother ran out of or had forgotten to order. It was at Rispens' that we usually traded: his store and butcher shop bore the likeness of all those independently owned establishments that dotted the landscape before the conglomerate supermarkets began to appear. Most things came in bulk lots. Cookies, crackers, flour, rice, coffee, and other commodities stood in boxes and bags on the floor, and the grocer withdrew from these containers the amount a person ordered. Butter and lard came in large tubs, from which he scooped the required amount into boat-shaped, paper-thin wooden containers. Margarine came uncolored and was made to look like butter by mixing a capsule of food dye into it at home. Bread came unwrapped and unsliced. Barrels of dill pickles and salted herring stood temptingly in a corner. Canned goods were up on the higher shelves, and the grocer retrieved them by mounting a sliding ladder or using a long-handled grasping tool. He figured the bill by adding up penciled figures on a pad of paper. One brought a shopping basket in which to take things home.

To signify our Dutchness, we frequently bought Dutch rye bread, an assortment of Dutch cheeses, and quantities of pickled herring. We also bought such favorites as kale and grey peas. We ate kale in a mixture with mashed potatoes and attended with sizable slices of pork steak; grey peas with bacon and quantities of bacon fat. What we usually bought in the butcher shop was pork chops and round steak. Chickens were expensive and eaten only on holidays. Liver was considered unfit for human consumption, and spare ribs were uniformly held in disdain. Frankfurts were cheap; I was given one whenever I made a purchase of meats.

But I did more than shop; I also worked at things. On several occasions I helped Mr. Rispens make sauerkraut in the dank basement under his store. I folded issues of *De Toekomst*, which was published by Dr. Van Lonkhuyzen in the small print shop adjoining the parsonage. I took woodworking classes at the nearby Church of the Brethren. I even took piano lessons for a while, though for fear of being called a sissy I discontinued the instruction after half a year. My

39

Eighth Grade Graduation
First row: Dena Rozema, Cora Vander Molen, Henry Kuiper (Princi-
pal), William Kooistra (teacher), Kate Van Byssum, Ella Mulder. Second
row: Tena Holtrop, John Vander Velde, John W. Blauw, Bertha Blauw,
Tracy Hoffman, Anne Decker, John Stowie, William Norlag, Henry Stob.

chief occupation was with the Jewish people in the neighborhood. Since orthodox Jews may not work on the Sabbath, they hired me to light their Saturday morning fires during the winter. I usually found the stoves already laid with paper and kindling; I needed only to light a match and ignite the flammable materials. I had ten customers and each paid me ten cents for my weekly services.

Honesty compels me to report some naughtinesses. John Vander Velde and I sometimes took our lives into our hands by climbing the high El structure near his house, vaulting over the electrified rail, and after mounting the platform stealing a free ride to the Loop and back. Of this I gave no account to my parents, who would certainly have disapproved of this adventure.

More innocent, but fraught with consequences less pleasant, was an action I took in the summer of 1919. My brother Neal was in the army of occupation on the Rhine, and we looked forward eagerly to his return. One day I espied on the nearby elevated B&O tracks a stalled train, whose cars were filled with soldiers about to be mustered out. Wanting to greet the tired-looking, khaki-clad men, and hoping that Neal might be among them, I managed somehow to climb the steep protective wall and land at last on the tracks. I had been there but a moment when a railroad guard took me in hand for trespassing and walked me to the roundhouse on Wood Street. From there he called the police, and when they arrived, I was driven in a paddy wagon to the Maxwell Street Station. There I was severely reprimanded by the officer in charge, though not booked. I walked home disconsolately. But when I told my parents of the incident, they applied no censure. Indeed, they thought that a certain eleven-year-old boy had been unduly harassed and mistreated.

The course of study at Ebenezer school finally came to an end. I had done satisfactory work and was asked by the principal to give the student graduation oration. On the evening of January 26, 1922, we were given our diplomas at the exercises held in church, and I said some words in praise of George Washington, the father of our country. Our graduating class was much smaller than the one that had left school in June of the previous year: we numbered five boys and eight girls. I was thirteen and a half years old at this time and still quite uninterested in girls; but to celebrate the occasion I asked the prettiest one in the class to accompany me to the ice cream parlor on 12th Street. After we had had a banana split, I walked her home. And that was that.

*   *   *   *   *

The nineteenth century did not end in 1900 or even in 1908. The robust optimism of that century, its firm belief in human progress, and its Victorian lifestyle lived on for nearly two decades after the calendar had ostensibly signaled the century's demise. Its hopes and aspirations were still alive when in 1911 men confidently erected a Peace Palace in The Hague, and when in 1912 they launched a presumably unsinkable ship. It was only after a floating piece of ice arrested the *Titanic's* maiden voyage and sent a supposedly invincible vessel to the bottom of the sea, and after the dreams of empire led misguided humans to plunge the world into four years of death and destruction in the course of a global war, that a new era dawned and another age arrived on the scene.

41

So I lived for at least ten years in a waning nineteenth century and for several more in a still emerging twentieth. It is true, of course, that the scientific advances of the present age and the technological marvels that now surround us and significantly shape our lives had been adumbrated and in some cases had materialized decades before my birth. Before my father arrived on these shores in 1880, the country had already come into possession of Morse's telegraph, McCormick's reaper, Singer's sewing machine, Pullman's sleeper, Bell's telephone, and Edison's incandescent electric light. By then, the railroads had also spanned the continent and had woven a web of rails in every region of the country. The ubiquitous telephone became a familiar household instrument, and horse-drawn streetcars were replaced by electrified trolleys. In 1891, Edison patented the kinetoscope, and its invention engendered a burgeoning movie-making industry. Henry Ford put out a two-cylinder car as early as 1892. The typewriter came into general use in 1895. In 1901, the first wireless signal was sent from Europe to America. And in 1903, Orville and Wilbur Wright initiated the age of modern aviation by flying a heavier-than-air machine at Kitty Hawk. During my infancy and youth further developments took place. In 1909 Henry Ford began to market his popular Model-T. In 1910 Glen Curtis flew a plane from New York to Albany at fifty miles an hour. In 1914, when flying boats were already traversing the sky between Tampa and St. Petersburg, the Navy established at Pensacola a training school for aviators. In 1916 the tank made its debut in the Battle of the Somme. In September 1917, a United States Army aero squadron arrived in France to do battle in the air. And modern radio broadcasting began in 1920, when station KDKA transmitted over the airwaves the returns of the Harding-Cox presidential election.

Yet, while I was growing up, very few of these developments impinged significantly upon our lives. I knew, of course, about railroads, telephones, trolley cars, Els, and the like; but for the most part my neighbors and I lived in a period of unsophisticated transition, unenriched by modern gadgets and conveniences. We saw no planes, used no typewriters, went to no movies, had no electric lights, listened to no radio, and possessed few cars. Ours remained to a very large extent the "horse-and-buggy" days. Mr. Rispens eventually acquired a Model-T, which became the cynosure of curious eyes and rather a thing to be gawked at than to be driven in. Occasionally, a truck with hard rubber tires and a visible chain drive appeared on the streets. Equipped with governors, these early trucks were not able to go very fast, and when we were on our roller skates, we kids could hitch on with ease. But what we normally saw on the streets were horses and wagons. All house-to-house deliveries were made from horse-drawn vehicles. The Chicago Fire Department began to motorize about the time I was born, but wailing fire engines drawn by horses and accompanied by spotted Dalmatians were still to be seen rushing down the streets when I was growing up. Large wagons laden with barrels of beer and drawn by handsome Belgians or Clydesdales appeared everywhere. The street sweeper with his cart and stiff, long-handled brush, who was charged with picking up what were euphemistically called "road apples," was a familiar sight. Iron hitching posts and judiciouly placed water troughs stood at intervals along the curbs, and a "wooden Indian" could often be seen standing outside a tobacco shop. As for the railroads, the locomotives were steam-driven, and water towers and reserve coal bins dotted the landscape along the rails to facilitate their refueling. What particularly fascinated youngsters like me were the hand-propelled carts on which the railroad's maintenance men sped to accomplish their mission. All of us hoped one day to ride on one of those carts or to sit in the caboose.

The nineteenth century also reflected itself in the clothes we wore. Until their midteens, boys wore knickers and long black stockings that were held up with rubber bands; they invariably wore caps, even in summer. On Sundays they donned button shoes that were fastened with a metal buttonhook. Men wore high, stiff, detachable collars and derby or fedora hats; the vests of their three-piece suits invariably sported a gold chain attached to a usually massive gold watch. Men shaved with straight-edged razors that they sharpened daily on a leather strop. The women wore bone-ribbed corsets and high-necked, floor-length dresses, and in our circle at least, they eschewed lipstick and rouge. Pregnant women who were already great with child avoided public exposure and remained in waiting until the time of their delivery.

The prevailing etiquette preserved the manners and mores of the Victorian age. Children did not interrupt their parents' conversation or intrude on an adult gathering. Young people called older folks, and especially married persons, by their surnames prefixed by Mister, Missus, or Miss. No one of any age presumed to address a relative stranger

Brother Neal

or a casual caller by his or her first name. This unseemly practice, which in the twentieth century has come to project a friendliness obviously artificial and spurious, was then rightly regarded as a belittling discourtesy.

*   *   *   *   *

The year 1917 was a year to be remembered. I was then nine years old and in fourth grade. Of parochial interest, and a cause for thanksgiving, was the fact that Calvin College, the denominational institution my father always called with great fondness "Onze School," had in

September established itself in a spacious new building on a nine-acre Grand Rapids campus. But of more immediate interest and concern was the ongoing European war. Russia, whose military might was not great, and whose forces on the eastern front were in any case ineffectually deployed, signed a peace treaty with the Germans in December of that year and withdrew from the war. This hurt the Allied cause: Germany now not only had one fewer enemy to fight; she was able to shift large forces westward to engage her remaining foes.

But more important than this were the events that were occurring within Russia itself. I don't know how statesmen of the time assessed these goings-on. I know that we in our small corner barely took notice of them. But they proved to be of great significance, and the forces they loosed have to a large extent directed the course of twentieth-century history. In March 1917 the so-called "White Russians," or "Mensheviks," revolted against the czar and set up a moderate socialist government under Prince Levov, and in May under Alexander Kerensky. Emperor Nicholas II abdicated on March 15. An internal struggle followed his dethronement, and on November 6 the Petrograd Soviet under Lenin and Trotsky overthrew the Kerensky government and established a communist police state. With the Bolsheviks in control, Russia stepped out of the war. In time, the powerful Soviet Union was formed, and its political, economic, and religious policies and stratagems have had world-shaking effects. But I suppose that at the time few, if any, thoroughly understood what was happening or envisioned the global consequences the Communist Revolution would produce.

What engaged the attention of Americans, as well as the members of our family, was America's own participation in the war. The United States had affirmed its neutrality from the beginning of the war; but its armed cargo ships had for some time been surreptitiously delivering goods and equipment to the beleaguered British. This led Germany to declare, in February 1917, that after March 1 any armed merchant vessel plying the high seas would be considered fair game for its ubiquitous U-boats and would be sunk without warning. After the United States had suffered some losses, and the seas were no longer safe, President Wilson, with congressional concurrence, declared war on Germany on April 6. The act was enthusiastically endorsed by the general public, and all across the country young men appeared eager to enter the fray. In some German and Dutch settlements in the

Midwest, however, approval was muted or unexpressed, and people there sometimes suffered under the chauvinistic ardor of their neighbors. Indeed, one bad feature of the war years was the hate hysteria that swept the nation not only against innocent and patriotic German citizens but also against the German language and all things Germanic.

On May 18, 1917, Congress passed the Selective Service Act, and early in June Secretary of War N. D. Baker drew slip number one to begin the draft. My brother Neal, then twenty-two years old and in love with a young lady from Englewood, was one of the earlier draftees. I shall not forget the day he left the house to join the army. I myself became a member of the armed forces during World War II; but in the early 1940s we went in solitary privacy to our appointed posts. Things proceeded differently in 1917. The papers announced that the young draftees from a designated neighborhood would assemble on a certain street at a certain time and be marched in a group to the waiting train, which would carry them to their destination. Citizens gathered to cheer the recruits on; and to the accompaniment of flag waving and applause, the civilian-clad boys marched awkwardly but cheerfully off to war with the boisterous acclaim of the crowd ringing in their ears.

Neal was sent for training to Camp Grant near Rockford, Illinois, where members of the family were allowed to visit him on occasion. Having gone through the bare basics, he was shipped overseas in late 1917 and assigned to the army's Eleventh Machine Gun Battalion, a unit of the Fourth Division. My brother George, then but 17, had wished to join him; but he was not subject to the draft, and the officials would not accept his offer of enlistment.

Naturally, it was with some trepidation that my parents saw their son put on the khakis; yet the family shared in the general excitement engendered by the declaration of belligerence, and all of us did what we could to support the war effort. We patriotically heeded Herbert Hoover's admonition to preserve essential foods, and upon his advice we normally observed wheatless Mondays and Wednesdays, meatless Tuesdays, and porkless Thursdays and Saturdays. We planted no victory garden, as many people did, but Father bought some "Liberty Loan" bonds, and Mart and I bought a few "Thrift Stamps." We boys even put our alley junking habits into the service of our country. We had been told that peach pits were needed for the production of gas masks, so we scrounged as best we could to gather a supply of them.

My sisters helped the cause by assisting the Red Cross in preparing bandages for the wounded; and, though Father and Mother did not usually join the chorus, the rest of us often sang the war songs that could be heard everywhere — "Johnny Get Your Gun," "Goodbye Broadway, Hello France," "Keep the Homefires Burning," "The Yanks Are Coming," "Over There," and others.

Neal soon earned his sergeant's stripes, and while in command of a machine gun unit he fought at Chateau-Thierry, in the second battle of the Rhine, and at the St. Mihiel Salient. In one of these encounters he was gassed and subsequently briefly hospitalized; but he nevertheless took a belated part in the Meusse-Argonne offensive, which sealed the fate of the German forces.

The end of the war was signaled by Kaiser Wilhelm's flight to Doorn, The Netherlands, on November 9, 1918. On November 11 the armistice was signed in Marshal Foch's railway car in the Compiegne Forest. The jubilation that greeted that act knew no bounds. People in our neighborhood went berserk: they built a large bonfire late at night on the corner of 14th Place and Ashland, within a stone's throw of our house, and supplied fuel for it by gathering together every scrap of wood to be found in the vicinity and even by seizing unchained carts and wagons and wheeling them onto the fire. Gangs blocked the progress of the streetcars by sitting on the rails or by cutting the trailing trolley ropes with knives and scissors. Though none of our family participated in the destructive activity, as far as I know, we remained awed spectators of the scene for a very long time, and it was early morning when we retired to our beds.

When the turmoil of war had died down and winter had set in, the dreadful influenza of 1918 spread among the people. Our family fortunately escaped the worst effect of the disease; but there were several in our neighborhood who were laid low by the flu-induced pneumonia, and a number of them died.

*   *   *   *   *

The year 1919 can be said to have ushered in a new age. Woodrow Wilson's Fourteen Points relating to the establishment of democratic freedoms, the security of treaties, the cessation of war, and the reconstruction of Europe had already been ignored in the previous year by Britain's Lloyd George, France's George Clemenceau, and Italy's Vit-

47

torio Orlando. The harsh Treaty of Versailles that these three and a weakened Wilson imposed on the Germans proved to be the seedbed in which Hitler's Nazi tyranny later sprouted. An omen of coming days was the rise in Italy of Benito Mussolini in 1919: in the course of that year he organized his Fascists into a military force known as the "Black Shirts."

What did much to create the so-called Roaring Twenties was the October 1919 passage of the Volstead Act, which the following January imposed Prohibition on an unreceptive and uncooperative populace. There were no blacks in the immediate neighborhood of my youth, but their presence in Chicago and their sorry plight came vividly to our attention when, in July 1919, a four-day riot killed forty-two persons and injured 514 more. Although Jack Dempsey had not been in uniform during the war and was considered a "slacker" by some, most sports fans were elated when he won the world's heavyweight boxing crown that year. They were deeply saddened, however, when that fall the Chicago White Sox became the "Black Sox" by throwing the World Series through the gambling defection of key players. The Fundamentalist-Modernist controversy, which would dominate church life in the 1920s, was presaged by the establishment in 1919 of the World's Christian Fundamentals Association, and a certain denominational polarity came to expression with the appearance in the Christian Reformed Church of the magazine *The Witness* and its counterpart *Religion and Culture*. A personal highlight of the year was the September return of my brother Neal, who had served in the army of occupation until late August 1919 in Coblenz on the German Rhine.

Family festivities took place in the year 1920: on June 16, Neal married his long-time fiancée, Jennie Hoffman; and on August 25 my sister Gert married John Zeilstra. That year saw Warren Harding and his running mate, Calvin Coolidge, defeat the Democrat James Cox and the Socialist Eugene Debs for the presidency of the United States. It also witnessed the establishment of the League of Nations, as well as the growth of Calvin College into a four-year, degree-granting institution. Church life was disturbed in June by the deposition of Rev. Bultema for holding and publishing unacceptable premillennialist views.

On May 11, 1921, my brother George married Ann Rispens, and the couple took up residence in an apartment above Mr. Rispens' store.

The newspapers that year gave great publicity to the Sacco-Vanzetti murder case. Nicolo Sacco, an Italian shoe factory worker, and Bartolomeo Vanzetti, an Italian fish peddler, had been convicted of the murder of a Massachusetts paymaster and his guard; but charges of racial prejudice and judicial bias kept the matter in the courts and in the public domain for six long years thereafter. Of religious interest was the emergence that year of Frank Buchman's "Oxford Group," later named "Moral Rearmament"; and of parochial interest was the establishment of a missionary training school in Chicago that would in time develop into the Grand Rapids-based Reformed Bible College. In the early years of this institution, my brother George served as its treasurer.

On January 1, 1922, my father assumed the vice-presidency of the First Church consistory. I graduated from the eighth grade on January 26, and on August 2 my sister Jen married Henry Vander Molen. Seven of my brothers and sisters were now married, all of them to persons of Dutch extraction who held full membership in the Christian Reformed Church. All of them, except George and Ann, lived in the Crawford Avenue area, about three miles west of us, where they attended the Douglas Park Christian Reformed Church. Father and Mother were now grandparents of ten children, and I, at the age of thirteen, was an uncle ten times over.

So ended my grammar school days.

3

THE BUSINESS WORLD
(1922-1925)

All my brothers and sisters entered the work force immediately upon finishing grammar school. Except for Tom, who seems to have taken some evening classes while holding down his first job, none of them received a formal education extending beyond the eighth grade. This was not unusual in our community; indeed, it was the rule. I myself might very well have exemplified the rule had not a representative of a commercial school called on my parents and convinced them that what I needed was a business education.

Up to that time I had not much thought about what I would do after graduation. I simply supposed that I would find suitable employment somewhere. When I was still very young, I thought it would be nice to be a fireman and squirt volumes of water from large hoses, or to be a policeman and wear blue. When, somewhat later, I saw how cheerfully and expectantly the postman was greeted on his daily rounds, the delivery of mail appealed to me. I had noticed that to be a janitor in a church one needed to be old, and I therefore did not at this time contemplate assuming the role; but I did think it would be pleasant to move in solitude through every precinct of the church's cavernous interior and, between dustings, find time for meditation and reflection. But now that further education was in the offing, I cheerfully turned my mind in that direction.

Since I liked numbers, bookkeeping seemed suited to my talents;

and, since I found school life quite agreeable, I readily concurred in my parents' decision to send me for further development to the Chicago Business College. The institution with this pretentious name was, of course, not a college at all but a training school for adolescents seeking to acquire skills useful in the world of trade and commerce. It occupied the second floor of a large building located on the corner of 12th Street and Ogden Avenue. The school was about a mile from our house, and I reached it by foot along varying paths.

It was in mid-February of 1922 that I began my studies there, and I finished the prescribed course exactly one year later. I enjoyed the course in bookkeeping and the one in commercial law, but, being devoid of manual dexterity, I had some difficulty with the typewriter. I did finally learn the rudiments of typing, but I did not then, or ever thereafter, become proficient in it. This holds with greater force for shorthand. I learned how it was done, but I had no real aptitude for it, and I soon lost the meager ability that I acquired in it for want of practice and application.

For all of that, I do not consider that year wasted. I grew in appreciation for what stenographers and typists do, and I learned something of what goes on in business offices, although at that time neither I nor any of my instructors envisioned an office equipped with computers, word processors, copying machines, and other such mysterious instruments. I also gained experience in social intercourse. I had hitherto associated almost exclusively with boys of Dutch descent who shared with me a common faith. I was now thrown into a group of people of diverse national origins and creedal orientations. I mingled daily with Jews, Poles, Germans, Greeks, Italians, and others, many of whom lived by standards quite unlike my own. And then there were the girls. They greatly outnumbered us boys, and some of them were flirtatious. I possessed few manly charms and displayed no romantic inclinations, but a blond-haired Dutch boy must have appeared to a curious few as a creature from another world, and more than one of the girls tried to involve me in after-school activities. I was tempted several times to accompany a pretty Jewish girl on her way home, but I invariably thought better of it and went my solitary way. What I gained or lost by such behavior I have not tried to calculate.

The course of instruction drew to a close just after 1922 was spent, and in that year a number of things occurred that affected my life and my family's in various ways. I don't remember whether it was in 1922 or earlier that my father quit the cinder business and went in search of outside employment; in any case, he was now working as a custodian in Marshall Field's downtown department store, and he continued to do so until the day he died. We were gladdened when three more infants were drawn into the family circle during that year, but were all cast into sorrow in May, when Bill and Tillie's seven-year-old daughter Annie died after a lingering illness. In August we celebrated the marriage of my sister Jen in a gala reception held in the Stege house basement. Some time later, with only Mart and myself living with them in the large Stege house, my parents decided to move the family into smaller quarters. Accordingly, they bought a two-story frame house on 13th Street, between Robey (now Damon) and Leavitt Streets, and in mid-October we moved into it. It was a very modest dwelling, quite unlike the one we had vacated. It was close to adjoining houses, being separated from them by narrow planked gangways in need of repair. Two front doors led into the two apartments, and uncovered wooden stairs provided access in the rear. In a backyard of sparse grass stood a small cottage, which we rented out to a Dutch family by the name of Bos. We occupied the upper story, and George and Ann, who had vacated their Ashland Avenue apartment, soon moved into the lower. I now lived considerably closer to the school — and also closer than I would have otherwise to the place where I would shortly be working.

The First Church congregation to which we belonged had earlier moved into the Ashland Avenue building inherited from the Lutherans.It had also by that time introduced a Sunday morning English worship service, which Dr. Van Lonkhuyzen conducted with a noticeable Dutch brogue, his "brethren and cistern" often evoking our laughter. Among the organizations active in the church was a young men's society, which had taken for its motto the Latin "Ora et Labora." It enlisted young men ranging in ages from sixteen or seventeen to twenty-one and older. This left us younger fellows out in the cold, and we decided to do something about it. After securing consistorial approval, we organized a junior young men's society that consisted of fourteen- and fifteen-year-olds. Having kept the motto "Ora et Labora," we met biweekly for Bible study and capped the meeting with an after-recess period in which we discussed whatever issues happened to interest us. For no reason other than that I was vocal in proposing the organization of this new society, I was asked to serve as president of the group.

We were not unaware in 1922 of the things that were happening around us. We noticed, for example, the renewed flareup of the Fundamentalist-Modernist controversy. In May, Harry Emerson Fosdick preached a sermon in the First Presbyterian Church of New York and subsequently published it under the title "Shall the Fundamentalists Win?" This received a response in July from Clarence E. Macartney, who published an article in *The Presbyterian* entitled "Shall Unbelief Win?" An echo of this controversy was heard in the Christian Reformed Church: in June of that year, Synod removed Prof. Janssen from his chair of Old Testament Studies at the Calvin Theological Seminary on the grounds that he held and propagated liberal views concerning the Bible's presumed inerrancy.

In politics, suspicions arose about corruption in the Harding Administration when intimations of the Tea Pot Dome scandal became public. It was in that year, too, that the international community was stunned by the seizure of Italy's government by the Fascists under Mussolini. Some, if not all, of these developments came under review in our juvenile society.

*   *   *   *   *

I don't remember just how it happened, but sometime in February 1923 I found myself in the employ of Mr. Eisner, the proprietor and manager of the Chicago Machine and Washer Company. I most likely got the job after Mr. Eisner asked at the school whether a tolerable office boy could be found among its recent graduates. In any case, I was hired in that capacity.

The business with this impressive name had been established in a small one-story, flat-roofed shop located on a residential street near Ogden Avenue and 15th Street, in the shadow of the huge Ryerson Steel plant on Western Avenue. It employed no more than five or six shop workers, and it specialized in making metal washers, which were produced on manned punch presses activated by overhanging canvas belts. It made other things as well, such as angle irons and related steel and iron products, but washers were the mainstay. In the front of the shop and to one side was a small bedroom-sized office that contained a filing cabinet and two desks, a large roll-topped one for

54

the boss and a smaller flat-topped one for me. One office door opened to the outside, another to the shop, and a third to a small closet containing a toilet and a wash basin. The latter facility was reserved for use by the "office staff," since another larger one, together with a lengthy wash trough, was established in the workmen's area.

When I began my work at this company, I was a little over fourteen and a half years old and still in knee pants. Upon reporting for duty, I was courteously greeted by Mr. Eisner and always treated kindly thereafter. It was not long before the shop workers also adopted me as a full member of their small and rather close-knit working community. I walked to work, carried my lunch, and normally ate with the other employees during the noon break. I learned in these lunch sessions a good deal about how the shop operated, and this helped me in the performance of my office duties.

My chief responsibility at the outset was to man the phone and convey messages to the boss who, in his role as manager, spent a considerable part of the day in the shop. I took occasional dictation, typed some letters, and sent out monthly bills. But I was also charged with keeping the premises clean: this meant not only that I was to sweep the office floor, dust the furniture, and keep the closet toilet bowl and sink immaculate; it also meant that I was to keep on hand a sufficient quantity of soaps, towels, and hand rags to meet the workers' needs.

I stayed on the job for two and a half years. When I left, I was no longer a callow youth but a strapping young man who had already passed his seventeenth birthday. In the course of thirty months, things do not remain the same, and with the passage of time my duties and responsibilities gradually and quite naturally increased. In the end, I came to write checks for the boss's signature, to dun customers for the payment of bills I sent them, to order steel sheets and bars from Ryerson's and reproach them for shipping delays, to prepare schedules for the prompt fulfillment of orders, to make up payrolls, and generally to monitor production — all of this, of course, under the supervision of Mr. Eisner, with whom I enjoyed the most cordial relations.

I don't remember what I was earning toward the end of my stay, but I know that I was originally hired at $18.00 a week. This was, I thought, a generous wage, and though it did not make us rich, it helped the family to maintain a comfortable living. During the period of my employment — from February 1923 to August 1925 — I did not much heed what was happening in the larger business world, but the economy was apparently flourishing. The Harding administration favored big business, and the Supreme Court, dominated as it was by Harding-appointed justices, lent support to laissez-faire capitalism by, among other things, killing a federal child-labor law and invalidating a minimum wage law for women. Yet the workers did not seem to be hurting. Growing prosperity was everywhere in evidence. The land boom in Florida drew ever-increasing numbers of investors, and the rising stock market tempted many to play the Wall Street gambling game.

In these years the automobile was steadily replacing the horse-drawn carriage, with the result that the automobile industry — and especially the Ford Motor Company — experienced a phenomenal growth. Although our family could not afford a car, and never owned one, a Ford Roadster could be purchased in 1925 for as little as $260.00, and millions of these and other "flivvers" were sold during my working days.

The landscape changed when the motor car began crowding the wagons off the streets. Service stations and garages proliferated, and new roads were laid to accommodate the growing traffic. But beyond that, social customs also changed. Highways and country lanes drew people out of their houses, shifted romance from the front porch to the back seat of the car, and replaced the men-only corner saloon with the isolated roadside tavern, where the prying eyes of neighbors could be safely avoided.

*   *   *   *   *

In 1923, during the first year of my employment, I celebrated my fifteenth birthday and became the uncle of two more children born into the family circle. It was also in that year that George and Ann decided, with my father's reluctant approval, to sever relations with the First Christian Reformed Church and to join the newly organized English-speaking Chicago IV Church, then pastored by its first minister, Rev. Herman Bel.

What lifted our theological spirits was the publication in that year of J. Gresham Machen's *Christianity and Liberalism*, which laid bare the weaknesses of theological modernism and significantly advanced the orthodox Christian cause. But what mostly engaged our attention

56

was the Michigan proposal to outlaw all private and parochial schools. Several of our local leaders joined Calvin College's faculty and students in opposing the contemplated action, and we all rejoiced when the proposal was overwhelmingly defeated in a public referendum. It is interesting to observe that while this contest was raging in Michigan, the state of Maine passed a law requiring the reading of the Bible in all public schools.

On the national scene, the year 1923 saw the initial publication of *Time* magazine, the discovery of insulin, the first nonstop transcontinental flight, the emergence of a young tennis champion by the name of Helen Wills, and a movement on the part of the National Women's party to add an equal rights amendment to the Constitution. That year was also marked by the death of a national leader: an undistinguished and scandal-ridden presidency came to an end when, on August 2, Warren G. Harding died in San Francisco from the effects of an embolism. Calvin Coolidge, his taciturn vice president, assumed the presidency on August 3. Laconic in speech and somewhat somnolent in appearance, he presided over a placid and business-oriented administration until near the end of the decade.

Virtually unnoticed in the United States but ominous in its forebodings of the future was the 1923 publication of Adolph Hitler's *Mein Kampf.* Imprisoned after the failure of the Munich *Putsch,* Hitler composed the book while in custody, dictating most it to Rudolf Hess. In it he laid bare his plans for the conversion of a stricken, impoverished, and downcast Germany into a proud and powerful Aryan Reich from which all Semitic influences would be resolutely banned and in which the Judeo-Christian value system would, in Nietzsche-like fashion, be degraded or ignored.

During the early and middle twenties the American social scene displayed signs of moral retrogression and decay. The popularization of Sigmund Freud's work induced many persons, especially the young, to let themselves "go." It was widely believed that no natural instinct or random impulse should be repressed lest a psychosis develop. One was to live without inhibitions, according to no objective standard, and without an oppressive sense of guilt. No desire was to be suppressed, no pleasure denied. Self-expression was in, and restraint was out.

Perhaps most marked in this situation was a decline in sexual mores. Advertisers exploited the sexual allure of young women in order to sell their products. In appearance and lifestyle the more "advanced" among the young women bore little resemblance to their elders. Slimness was popular, and all strove desperately to acquire a boyish figure. They abandoned corsets, taped down their breasts, raised the hemlines of their skirts, bobbed their hair, rolled down their stockings, applied rouge and lipstick, smoked cigarettes in public, drank illegal gin in "speakeasies," and danced endlessly to the sound of blaring jazz saxophones. In all of this they were, of course, aided and abetted by "liberated" young men who, no less than they, had cast off the shackles of what they regarded as an antedated Victorian lifestyle and an outmoded and intolerable code of moral behavior.

This world of unrestricted license was not one that we inhabited. We observed it with distaste from a distance and lived as best we could in Christian "separation." But we could not wholly insulate ourselves from the power and attraction of changing fashion, and women in our community were before long bobbing their hair, using lipstick, and wearing abbreviated skirts. Dancing, night clubbing, booze swilling, and sexual promiscuity were, however, not in their style nor in that of their male companions. Speaking generally, the life of our community continued to be lived under the moral restraints imposed by God's law. We heard the Ten Commandments recited every Sunday morning, and it was hard for conscientious persons not to heed them.

*   *   *   *   *

In the year 1924 there were at least two developments in the religious world that came to the attention of our people and produced concern among them. The first served to widen the breach between fundamentalists and modernists, and it occurred when many "liberal" Presbyterian ministers signed the Auburn Affirmation. The second caused a split in the Christian Reformed Church; at issue was the "doctrine" of common grace. The Synod of 1924 elevated it to the level of dogma by making it a tenet of the church: Synod declared that a certain grace of God is imparted to all men, a grace that furnishes them with various gifts and talents, restrains the generality of them from committing the more heinous sins, and enables all of them to cultivate virtues and do civic good. Two ministers, Herman Hoeksema and Ralph Danhof, had for some years before this contended against the Kuyperian doctrine of common grace, and they now refused to endorse Synod's

58

affirmation of it, whereupon they were deposed by their respective classes. They took with them most members of their congregations and, together with a number of other ministers, formed the Protestant Reformed Church. An independently run magazine, *The Standard Bearer*, made its appearance in October 1924 and became the journalistic voice of the new denomination.

On the national front, the Teapot Dome scandal continued to make news. Albert B. Fall, whom President Harding had appointed Secretary of Interior, was charged with accepting bribes from oilmen Harry F. Sinclair and Edward L. Doheny, to whom he had leased lands holding vast oil reserves. All three of these men were indicted for criminal activity in 1924. H. L. Mencken, the "bad boy of Baltimore" who became the nation's chief literary debunker, burst upon the scene when his *American Mercury* made its appearance in January 1924. Russia was in the news when in that same month Nicolay Lenin died and was succeeded by Josef Stalin.

In June of that year I celebrated my sixteenth birthday, and my passing that milestone coincided with a deepening of my religious awarenesses and sensitivities. I dare not say that in the months before and after that turning point I underwent a conversion. I had been baptized into the Christian faith, I never doubted any of the Reformed tenets, and even when I went astray, I felt obligated by the Bible's moral prescriptions. But I had not hitherto made a conscious personal commitment to the Lord, and this I now did. The surrender was accompanied by struggle and deep emotion. For days on end I would rise from my bed in the middle of the night and kneel in fervent prayer beside the sofa in the living room. And I began to read the Bible regularly, John's gospel in particular. I also turned to books on theology and related matters: I read Bosma's *Reformed Doctrine,* Kuyper's *To Be Near Unto God,* Bryan's volume on evolution, and I searched diligently through Matthew Henry's commentaries.

Having experienced God's grace and found peace in my soul, I felt I should make public profession of my faith before the congregation. I had not attended any preconfessional training classes at the church; I doubt that they existed among us. In any case, it was arranged that I should be examined by the consistory on August 25. I appeared with some trepidation before a roomful of solemn men, one of whom was my father. But I must have given a tolerable account of my knowledge, sentiments, and intentions, for after a lengthy interview I was declared a candidate for admission to the church and to the table of the Lord. I made public profession of my faith in the First Church on Sunday morning, October 5, 1924. That day my parents presented me with a gold open-faced pocket watch, which, with matching chain, I wore in the vest pocket of the long-trousered suit into which I had by now graduated.

*   *   *   *   *

When Bruce Barton's book *The Man Nobody Knows* appeared in the book stalls during the course of 1925, I secured a copy of it but found little satisfaction in reading it. The book depicted Jesus as a salesman and his twelve disciples as trained admen who by persuasion and technical ploys gained for Christianity an almost universal hearing and adherence. Placed in the context of modern business practice, the veritable Christ of truth and grace was largely obscured in the book, appearing instead predominantly as a paradigm to be followed by ambitious purveyors of material goods.

The year 1925 also saw the organization of the League of Evangelical Students in Pittsburgh, the inauguration of Charles E. Fuller's "Old Fashioned Revival Hour" radio broadcast, and the platform antics of the noted evangelist W. A. ("Billy") Sunday. What, however, engaged the attention of almost everyone in the nation was the Scopes trial in Dayton, Tennessee. The state of Tennessee had adopted a law prohibiting the teaching of evolution in the public schools, and John T. Scopes, a high school teacher of biology, was indicted for breaking the law. Pitted against each other in court were two famous lawyers and prominent public figures, Clarence Darrow for the defense and William Jennings Bryan for the prosecution. Bryan won a guilty verdict, but the liberal press depicted him as a buffoon, and, because the distinguished protagonist of the Genesis account failed to distinguish between creation and development, the fundamentalist cause suffered a significant setback. Mr. Bryan, greatly taxed by the demands of a trial conducted in an overheated courtroom, died five days after the trial ended.

The Volstead Act prohibiting the manufacture and sale of alcoholic beverages had been in effect for nearly five years now, but the prohibition was observed largely in the breach. Liquor was smuggled into the country from Canada and the West Indies, and it was produced locally and clandestinely in the many undercover breweries that had sprung up all across the country. "Bathtub gin" was even made at home and peddled in secret to friends and neighbors. Most sales were made, however, in private clubs and in "speakeasies" secured behind barred doors. One gained entrance into the latter establishments by whispering a password through the grilled windows with which they were usually furnished. Hip flasks filled with bootleg liquor and home-made "rotgut" became a popular clothing accessory. People, it seemed, developed a thirst that grew in inverse proportion to its lessened availability on the open market, and they quenched it by barhopping in dark and secret places.

Control of the liquor traffic fell naturally into the hands of outlaws, who organized themselves into heavily armed gangs determined to protect their turf against any rival who might dare to invade their territory. Rivalry, competition, and aggrandizement existed, of course, and the consequence of this was gang warfare. In 1925 — and for six years thereafter — "Scarface" Al Capone was one of Chicago's most notorious gang leaders. But he was not alone. Others, like Johnny Torrio and Dion O'Banion, figured often in the news, and none of these gangsters hesitated to commit murder in order to corner the market in illegal booze.

*   *   *   *   *

It was sometime in the spring of 1925, when I was approaching my seventeenth birthday, that I decided to return to school and study for the gospel ministry. I did not take the decision lightly. I had thought about the matter for many months and had often discussed it with my parents, brothers, and sisters. All of these good people enthusiastically endorsed the plan and urged me to proceed. So I gave notice to Mr. Eisner that I would be leaving his employ in mid-August, and when the appointed time arrived, I bade him and my fellow employees a fond farewell — and never saw any of them again.

In an effort to secure additional funds for my education, I applied for aid to Classis Illinois, which was wont to financially support qual-ified students in its region who were preparing or about to prepare for the Christian Reformed ministry. I appeared before Classis at its meeting in May 1925. After being interviewed for a considerable time, I was handed some sheets of paper and a pencil and told to go to the basement of the church and prepare, in the course of one hour, an essay on the subject of "divine revelation." I worked on the assignment as best I could, and when the hour had elapsed, I presented the chairman with what I had written. After the paper had been read to the assembled delegates, I was voted a yearly stipend of two hundred dollars and cordially dismissed. It was sometime during that spring that I wrote a short piece on "Sorrow and Joy" and took some pleasure in seeing it in print when it appeared in the May issue of *The Young Calvinist*.

My parents and my brother Mart did everything they could to further my plans. They even uprooted themselves. In order to facilitate my attendance at the Christian high school, Father sold our house on 13th Street and bought another at 7130 South May Street, very near the school I was to attend. The four of us moved into our new quarters in August 1925, a short time before the September opening of school.

We did not feel like strangers in our new neighborhood. My father's brother (Uncle Martin) and his large family lived nearby, as did my father's sister (Aunt Nellie Rudinga) and her many children. We had in the past visited these relatives often, and my cousins George, John, and Bill Stob, as well as Bill Rudinga, had frequently played against us in the intracity church baseball league. Mart and I now made peace with our erstwhile opponents, offered them the benefit of our athletic talents, and did in fact join forces with them. What is more, my brother Neal and his family lived in the neighborhood, and it was a pleasure to be near him and his wife and infant daughter.

As soon as we were settled, we joined the First Christian Reformed Church of Englewood, and we took an active part in its proceedings. Rev. Isaac Westra was the pastor of the church, and my brother Neal was a member of the council, a deacon.

So ended my days spent in the business world.

4

HIGH SCHOOL DAYS
(1925-1928)

The Chicago Christian High School had been established in 1918 and graduated its first class of commercial students in 1920. The first class of students taking the four-year college preparatory course graduated in 1922; of the twenty-nine students graduating, four were immediately hired as grade school teachers, and two went on to college.

Mr. James De Boer was the first president of the board, and he may fairly be considered the founder of the school. Prominent in the life of the First Christian Reformed Church and president of the Ebenezer School Board for a quarter of a century, he early on recognized that the Christian educational system needed an institution of learning that would bridge the gap between grade school and college. Others shared his vision, of course, and after many years of discussion and planning, the Christian Reformed people in Chicagoland determined to establish a high school. Although the greatest push came from the people in my old neighborhood, the board decided to locate the school in an area calculated to attract students coming not only from the old West Side but also from Englewood, Roseland, South Holland, Evergreen Park, Lansing, Munster, Hammond, and other nearby Dutch settlements. Englewood was finally chosen as the site. This precinct of Chicago adjoined Roseland and was in reach of the outlying Dutch communities. Moreover, two large Christian Reformed Churches and a Reformed Church were located there, and these institutions, espe-

Chicago Christian High School

cially the former, could be counted on to provide strong support for the new venture.

The beginnings were modest. The first classes were held in a common dwelling. When the number of students increased, the school was moved into rented rooms situated above some stores on 69th and May Streets. The school was located there when I enrolled on September 8, 1925. The student body then numbered about 150, and it was served by six teachers. Mark Fakkema was the principal, and he taught Bible and citizenship; Jacob Sietsema taught Latin and elementary algebra; Henry Swets taught history, archaeology, and geometry; John De Boer taught grammar, composition, English and American literature, and speech; and Harry Mouw taught general science, physiology, botany, and physics. Adriana Hammekool was the only woman on the faculty. She taught commercial subjects and occasionally assisted in mathematics. I took no courses with her, thus retaining my record of never having been instructed by a female teacher.

Since I was already seventeen years old when I entered the school, I sought permission to take additional courses each semester with a view to completing the four-year college preparatory course in three years; permission was granted, and I was able to anticipate graduating in June 1928.

*   *   *   *   *

At the outset of the 1925-26 school year I knew very few of my fellow students. I knew Harold Vander Velde, a freshman like me, because we grew up together on the old West Side. He was three years older than I, but we became fast friends during our high school days. Two men in the junior class — John Vander Meer and John Smilde — were also advanced in years, and this tended to bring us together; and then

64

Englewood friends
L. to R.: Fred Tigchelaar, Neal Vander Schoot, Henry Stob,
Jake Tigchelaar, George De Vries

there was my cousin, George Stob, who at eighteen was a senior and would leave for college the next year. We knew each other well; I would often visit him and his brothers at his parents' house on 73rd and Aberdeen in Englewood. I had that year very little association with the rest of the students, although in later years I came to associate in varying ways with Harry Elders, Nick Blystra, Jack Zandstra, and Angeline Nydam. I enjoyed the instruction and addressed myself to my studies with diligence and élan. I have no memory of engaging in any after-school activities. There was a basketball team, I know, but I was not a candidate for it. Generously laden down with overnight assignments, I was wont in those days to return home right after school and repair to the room set aside for me there. Furnished with a desk and with ample book shelves, it was here that in undisturbed solitude I could prepare for the next day's class sessions.

I was sufficiently involved in the affairs of the school to prepare a short essay entitled "A Challenge" for publication in the school annual. I believe that I pleaded in it for an alliance between faith and reason or for what may be called "Christian Scholarship." Another small writing of mine appeared in the January 1926 issue of *The Young Calvinist*. Someone had earlier published a defense of the "flapper," maintaining that "making up" is an art that produces wonderful results — "the ugly are made fair and the comely are made pretty." I opined that to plant a red splash across one's mouth and to make one's cheekbones resemble a rose was ill-calculated to enhance one's looks. But that, I said, was a matter of taste, and I was not concerned to outlaw lipstick and rouge. What bothered me about the "flapper" was her disrespect for convention, her ostentatious revolt against custom, her scandalizing of community mores, her posturing independence, her scorning of traditional values, and her basic licentiousness. I did not put it quite like that at the time, but that was the idea, and I still think that the "flapper" of the mid-1920s was hardly a paradigm of Christian womanhood.

Our small family went to church regularly, and my brother Mart and I joined the church's active young men's society. Here we struck up close friendships, Mart with fellows of his age and I with those of mine. Five of us soon formed ourselves into a close-knit group — Jack Tigchelaar and his brother Fred, George De Vries, Neal Vander Schoot, and myself. We didn't see too much of each other during the week, but we invariably spent the whole of Sunday together. We met at church in the morning, went home for dinner, and gathered about two o'clock at one or another's house, where we later ate supper and thereafter walked in company to church for the evening worship service. We took turns. On a given Sunday either Mrs. Tigchelaar, or Mrs. De Vries, or Mrs. Vander Schoot, or Mrs. Stob could expect five hungry young men to sit at her supper table. What we did on summer afternoons was sit on the porch and talk, though we would sometimes walk and talk. On winter afternoons we talked indoors and sometimes gathered about the piano and sang songs. And we smoked. All of us had pipes and tobacco pouches, and quite often we even resorted to cigars. After the evening service, the romantically inclined occasionally sought the attention of some girl; but in that first year at least, we normally drifted singly or in pairs to our respective homes, there to visit with our parents and prepare for the coming week's work.

High School Days (1925-1928)

We discussed religion, world affairs, sports, girls, and whatever came to mind. In 1925, the Scopes trial and the problem of evolution drew our attention, as well as the rise of Al Capone and the emerging gang warfare in the city. We noted that Red Grange had joined the Chicago Bears under coach George Halas, and that the Tribune Tower had finally been completed. We witnessed the inauguration of Father Charles Coughlin's notorious and "rightist" radio broadcasts in 1926; and we were led to reflect on the sabbath question when we learned that a minister of the Christian Reformed Church, Rev. H. Wierenga, had been defrocked in June of that year for holding deviant views on sabbath observance.

I was not idle during the summer of 1926. My brother Tom was credit manager at the Thomas S. Smith wholesale produce store on Chicago's South Water Market, then located near 15th Street and Blue Island Avenue, and he secured a job for me at the store. I began working there as soon as school let out. I was given a desk in the upstairs office and was assigned the duties of an accounts clerk. For most of that summer I handled the asparagus accounts, thereafter those pertaining to peppers and tomatoes. Tom resigned his position in mid-August and established, with his brother-in-law, the real estate firm of Hendrikse and Stob. But I stayed on until Labor Day and was invited to return the next summer. As it turned out, I worked at Smith's every summer for the next nine years.

*   *   *   *   *

When my second year of high school began on September 7, 1926, we were still meeting in the old cramped upper rooms at 69th and May Streets, but a commodious brick building featuring spacious classrooms, a library, a laboratory, a gymnasium, and a large auditorium was in the process of construction on the corner of 71st and May Streets, and we looked forward to moving into it. In that academic year, I was listed as a junior and so had crept up on such seniors as John Vander Meer, John Smilde, John Rottier, Abe Van Kampen, Peter De Vries, and Ann Geerdes. My junior classmates included Harold Vander Velde, Syd Youngsma, Henry Evenhouse, George Vander Werken, Joe Jellema, Ray Hofstra, Bertha Prince, Cecilia Ottenhoff, and twelve other students with whom I associated less frequently and more casually.

67

Literary Club Officers
Peter De Vries, John Smilde, Henry Stob, John De Boer

Our new principal and Bible teacher, Mr. J. Bajema, had replaced Mr. Fakkema, who in June of 1926 had accepted an appointment as director of the recently established National Association of Christian Schools. Miss Hazel Bode was the other newcomer on the faculty; she joined Miss Hammekool in the commercial department.

I now became involved in the extracurricular affairs of the school. Early in the year, a literary club was organized, and Peter De Vries, who later became a distinguished novelist, was elected president; Mr. De Boer was the faculty sponsor, and I served as vice president. The ten members of the club held biweekly meetings at which we read book reports and considered the various phases of literary production such as style, content, setting, and so forth.

With the new gym on the horizon, the students anticipated a marked growth in athletic activities and decided to form an all-school athletic association. At an October meeting I was asked to serve as president of the association; Peter De Vries was elected secretary, and John Smilde was named treasurer. Part of the work of the association was to locate suitable places for basketball practice. When our new gym was ready for use, the association conducted a vigorous fundraising campaign and collected $900.00. The money was used to purchase needed gym equipment.

About this time, Mr. De Boer, the debate coach, issued a call for debaters, and I responded to the call. After tryouts, six of us were selected for the two three-member teams, and I was asked to serve as captain of the group; Peter De Vries, John Rottier, and I constituted the affirmative team, and Robert Van Kampen, Helen Zwiers, and Ann Geerdes constituted the negative team. At issue was the granting of immediate independence to the Philippines. Only two formal debates were held that year, both in Michigan, one against Grand Rapids Christian High School and one against Holland Christian High, on December 15 and 16, 1926. The negative team defeated Holland by a score of 3-0, but lost to Grand Rapids by a score of 1-2. The affirmative team beat both Michigan schools by a score of 3-0.

I was practiced in baseball, but I had never up to that time had a basketball in my hands. But I was 5 feet 11 inches tall and, because the junior varsity needed a center, I volunteered to play. I made my first appearance on the floor on February 4, 1927, just before our new gym became available. We played a number of games thereafter and my skills gradually improved, but the scores we posted that year would scandalize the present generation: we won and lost by scores of 11-8, 14-6, 4-19, 20-19, 15-12, 18-19, 9-30, 15-12, and 22-14. Members of the Junior Varsity were John Rottier, John Baan, Ray Hofstra, Syd Youngsma, Ray Prince, James Erickson, and myself.

I had nothing to do with the publication of the school annual that year — such work was reserved for seniors — but I did write a short piece for the literary section. It was entitled "Boys" and had something to do with the effervescence of young blood.

We moved into our spacious new school building on March 9, 1927, and we were all on hand when the dedicatory services took place on the 10th. It was a time of great rejoicing and an occasion for giving thanks to God, for the building was wonderfully adapted to our needs. Mr. L. Dykema was the school janitor, and the move into larger quarters had greatly increased his workload. We lived comfortably at home, but my family was not affluent, and to help defray the expenses of my present and future education I took on the job of assistant janitor. Beginning in mid-March, 1927, I helped Mr. Dykema by sweeping the floors every day after school. When basketball practice

*Henry
the Haberdasher*

or a committee meeting intervened, I either hired a replacement or worked overtime.

Eager to reduce the financial burden on my parents, I had previously taken on another job. Early in that academic year I learned that the owner of a men's haberdashery shop on 69th and Halsted Streets was looking for a salesperson to help him serve the Saturday trade. I applied for and got the job. Beginning in October 1926, I worked in the store every Saturday from nine in the morning until nine at night. We did not stock suits but dealt in such clothing accessories as shirts, ties, belts, suspenders, hats, gloves, handkerchiefs, scarves, socks, spats, and the like. I stayed on the job until the school term ended, at which time I resumed my full-time summer employment at Thomas S. Smith's.

My association with the church's young men's society continued

70

*Henry
the Basketball
Player*

that year, and I was privileged to be sent as a delegate to the seventh annual convention of the American Federation of Reformed Young Men's Societies, held in Grand Rapids on November 3 and 4, 1926. Here I met young men from across the country and also such church leaders as H. J. Kuiper, Louis Berkhof, and Henry Keegstra.

My life at home during that year was quite uneventful. I continued to associate with my friends from church, and we tended to carry on as we had before. Our family circle increased when John Vander Meer joined us as a boarder. He was then a senior at the high school and was preparing for the ministry; he was a kind and gentle man and we profited from his presence. Mart entered on a new career when he began to cut and sell meat in Mr. Kamp's butcher shop at 72nd and Sangamon Streets. Mart had also formed new friendships, and he often brought his friends home for coffee and games. Guest traffic was indeed constant at our house, especially since my married brothers and sisters and their children frequently came to visit.

Our daily occupation did not keep us from observing the happenings around us or from sensing the drift of things and being alerted to the current climate of opinion. We noticed, for example, that the Ku Klux Klan was growing in numbers and influence, and we deplored its reign of hooded violence and black lynchings in the South. Although we ourselves were not the beneficiaries of the growing prosperity, we were aware not only that business was flourishing but that, governed by a laissez-faire mentality, it was characterized by cutthroat competition, uncontrolled speculation, and a lust for gain untempered by moral considerations. I had earlier read Sinclair Lewis's *Babbitt,* and at school we had been introduced to F. Scott Fitzgerald's *The Great Gatsby.* The pictures these books painted of our achievement-oriented society were not heartening.

What characterized the middle years of the 1920s more than anything else was a fervent and outspoken pacifism. I myself fell under the spell of the antiwar propaganda, partly because it was vociferous and widespread and partly because my teacher, John De Boer, was a persuasive spokesman for the abolition of war and for the rise of a weaponless society. Government action reflected the spirit of the times. The nations that had been allied against the central powers in the Great War were busily engaged in dismantling their war machines and confidently proclaiming a holiday on the manufacture of munitions and the construction of new implements of war. This was taking place just when Italy was growing in military might and when Hitler was planning to transform Germany into a totalitarian state bent on conquest.

Sports happenings of some significance occurred that year. Gene Tunney won the heavyweight boxing crown by defeating Jack Dempsey on September 4, 1926, and in 1927 Babe Ruth hit a record-making sixty home runs. More importantly, on May 20-21, 1927, Charles

Lindbergh flew solo and nonstop from Long Island to Paris in the single-engine *Spirit of St. Louis;* and sometime during that year Henry Ford introduced to the public his Model-A motor car. The year also witnessed the electrocution of Sacco and Vanzetti.

* * * * *

On September 7, 1927, I reported for my third and final year of high school instruction. After working all summer and riding long distances in crowded streetcars, it was a joy to be back at school. I was happy to see old friends, to greet new students, and to be engaged again in study and play. The imposing new building, unsullied in its newness, was in itself attractive, and it stood only a short half-block from our house, a fact that carried with it a number of obvious advantages. Also, college was now but a year away, and the prospect of entering it in the not-too-distant future lifted my spirits.

There were changes in the faculty. Mr. Bajema had left, and Dr. Frederick H. Wezeman had assumed the principalship. Miss Bode had also left and had been replaced in the commercial department by Mr. Arthur Lanning. The number of faculty members rose to nine with the accession of Mr. William Kooistra, who had been appointed to teach mathematics, and of Miss Effie Zwier, who was engaged to teach English and German languages. The janitorial staff had also increased in size. Assisting Mr. Dykema that year was Mr. Busch and, on a part-time basis, the aged Mr. Koelikamp. With these additions, my mopping and dusting came to an end. This was a boon, for I was about to take on more work than a sensible student should. That year I took twenty hours of English with Mr. De Boer, mostly in English and American literature, ten hours of Latin II with Mr. Sietsema, ten hours of History III with Mr. Swets, twelve hours of physics with Mr. Mouw, and one hour of Bible with Dr. Wezeman.

There were now about 200 students enrolled in the school, forty-three of them in their last year of residence. At a class meeting held to elect officers, the seniors chose Harold Vander Velde as vice president and Sydney Youngsma as secretary, and I was asked to serve as class president. The school had hitherto had no student council, and it was now decided to establish one. Five members from each of the four classes were selected to constitute the council, and for no reason other than that I was a senior in office, I was chosen to act as president.

In the wake of these developments, a roller-coaster effect dragged me irresistibly into additional student offices. Since I had been president of the all-school athletic association the year before, the students found it easier to keep me on the job than to seek the improvement that others could provide. Something similar could be said about the boys' literary club. I had previously been vice president of this thirteen-member body, and now my kindly associates felt that the only courteous thing to do was to elevate me to its presidency. I balked a little when I was asked to be editor-in-chief of the school annual, but I was honored by the appointment, and after some hesitation I accepted the assignment.

While all this was going on, Mr. De Boer appointed me captain of the debating teams, and Mr. Swets was about to put me at center on the varsity basketball squad. What these extracurricular activities would do to my curricular standing I didn't know; but there was a backlog of decent grades and I thought I could squeeze by even though Saturdays afforded me no leisure because I had already resumed employment at the Halsted Street haberdashery.

The newly established student council got off to a good start. Twenty members sat on the council, and the presence of so many representative students at every sitting was in itself conducive to class intimacy and cooperation. What made the whole thing work as well as it did was the presence at our meetings of the faculty sponsor, Dr. Wezeman. He not only instructed us in parliamentary procedures but also raised many issues bearing on the relation between faculty and students.

The athletic association, with Alice Bos as vice president and Grace Dykstra as secretary, served the school by again conducting a fundraising campaign. With the money collected that year we were able to furnish the gym balcony with a considerable number of spectator seats. The association also brought into existence a girl's basketball team, the first in the school's history. The boys' literary club, with Raymond Hofstra as secretary and Mr. De Boer as faculty sponsor, held regular biweekly meetings, at which we learned quite a bit about English composition and literary criticism. One feature of our meetings was the "open forum," in which any member could introduce for discussion whatever subject he chose.

The production of a school annual is an arduous and time-consuming task, and one is unlikely to undertake it twice. Fortunately, I was assisted on the editorial side by ten willing workers, and Harold Vander Velde, who managed the business end, had three competent assistants. The book was dedicated to John De Boer, the memory of whom still inspires those who sat in his stimulating English classes. A "nonsense rhyme" in the annual represented my first feeble attempt at writing poetry.

Owing to the excellence of Mr. De Boer's coaching, the debating teams enjoyed a successful season. The proposition that year was "Resolved that the House endorse the governmental principles of Benito Mussolini." The negative team, arguing against the proposition, consisted of Sydney Youngsma, Elizabeth Ottenhoff, and Grace Dykstra. The affirmative team, arguing for the proposition, consisted of Bertha Prince, Elizabeth Geerdes, and myself. We engaged in eight debates against four schools — the Luther Institute of Chicago, the Central YMCA Preparatory College, Holland Christian High, and Grand Rapids Christian High — and we won eight victories, seven of them by a 3-0 score.

Under Mr. Swets's coaching, the basketball team also grew in stature: it won fourteen of the twenty games it played. Particularly gratifying were the team's victories over the Holland and Grand Rapids Christian high schools on their home floors. This had not occurred before, and, though these schools beat us in return matches, those defeats could not erase the memory of our earlier conquests. There were eight men on our team: playing at forward were Albert Dekker, James Erickson, Raymond Hofstra, and Cornelius Kostelyk; at guard were Henry Smith, John Vanden Berg, and Sydney Youngsma; I held down the center post. What may be of some interest to modern statisticians is the fact that we beat Holland by a score of 14-8 and Grand Rapids by a score of 16-14. Obviously, the game was not played then as it is today.

The Christian high schools of Chicago, Holland, and Grand Rapids had for some time been holding interschool oratorical contests in which one girl and one boy from each school competed for the year's two prizes. At the tryouts held in our own school, Bertha Prince emerged as the school's female orator and I came to represent the boys. At the trischool meet held in Holland, Bertha came in first in her division and captured the girl's prize. The Holland representative, Ed Visser, won the boy's contest, and I had to be content with second place.

While all these things were going on, I remained, of course, a student under instruction and tried my best to keep abreast of curricular affairs. Under the circumstances, however, I could not—or did not — address myself to my studies as diligently as I should have. I remember that I quite frequently skipped classes, and this, combined with a certain inattention to what I considered peripheral class assignments, came to be reflected in my grade standings. Although my average declined somewhat, I did finally emerge as the class valedictorian, and at the commencement exercises I was called upon to deliver the farewell address, which had earlier appeared in the annual under the title "Vale."

I look back on those high school years with nostalgia and considerable satisfaction. The school I attended was relatively young and small, and the number of teachers was not large; but the instruction was in general good and in some cases masterful. I remember with delight Mr. Mouw's course in botany; but my favorite subjects were history and literature, and I owe to Mr. Swets and Mr. De Boer a debt I can never quite repay.

I met Henry A. Swets not only in the classroom but also in the gym and in the locker room, and I found him to be everywhere and always a Christian gentleman. An excellent teacher of ancient, medieval, and modern history, he engendered in me an abiding interest in those subjects, and on the playing field he was a model of the true sportsman to all of us. His name led us to refer to him at times as "Henry Always Sweats," but this was meant to be a tribute to his earnestness and zeal. Most of us not only respected him but loved him, and we did so because he exhibited in his person and bearing the distinguishing marks of an authentic human being and a veritable man of God.

John De Boer was a brilliant lecturer and an acute critic of affairs. His course was invariably a stimulus to thinking and reflection, and I owe him thanks for introducing me to many English and American literary classics, from Beowulf and Chaucer down to Henry James. He also helped me to acquire whatever facility I have for speaking and writing in an intelligible tongue. His pacifism resonated in my soul, but I was not wholly convinced that war could finally be banished from a fallen and fragmented world. His theory that language was shaped by usage seemed to make sense, but even at this early stage of my development I thought that objective rules should govern grammar inasmuch as the *logos* linked words to reason. I learned from him that Christianity had a horizontal dimension, but I could not even then equate love of God with love of man. And I regret that his often expressed distaste for Latin led me to pay less than adequate attention to that language. Yet, when all is said and done, I must acknowledge that he was one of the most formative and wholesome influences in my early life.

*   *   *   *   *

There was life, of course, outside the confines of the school. Early in that academic year, Harold Vander Velde and I were absent from school for a period of two weeks. Harold had been delegated by his church society, and I had been delegated by mine, to attend the eighth annual convention of the American Federation of Reformed Young Men's Societies, which was to convene in Passaic, New Jersey, on October 10 and 11, 1927. With a number of other delegates from the Midwest we began our journey by car on the seventh or eighth and did not return to school until the twenty-first. This was our first visit to the East, and we seized the opportunity to visit as many historic places as we could on the way up and back. We stopped in New York, Philadelphia, Gettysburg, Watkins Glen, and other places, and we lingered in various scenic spots whenever their allure attracted us. The convention was an education and so was the trip, enabling us to justify our long absence from the classroom.

I had not hitherto paid much attention to girls, but during my last high school year I formed a kind of romantic attachment to a fine young lady who lived in Cicero. My friends from church, particularly Jack Tigchelaar and Neal Vander Schoot, had girlfriends in that remote locale, and I occasionally accompanied them in order to spend an evening with Tena D. I liked her, and we spent some holidays together; but our relationship stayed casual and unfettered, though I did write her on several occasions in my first college year.

A highlight of the year was the celebration that took place when my parents commemorated their fortieth wedding anniversary on March 6, 1928. All the children and grandchildren came together for the event, as well as more distant relatives and a large group of friends. My brother Bill, the firstborn, paid tribute to Father and Mother on behalf of all of us, and a friend of Father read a Dutch poem he had

High School Graduate

composed extolling the virtues of the celebrants. It was a memorable occasion, and we all lifted our hearts in praise toward heaven for providing us with gifted, loving, and God-fearing parents.

During that year the world, of course, revolved around us, as it always does. In the autumn of 1927, Harry Emerson Fosdick's "National Vespers" appeared on radio, and about that time the second Tunney-Dempsey fight took place. Of greater interest to us as church members was, however, the adoption of a statement by the June 1928 Christian Reformed Synod that declared dancing, card playing, and movie attendance to be "worldly amusements" in which no true Christian ought to participate. That body's mood relative to this issue came to expression when Synod, having learned that Professor B. K. Kuiper had attended some movies, revoked his appointment as church historian and dismissed him from the seminary.

My high school days came to an end when on June 21, 1928, three days before my twentieth birthday, I was handed my diploma at the commencement exercises held in the First Reformed Church of Englewood (located on 62nd and Peoria Streets). There were forty-three graduates, nine from the two-year commercial course, twelve from the three-year commercial course, and twenty-two from the four-year general course. Of the latter, seven students would go on to college that fall, and I was numbered among them.

Immediately upon graduation I reported to work at Thomas S. Smith's. I stayed at my accounts desk until just before Labor Day, after which I turned my eyes toward Grand Rapids, Michigan, and Calvin College.

5

COLLEGE DAYS
(1928-1932)

I entered Calvin College as a freshman in September 1928, and was promptly enrolled in the pre-seminary course. The nine-acre college campus was located in southeast Grand Rapids and was bounded by Franklin Street on the south, by Giddings on the east, by Thomas on the north, and by Benjamin on the west. The campus grounds had been bought in 1909 for $12,000, and the first building erected on it — the so-called administration-classroom building — was dedicated on September 4, 1917. This building stood near the center of the small campus, and the life of the college community was focused on it. It was a large red-brick building adorned at its main entrance with several tall Grecian pillars; it was topped by a cupola that was visible for miles around and served to give the campus its identity. Its main floor contained a chapel with 700 seats, a faculty room, the office of the President, an adjoining space in which the registrar, the treasurer, and a clerk-typist held sway, and several classrooms. The upper floor contained more classrooms and also afforded entrance into the chapel balcony. The locker-laced basement contained rest rooms, a boy's lounge, a girl's lounge, and two small laboratories, one for chemistry and the other for the organic sciences. All in all, it very adequately met the needs of the college community. A second building, a men's dormitory able to accommodate eighty students and containing in its basement a small, sparsely furnished gymnasium, arose on the corner

President Johannes Broene

Freshman Class of 1928-29

of Giddings and Thomas in 1924 (a large portion of the money needed to erect it was contributed by Mr. Van Achthoven of Cincinnati, Ohio). On May 8, 1928, a mere four months before I appeared on the scene, the Hekman Memorial Library had been dedicated, and this attractive building graced a corner of the campus at Franklin Street and Giddings. Its books had formerly been housed in a basement room in the classroom building. It was in and around these three buildings that student life revolved during my first years at college. There was no hint in those days of snack bars, playing fields, theaters, music rooms, swimming pools, and other such extravanganza.

The college traces its lineage back to 1876, but this dating is misleading. What was established in 1876 was a theological seminary charged with preparing ministers for service in the Christian Reformed Church. At the seminary's beginning there was only one teacher, the Reverend G. E. Boer, and he taught everything from grammar to eschatology. The staff gradually increased, and, in order adequately to prepare the students for ministry, the teachers, besides giving instruction in theology, provided courses in history, philosophy, languages, and literature. The course of instruction embracing those subjects eventually came to be known as the seminary's literary department; but it was not until 1894, when two laymen, A. J. Rooks and Klaas Schoolland, were appointed to the staff, that nonseminary students were permitted to take classes in this department. Ten years later, in 1904, the seminary's literary department was so far divorced from the seminary as to be called the "John Calvin Junior College," and it could be argued that it was in this year that Calvin College really came into existence. The two-year junior college added a third year in 1910, but it was not until 1920 that it became a full-fledged four-year, degree-granting college. It awarded its first baccalaureate degrees to eight students in 1921, seven years before I entered its halls.

Rev. J. J. Hiemenga was the first president of the school (serving from 1919 to 1925), and he was succeeded by Professor Johannes Broene (1925 to 1930). The latter amiable gentleman was in charge of the college when I entered it. In 1928 sixteen professors constituted the all-male faculty; in general, each of these teachers was the sole instructor in the subject he professed. Ralph Stob taught Greek; Albertus Rooks taught Latin and served as academic dean; Albert Broene taught French and German; Henry Van Andel taught Dutch and art; Jacob Vanden Bosch taught English; Harry Dekker taught chemistry and served as registrar; John Van Haitsma taught organic science; Edwin Monsma taught physics and assisted in biology; James Nieuwdorp taught mathematics; Peter Hoekstra taught history; Harry Jellema taught philosophy and psychology; Henry Ryskamp taught sociology and economics; Henry Meeter taught Bible and Calvinism; Seymour Swets taught speech and music; and Henry Van Zyl and Lambert Flokstra engaged jointly in teacher training. Two women served in an auxiliary capacity: Johanna Timmer was the librarian and "advisor to the girls"; and Elizabeth Vertregt, a recent graduate, assisted in the library. This was the staff. The salary scale adopted by the board in May of 1928 stipulated that instructors were to be paid from $2,000 to $2,400 a year, associate professors were paid a little more, and the salary of a full professor ranged from $2,600 to $3,300. The president's salary was set at $4,000. This salary scale was established, it should be noted, when the business boom of the 1920s was in full swing and postwar prosperity was at its peak.

Being a denominational college, Calvin attracted students from every sector of the nationwide church. On its campus one could meet young men and women from Washington and California, from the plains states and the Midwest, from Massachusetts and New Jersey, and from several points in between. This rich and enriching amalgam made Calvin a most desirable place to be, and I found it exciting to be in contact with persons of common faith who nevertheless represented diverse cultures and followed differing social customs. What enriched the mixture, too, was the presence on campus of the theological students. The seminary did not yet have its own building. Its classes were held in the administration building on weekday afternoons, and one frequently met seminarians on the grounds. In addition, a goodly number of them lived in the dorm and associated there with members of every college class. This mingling of theological and liberal arts students cemented the bridge between college and seminary and considerably enhanced the quality of life on campus.

I was one of the 89 freshmen who joined the student body in September 1928, and the coming of our class brought the number of registered students to 325. In a school of this size it was easy to become known and to learn to know others, and I felt immediately at home in my new environment. Present were several members of my high school class, as well as a number of people from the Holland and Grand Rapids schools whom I had come to know through our debating and basketball encounters. Then, of course, there were old friends like George Stob, Peter De Vries, John Vander Meer, and others who had come to the college from Chicago earlier.

During my first year at school I did not live on campus. My brother Mart had earlier made friends with Bill Pastoor, who had come to Chicago from Grand Rapids in order to gain additional experience in the butcher trade. Bill visited us often in Chicago, and sometime during the summer of 1928 it was arranged that I should take up residence in the fall with his parents. Upon my arrival in Grand Rapids, I accordingly became a full-fledged boarder in the Pastoor household and a veritable member of the family. Mr. and Mrs. Harm Pastoor lived at 911 Prince Street, within easy walking distance of the college. Living at home besides myself was a son, Don, and two daughters, Edith and Hildred. These children of the house were near my own age, and I very much enjoyed their presence and companionship. Of more than passing interest is the fact that Hildred, the younger of the girls, soon became engaged to my nephew, John Stob, my brother Bill's oldest child, and the two were eventually married. Mr. Pastoor owned and operated a butcher shop at Leonard and Pine streets on the city's west side, and during that first academic year I worked every Saturday in his shop defeathering and disemboweling chickens, making hamburger, and, somewhat later, carving out and selling cuts of beef and pork.

The Pastoors were followers of Herman Hoeksema and members of the Protestant Reformed Church, and I did not join them at worship on Sundays. I joined the nearby Neland Avenue Christian Reformed Church and soon became active in its adult Sunday School class. Rev. D. H. Kromminga had until that point been pastor of the Neland Avenue Church, but in June of 1928 he had been appointed to succeed the ousted B. K. Kuiper as professor of historical theology at the seminary, and soon thereafter he vacated his pulpit. Rev. H. J. Kuiper, who had been appointed editor of *The Banner* that same June, assumed the Neland Avenue pastorate some months later.

Because the pre-seminary course was prescribed and rigid, I experienced no difficulty with registration: there were no options to baffle or confuse a registrant. During the academic year 1928-29, I took eight hours of Greek with Prof. Stob, my second cousin; six hours of Latin with Prof. Rooks; eight hours of Dutch with Prof. Van Andel; six hours of English composition with Prof. Vanden Bosch; and three hours of logic and three hours of psychology with Professor Jellema. My performance in Latin was poor, but I received creditable grades in other subjects, and I was greatly attracted to philosophy. I found Jellema to be a fascinating teacher and his course in logic a delight; I was to be in every one of his classes thereafter and major in his field. But I should also pay tribute to Prof. Vanden Bosch: in his course in composition he made us submit for evaluation one piece of writing every week, and these exercises in literary creation did much to hone our communication skills. Classes were held only in the mornings, many of them beginning at 7:30. That left us with generally unencumbered afternoons and evenings, and in my first year I was able to devote much of this free time to my various studies.

I made a number of new friends that year, perhaps the closest bonds being with two fellow preseminarians, Rod Youngs and Ed Borst. We would sometimes study together, but more often we simply met for small talk spiced at times by serious discussion of certain controversial subjects.

The social life of the school also brought me into contact with the female students, but I formed no steady attachment to any of them.

The whirl of things involved me in a number of extracurricular activities. I naturally participated with the whole student body in the "Soup Bowl," an afternoon of fun and games and an evening of banqueting that inaugurated the school year and was designed to foster student fellowship. It seems that it was customary for the freshmen to repay the sophomores for their staging of the Soup Bowl by giving them a party. For some unknown reason I was asked to organize and chair the party, and since the party was judged to be a success, I came quite accidentally into the good graces of many of my classmates.

Some of us who were pursuing the preseminary course believed we should do something to master the Dutch language, so we decided to establish what came to be known as the Freshmen Dutch Club. At our rather irregular meetings we tried to help one another unravel the intricacies of Dutch grammar and to traverse safely the labyrinthine ways of its arbitrary genders. Prof. Van Andel was the faculty sponsor of this fourteen-member club, and at its first meeting I was elected president of the group.

There existed on campus a much larger Knickerbocker Club, also sponsored by Prof. Van Andel and designed to perpetuate the Dutch tradition on campus and to preserve its heritage. It turned out that year to be a sort of drama club, for its main activity was to stage a lengthy play called *The Siege of Leyden,* in which I played as one of a small number of alderman.

Judging that I could not spare the time for basketball, I made no effort to make the junior varsity team, but I did go out for debating. In the intraschool contests held to assist Prof. Vanden Bosch in selecting members of the varsity inter-collegiate team, George Stob, Peter De Vries, and I argued on the affirmative side of the proposition "Resolved that our jury system be abolished." We met a team that had previously eliminated another. On January 24, 1929, we debated William Frankena, Vernon Roelofs, and Jack Westra, and in the opinion of the *Chimes* reporter we bested the opposition; but the faculty judges ruled against us and we meekly accepted their verdict. George Stob and Peter De Vries were subsequently made members of the varsity team, and I was made a member of the freshman team. On March 18, 1929, Peter Eldersveld, Henry Dobbin, and I debated a veteran

Ferris Institute team that had already scored eleven victories, and we went down by a score of 0-3.

The student body was normally a law-abiding group, but in November 1928 it went on a rampage. Word had been received that Herbert Hoover had defeated Al Smith for the presidency of the United States, and on the next day the students declared a holiday. President Broene urged students to return to classes, but most refused, and a few of the leaders, mostly seniors, were subsequently roundly censured.

Grand Rapids was a picture in the first fall of my residence there. Its tree-lined streets contrasted markedly with the shadeless pavements of Chicago, and I remember vividly the sensations of sound and smell that accompanied my walking on the leaf-strewn sidewalks of the city. These sensations prompted me to write in November 1928 a tribute to

A Leaf

I could not help noticing it. It fluttered down beside me, grazing my cheek in its precipitous descent, and fell prostrate at my feet. The wind had done it — had dethroned a king, had shattered a masterpiece. As I watched, it made convulsive starts in haughty protest to its deposition. Through its contortions its delicate outline only whispered the excellence of its former architecture. The tender nourishing fibers, retaining a suggestion of their original green, were imbedded in a field of gold that deepened toward the edges into a blush. The harmonious blend of tints was a symphony. A gust of wind swept it into the gutter.

During the course of that year I wrote my parents regularly and returned to Englewood as often as I could. I spent Thanksgiving Day and the Christmas holiday at home, but I would thereafter not go back to the home on May Street, for in the spring of 1929 my parents moved into a house built for them at 1330 South 57th Street in Cicero. It is there that I lived during the summer of 1929, and it was from here that I traveled each day to my desk at Thomas S. Smith's produce house, where I continued to be employed.

* * * * *

With Art Kaptyn

I began my second year of college in September 1929. Having earlier informed the Pastoors that I would be living on campus that year, I found myself at the start of school sharing a dormitory room with Arthur Kapteyn, a classmate whom I had not previously known but with whom I enjoyed a pleasant association as long as we lived together. We each paid six dollars a week for our room and board. The room we occupied was suitably furnished, and, with our bunks properly stacked and our desks judiciously placed, there was ample space in which to move around and accommodate guests. The room boasted no wash or toilet facilities; for our ablutions we had to resort to the communal lavatories located at the end of the hall. Three meals a day were served cafeteria-style in the basement dining room, and, although some complained at the repetitious fare, we ate, I judge, as well as most of us would have at home, and the company at table was not a thing to be despised. Security regulations were nonexistent: doors were never locked, and there were no curfews; we were free to come and go as we pleased.

The dorm was under the jurisdiction of a faculty committee on housing, but its internal affairs were governed by student officers appointed by that committee. During that year, Frank De Jong, a senior seminarian, functioned as president: he was charged with preserving order, with licensing in-house programs, and with maintaining good relations with the students, the resident matron, and the kitchen staff. He was also obliged to keep in touch with the faculty supervisors and report to them any misdemeanor thought worthy of corrective discipline. As befitted his office, he lived alone in a private room which, being unattended in his absence, was on occasion roughed up by pranksters. Yet he was a friendly fellow and well-liked, and he served us admirably.

There was, I believe, a washing machine in the basement of the dorm, but it was not much used. I followed the example of many and sent my laundry home by parcel post in a sturdy cardboard box suited for the purpose. The box of clean clothes that my mother returned was invariably stuffed with fruit and cookies and sometimes with a bit of money or a new item of apparel. And, of course, it always contained a reassuring and admonitory letter. The dorm also boasted a barber shop of sorts: senior student Gerrit Vander Ziel occupied a private ground-floor room just off the lounge that was equipped with a barber's chair, and it was he who cut our hair for a nominal fee while discoursing learnedly on topics philosophical. We had similar interests, and I found my visits to his shop both diverting and instructive.

It is fair to say that a generally Christian atmosphere prevailed in the dorm. All of us had been brought up in the church, we had come to this school because of its Christian stance and witness, and most of us were preparing for Christian service in one field or another. Our life together largely reflected these facts. Meal times were accompanied by devotions; and we were expected to attend church on Sundays as well as participate in the morning chapel services held daily in the college auditorium, and this we normally did. Dancing and card-playing were forbidden, and the rules against these things were generally observed: I know of nobody who visited ballrooms, and except for an occasional game of rook, few of us spent our time at cards. Movie attendance was banned, but this proscription met with little favor and was widely ignored. In the tradition of the Dutch, almost everybody

89

smoked, and some of us did not disdain an alcoholic drink. We were not allowed, of course, to bring beer or liquor into the dorm, and in any case the national prohibition law was still in effect; but there were "speakeasies" in Grand Rapids, and the purchase of a pint of smuggled gin occasionally occurred. But the practice was not widespread or in any given case habitual.

In other respects, we residents of the dorm behaved, I suppose, as students so domiciled have always behaved. We burst into each other's rooms without notice and at inconvenient times. We engaged in idle banter. We hazed pretentious freshmen. We knotted the bed sheets of disfavored persons or, for their dousing, balanced a bucket of water atop their doors. We simulated warfare by exploding firecrackers at midnight. We mounted an occasional raid on the unguarded kitchen pantry, and we often slept too little. But it was not all horseplay. We studied, too, and in small groups we often engaged in serious discussions of important matters. And we formed lasting friendships.

I was fortunate that year to come into close association with Henry Zylstra and John Hamersma, to whom I remained firmly and affectionately bound until in later years their untimely deaths wrenched them from my side. The three of us formed with others a small band that came to be know as the "Friggers": included in the group were Gus Frankena, Leroy Vogel, Don Stuurman, Rod Youngs, and Art Kapteyn. We stood on campus in friendly rivalry with another, somewhat "bohemian," group known as the "Conblos," which included among its members George Stob, Peter De Vries, Syd Youngsma, Red Huiner, Peter Lamberts, Ted Jansma, and Herb Brink. Challenged to a basketball game, we once played against the Conblos in rented tails before a large crowd of appreciative spectators. For a while we had a mascot, a garden snake we called Adolph, which reptile made its home in a large jar I kept in my room. But it came to land one day — whether by accident or design, none seemed to know — in the dorm matron's bathtub, where it was "done in" by Mr. Norden, the school custodian. We were, of course, saddened by Adolph's demise, and in a November 1929 issue of *Chimes,* I wrote a fitting epitaph for him.

But we normally engaged in more intellectual pursuits. I was now a sophomore, and at a meeting held early in the year, I was elected president of the class and by virtue of my office made a member of the student council. The council was composed of eight members, two from each class. As a mediator between faculty and students, the

Debating Team, 1929-30
Henry Zylstra, Gerrit Vander Ziel, Henry Stob, Roderick Youngs

council undertook to strengthen intraschool relationships, to foster mutual understanding, and to assist in the reparation of such breaches as might occur in a school where numbers are small and contacts frequent.

The membership of the council underwent a change early in the year, and thereby hangs a tale. George Stob, a senior, had been elected president of the council in September, and Peter De Vries, a junior, had been elected vice president; but they unfortunately did not remain in office long. It seems that Leo Peters, a sophomore at the time, decided to build a "safe" fire on the dorm's flat roof as a prank and thus provide the populace with a harmless "scare." He required for his purpose a large sheet of protective asbestos and, of course, the fuel for burning. But having at the time no means of transportation, he enlisted the services of Peter De Vries, who owned a car and who happened to be in the company of George Stob at the time. The three of them set out on their errand, procured the required materials, and brought them back to the campus. Stob and De Vries then left the scene and took no part in the ensuing conflagration. However, Peters and some companions started and manned a roof fire of some proportions which, being seen and reported by

91

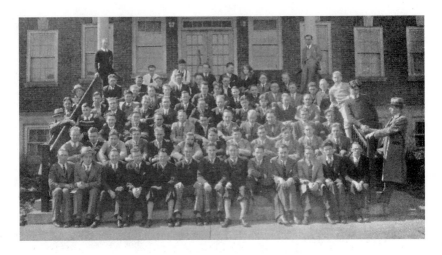

I bid goodbye to the dormitorians

fearful neighbors, brought out the fire department and caused considerable excitement. No damage was done, except to the composure of the neighbors and to the sensibilities of the faculty's discipline committee. What punishment Peters received I do not recall, but George Stob and Peter De Vries were held to be accessories to the "crime" and were deprived of their offices. John Dolfin was thereupon elevated to the presidency, and Henry Zylstra became vice president; I served the council as secretary.

I also became a member that year of a campus literary club. We called ourselves the Pierians since our purpose was to "drink deeply of the Pierian Springs," as Alexander Pope advised. We met monthly under John Timmerman's presidency and Prof. Vanden Bosch's sponsorship, and at every meeting we discussed the latest *Literary Guild* and by turns presented a paper on anything from poetry to drama.

I was elevated that year to a position on one of the two varsity debating teams. The affirmative team consisted of Bill Frankena, Vern Roelofs, and Henry Dobbin; Hank Zylstra, Rod Youngs, and I composed the negative team. The issue we addressed was unilateral disarmament, and our team argued against it. We engaged in three debates: one against Central Michigan College at Mt. Pleasant, one against Michigan State Teachers at home, and one against Hope College in Holland. We were fortunate enough to win all three contests. The highlight of the debating year, however, was marked by the appearance on our campus of a team from Purdue University. Prof. Vanden Bosch, our coach, shuffled his lineup and appointed Bill Frankena, Hank Zylstra, and me to engage the visitors in debate. Dressed in rented tuxedos, we conducted the debate before a large audience in the college auditorium, and three outside judges were unanimous in their judgment that we had won.

Two additional events of some significance shaped the contours of my life that year. Both were connected with trips to Hope College. One day three of us traveled to Holland for a debate only to find that we had misread the calendar: no debate was scheduled for that day. What then to do? Time was on our hands, and we were reluctant to return immediately to Grand Rapids. Some one of us then espied a movie house on Main Street and suggested that we enter and discover what went on in there. I was now twenty-one years old and had never seen a movie. Indeed, a short time earlier I had ridden to Chicago with a group of students, and when, in the middle of our trip the car broke down and had to be towed to a garage for repairs, I had refused to join my companions when they decided to attend a local movie. I preferred, I had said, to preserve my innocence. So I had sat for four long and solitary hours in a cluttered garage sheltering myself from the contagion of that which I had been taught to consider "worldly." But now, with some trepidation and yet with a certain resolve, the three of us — Hank Zylstra, Rod Youngs, and myself — bought a ticket and went in to see a movie. I don't remember what it was about and who played in it, but on our trip home we judged that we had been pleasantly entertained and had suffered no ill effects from our fall from grace.

A week or so after this adventure, our scheduled debate with the team from Hope College took place and we emerged the victors. Upon arriving home from Holland, Hank and Rod repaired to their own quarters and I entered the dorm with the news of our victory. A number of my friends thereupon suggested that we celebrate by lighting and tossing a firecracker that some enthusiast had produced. Emboldened by the victory, I consented. I don't remember whether I held the firecracker, or lit it, or simply threw it; the whole thing was a communal affair and my involvement in it was only partial. But the dorm president heard the loud report, and the next day Don Stuurman and I were summoned to appear before the faculty's

93

housing committee. Finding us guilty of a serious offense, the committee ordered us to vacate the dorm forthwith. So in March 1930, Don and I moved into a shared room that we rented from a widow lady who lived on Benjamin Avenue near Alexander. The irony of the situation came home to a number of us when, near the end of the school year, the chairman of the faculty's committee on housing, Prof. Henry Ryskamp, accosted me on campus and informed me that I had been selected to be president of the dorm the following year. When Prof. Ryskamp urged me to accept the appointment, I thanked him for the trust and confidence the committee had placed in me and said that I would gladly undertake the task. So ended the firecracker episode.

There was on campus a chapter of the League of Evangelical Students. This league had been organized in Pittsburgh in the spring of 1925 by Princeton Seminary students who were inspired and sponsored by Professors Machen and Wilson. In the ensuing years, chapters of the league were established at a number of colleges and universities on the east coast and in the midwest. The Calvin chapter embraced very nearly the entire student body, and at a meeting held at year's end I was asked to head the group and preside at its meetings during the next academic year.

While all these things were going on, college was, of course, in session. Books had to be read, assignments completed, and requirements met. This kept me busy. During that academic year of 1929-30, I took four hours of Reformed Doctrine with Dr. Meeter, six hours of Greek with Prof. Stob, six hours of Latin with Prof. Rooks, six hours of Dutch with Professor Van Andel, six hours of English and American literature with Prof. Vanden Bosch, six hours of philosophy (introduction to philosophy and Greek philosophy) with Dr. Jellema, and four hours of what was called physical education (but which consisted of little more than calisthenics and team play in the gym).

Campus life was not insulated from the outside world, and many of us kept in some touch with what was going on there. We took note of the 1929 St. Valentine's Day massacre of seven gangsters on Chicago's North Clark Street by Al Capone's henchmen. We read in the papers that Richard E. Byrd had flown over the North Pole in a tri-motored plane, and we were told in news reports that Albert Einstein had recently propounded a radical new theory about the space-time universe. Walter Lippmann published *A Preface to Morals* in 1929, and when it came into my hands during that academic year, I read it with great delight. Of religious interest was the 1929 Lateran Treaty, by which the Vatican was established as a city state and the Pope was recognized as a sovereign prince. So was the September opening of Westminster Theological Seminary, with a teaching staff that included three sons of the Christian Reformed Church — Cornelius Van Til, Ned Stonehouse, and R. B. Kuiper.

Momentous, of course, was the Wall Street stock market crash of October 27, 1929. Herbert Hoover had been inaugurated as president in March and, with business booming, he had promised a car in every garage and a chicken in every pot. But things did not turn out that way. By the end of 1929, stockbrokers had lost forty billion dollars in paper value, hosts of speculators went broke, and thousands of little people lost their jobs. The Great Depression that followed the crash was not to reach its depth until 1932, but within three months of the market's collapse a blight fell over the land. The members of my family did not deal in stocks, and having no wealth to lose they lost no fortunes. But they, like most other people, were to suffer from the Depression through unemployment, lessened income, and in various other ways. We who were students did not stand in the eye of the storm and suffered no real hardships. With our stipends intact, we may have even gained by the radical fall in prices. But as time went on and the Depression deepened, we could not but observe how great and painful was the distress of the general populace.

In the summer of 1930 the Thomas S. Smith establishment still stood firm, and when school let out I was back at my desk at the South Water Market for my fifth summer of employment. I have no vivid memories of how I spent my summer evenings, though I seem to recall that I went out a few times with a young lady from a neighboring church and once with a high school classmate. These liaisons were, of course, casual and I was able to return to school unencumbered by romantic ties.

I lived all summer with my parents and Mart, and most of my married brothers and sisters were near neighbors. This afforded me plenty of good company, and I must have spent a good deal of time with them. I was probably indisposed to undertake great adventures, for work at Smith's was somewhat exhausting. I led a sedentary existence there, but with the years my responsibilities seemed to increase. I was required to balance all the accounts of which I had been put in charge, and this was not always easy. Shipments sometimes went unrecorded by the receiving clerk; at other times manifests were mislaid or bills lost, and this made it difficult to adjust claims. But things were normally put to rights, and on the whole I enjoyed my work. I rode the 12th Street trolley car to and from work, and in my coming I read *The Tribune* and in my going *The Daily News*.

We had an hour for lunch, and I ate my bagged sandwiches on the fire escape out back, together with a green pepper and perhaps a peach or apple that I "borrowed" from downstairs. I usually took a walk along the busy street at noon, wandering often into the adjoining black neighborhood, where I was met on every side by dilapidated dwellings, unemployment, poverty, prostitution, and delinquency. The scene was inherently depressing, but I'm ashamed to say that it did not arouse in me the degree of compassion and concern that it should have. Years later I would plead the cause of the disfranchised and deprived people of the ghetto, but at this time a somewhat calloused and unresponsive conscience tended to contemplate these people more as objects of interest than as divinely entitled human subjects bereft of their dignity and suffering from discrimination and abuse.

*   *   *   *   *

I began my third, or junior, year of college in September 1930. The first thing a student wants to do upon returning to school after a summer's absence is to secure his lodgings and settle in for the long grind. On this score I experienced no difficulty that fall. Because I had been selected as president of the dorm, a pleasant private room in it had been reserved for me. It was located on the second floor, at the northeast extremity of the building, and from my window I could overlook a fair stretch of Giddings Avenue. The room was smaller than the one I had shared with Art Kapteyn the year before, but there was ample space in which to move around and entertain guests, and it was rent free. It contained the usual furniture, but it boasted in addition a comfortable lounge chair that I used for light reading and frequently for napping.

Dorm life proceeded peacefully during my year's tenure in office. I fielded the usual complaints against this or that regulation; sometimes I had to express to the kitchen staff the residents' dissatisfaction with the meals; and on occasion I had to quell a minor disturbance or silence a too vociferous crowd of disputants in one or another room. But nothing occurred to seriously ruffle the surface of our communal existence, and no prankster undertook to disarrange my living quarters or discomfit me in any way. I can recall only one occasion on which I had to confront a student in a semi-disciplinary fashion. A somewhat arrogant and pugnacious individual once insolently challenged my authority when I asked him to moderate his behavior. I am perhaps somewhat competitive, but I don't believe I tend to be combative. But in this instance I backed my adversary against a wall and warned him that admonitions left unheeded might lead to unpleasant physical consequences, and that in order to keep his facial features unaltered and intact, he would be well advised not to puncture my composure further or tax my patience beyond endurance. Although this young man was quite my size and I cannot accuse myself of bullying him, I am not proud of my behavior in this instance: violence or the threat thereof is unsuited to social intercourse and is not the preferred way to bring about compliance even in other contexts. Yet the procedure did prove effective, and this perhaps goes to show that by the employment of second-rate tactics one can reach desired ends. It may even indicate that from relative evil good may come.

There was a scattering of sophomores living in the dorm, and some of them participated with their fellows in putting freshmen down and impressing on the consciousness of the latter an awareness of their inferior status. Hazing did not take place in the dorm, and its existence elsewhere was consequently not one of my official concerns. But an instance of it came to my attention when a freshman dormitorian from the Iowa midlands fell into Red Huiner's hands. That freshman was Feike Feikema, an extremely tall and muscular fellow fresh from a farm near Doon, and he could have laid Red and his companions low with one swipe of his strong hands, but he heeded his mother's admonition and practiced submission. Feikema, who came to be employed as an assistant to the janitor and who in the course of that year could frequently be seen in our halls with broom and mop in hand, later became a distinguished novelist and, as Frederick Manfred, came to join David Cornell De Young ('29) and Peter De Vries ('31) as one of the three brightest literary stars that Calvin has produced. In a delightful piece written for the *Calvin Spark* in 1985, Feikema tells of his initiation into college. He reports without rancor and with evident

97

nostalgia that he and a few of his classmates were waylaid one evening by stalking sophomores. "We were bound," he writes, "with ropes, carried to the unfinished attic of the new Seminary building, splashed with red paint on our backs, and tied to 2" × 6" uprights. We managed to wiggle loose; then spent several hours in the dorm shower room scraping off the paint." This sort of thing went on at Calvin in those days, but it was done in fun, and the few victims of this horseplay took things in stride and harbored no resentment.

Although the number of faculty members remained constant at eighteen and the student enrollment figures still hovered slightly below the 400 mark, a number of changes took place at Calvin in 1930: by an act of Synod, the school's official name was changed to "Calvin College and Seminary"; Miss Timmer functioned no longer as "advisor to the girls" but had become dean of women; and Elizabeth Vertregt was elevated to the rank of chief librarian. But the biggest change took place in the president's office: Johannes Broene had with great reluctance assumed the college presidency in 1925, and in May of 1930 he asked to be relieved of his official duties and restored to the faculty as a full-time professor of psychology. The Board honored his request and appointed in his place Rev. R. B. Kuiper, who a year before had joined the faculty of Westminster Seminary as professor of systematic theology. Mr. Kuiper took office in September 1930 and was replaced at Westminster by John Murray. Worship services in the college chapel were much improved with the installation of a Wangeren organ during the summer of 1930. This three-manual instrument, which Prof. Van Andel played daily with great gusto, was the gift of Mr. and Mrs. William B. Eerdmans, successful local publishers and ardent friends of the school. The number of campus structures grew to four when there arose at the corner of Franklin Street and Benjamin Avenue a spanking new seminary building. The faculty and students of the theological school had since 1917 been quartered in the central administration building; they were now able to take up residence in their own spacious and well-equipped edifice. A gift of the Hekman brothers — John, Henry, and Jelle — the building was formally dedicated on October 29, 1930, and for thirty long years it served the seminary well.

Things were happening off campus as well. In the course of that year, William Howard Taft died, General Douglas MacArthur became the Army's chief of staff, Mahatma Gandhi challenged British rule with civil disobedience, and Hitler's Nazi party grabbed 107 seats in the

German Reichstag. But for me and my family these things faded into the background and seemed of little consequence when word was received that my brother Neal had been in an auto accident and now lay dead in a Chicago hospital. The van Neal had been driving was struck and demolished by a train at a railroad crossing, and Neal died enroute to the hospital of the massive injuries he sustained in the crash. He had survived the war, but now, on November 19, 1930, at age 36, he was taken from us and we deeply mourned his passing. He left a wife and three small children. I, of course, attended the funeral with my stricken parents and did what I could to console my grieving sister-in-law. Services were held in the First Christian Reformed Church of Englewood in the presence of a large crowd of friends and associates. Neal had served the Englewood congregation as deacon and as leader of the men's society, and he was held in high esteem for this as well as for his personal qualities. His sudden and tragic death affected many, and he was deeply mourned by all who knew him. Our grief, however, was assuaged by our assurance that Neal had gone to be with the Lord whom he had faithfully served in this life and would now eternally enjoy.

I returned to school chastened by the specter of death and addressed myself with renewed seriousness to the pursuit of learning. In the academic year 1930-31, I studied Reformed doctrine and cultural Calvinism in four semester hours with Dr. Meeter, pursued Greek with Dr. Stob for another six hours, took three hours of medieval history and three hours of Dutch art with Prof. Van Andel, began an eight-hour study of German with Prof. Albert Broene, took six hours of modern European history with Dr. Peter Hoekstra, and continued to work in my chosen field by taking three hours of medieval and three hours of modern philosophy with Dr. Jellema. In addition, I took two hours of public speaking with Mr. Seymour Swets.

I did tolerably well in my assigned courses, particularly in Greek, history, and philosophy, but I nearly failed in Calvinism. Dr. Meeter was an estimable person, and he later wrote an excellent book on Calvinism; but there was something in his posture and tone of voice that turned me off, and I regularly skipped his classes. Aware of my absences, he confronted me at year's end and said, "You should take the exam and get a decent grade, but, if you choose not to, I have no recourse but to give you a *D*." I thanked him and said, "I'll take the *D*," and that dark blot on my record still stands for all to see.

The Student Council, 1930-31
Standing: Leo Peters, John Hamersma, Ted Jansma,
John Timmerman, William Swets. Seated: Gilmer Van Noord,
Henry Stob, Henry Zylstra, Evelyn Van Appledorn

My course work combined with my duties at the dorm kept me busy. I therefore attempted to restrict my extracurricular activities as much as possible. If I was not very successful in that endeavor, it was not for lack of trying. I knew from four years of experience that high school and collegiate debating requires a large amount of preparation and consumes a good deal of time. I therefore determined to sever my connection with the varsity debating team. By this action no harm was done to the school's forensic program, for Prof. Vanden Bosch had a number of excellent debaters at his disposal, and from these he fashioned teams that performed that year with great distinction and remarkable success. Meanwhile, I was free to devote myself more fully to my studies.

The production of the school annual was the responsibility of the junior class, and when it was proposed in an early meeting that I act as editor-in-chief, I demurred. I distinctly remembered the stress I was under to produce the high school annual, and I had no desire or

The Chimes *Staff, 1930-31*
Standing: Jack De Vries, Abel Poel, Henry Dobbin, Cornelia Kloet, Jack Lamberts, John Timmerman, Marion Reitsema, Don Sherfey, Henry Stob, Sydney Youngsma. Seated: Gus Frankena, Norman Goldsword, Leo Peters, Henry Zylstra, Mildred Reitsema.

inclination to repeat the experience. I therefore stoutly resisted every attempt to get involved in the collegiate venture. To my great satisfaction, Gus Frankena was chosen to edit the annual. By way of concession I agreed to serve with Mildred Reitsema as literary editor.

I held no class office that year, but because I had held office the previous year, I was by statute given a seat on the student council. Henry Zylstra, now in his senior year, was elected president of the council, and I was chosen to be vice president. The two of us spent a lot of time revising the constitution in an attempt to give the council more authority in regulating student life, but it was not until the following year that an improved document was adopted.

The student publication, the Calvin College *Chimes,* underwent a transformation at the beginning of that school year. Established in 1907, the *Chimes* had up to that time been largely a literary magazine

101

The Neo Pickwickians, 1930-31
Seated, front: John Verbrugge, Peter De Visser. Seated,
2nd row: Jack De Vries, Prof. Ryskamp, Lewis Grotenhuis,
Case Plantinga, Gus Frankena, Don Stuurman.
3rd row: Aldert Venhuizen, Clarence Pott, John Timmerman,
Henry Zylstra, Jack Lamberts
Back row: Henry Stob, John Hamersma

that was published monthly in pamphlet form. Under the aegis of Peter De Vries, its current editor, and with the assent of several on the staff, the format was radically changed: *Chimes* became a biweekly newspaper. Editorials and comments were still to be found in it, but the essays, poems, and other literary productions that had earlier graced the publication were conspicuous by their absence. The change did not meet with universal approval, and I myself wondered out loud whether it represented an improvement; but in a plebiscite conducted at year's end, the student body endorsed the alteration, and *Chimes* never thereafter reverted to its former self. I became a member of its staff, serving with Mildred Reitsema, John Timmerman, and Henry Zylstra as one of the four associate editors charged with producing periodic editorials. Peter De Vries resigned as editor on December 18,

The Knickerbocker Club, 1930-31
Standing: Vander Ploeg, Marvin Schans, Nieuwdorp, Edith Dykstra,
Marcellus Vertregt, Stob, Peters. Seated: Anne Zylstra, Theresa Bouma,
Hamersma, Spoelhof, Ruth Roelofs, Alyce Damkot

1930, ostensibly for health reasons, but more probably under pressure from an administration that took no delight in his acerbic wit and his sometimes vitriolic attacks on what he regarded as a comatose and moribund tradition. Leo Peters completed De Vries's term.

The Calvin chapter of the League of Evangelical Students had a membership that year of over two hundred. As president, I was charged with giving the organization some direction, and I was ably assisted by many willing workers. We collected funds through solicitation, did deputation work at neighboring colleges, and on January 23, 1931, held a daylong regional conference featuring prominent religious leaders. The assembled students, representing several colleges and seminaries, were treated that January day to three major addresses by distinguished speakers and were led by knowledgeable persons to consider a variety of subjects relating to Christian witness in five different sectionals. A public meeting held that evening topped off the day and enriched our coffers. The sixth annual national convention of

103

the League of Evangelical Students was held in Philadelphia in February 1931, and I was in attendance as a delegate from the Calvin chapter. For three days, many students from various colleges were led in devotions, speeches, rallies, and discussions by such leaders of the evangelical community as Machen, Craig, Sloan, Glover, Gray, Lenton, Murray, Kuiper, and others. I was privileged to chair the nominating committee, to take lodging in John Murray's house, and to spend a delightful evening with a few others in the company of J. Gresham Machen. I returned to school enriched by the Philadelphia experience.

I retained my membership in the Knickerbocker and Pierian clubs that year, but I was irregular in attendance at their meetings and did not get deeply involved in their proceedings. I focused instead on two other clubs, one a venerable establishment — the Plato Club — and the other a quirky new creation with bohemian-like tendencies — the Neo Pickwickians. The Plato Club, sponsored by Dr. Jellema, was designed to bring together a small group of people who were interested in philosophy and were ready to prepare discussable papers on a variety of philosophical themes. The club was open to juniors and seniors only, and the number of members was limited to twelve. I joined the club in September. During that year we devoted ourselves to a study of Wallace's *Prolegomena to the Logic of Hegel,* a difficult book that taxed our minds but evoked stimulating discussions on a wide range of logical, epistemological, and metaphysical issues. The Neo Pickwickians were a group of friends interested in literature but disposed to pursue belles-lettres in an unconventional way. We incorporated ourselves that year, secured Henry Ryskamp as faculty sponsor, gave ourselves literary names, held our meetings in outlandish places, prepared some serious papers, ate midnight snacks, and had fun. There were fourteen members in the group: of that number, one became an outstanding preacher, two became business executives, one became a lawyer-judge, seven became college and university professors, and one became an editor-publisher.

To top these things off, I entered into a business partnership that year. The furnaces of the day burned coal, and the ashes had to be disposed of somehow. To ease the burden of the householder, John Nieuwdorp and I offered to remove each tub of ashes for the sum of ten cents a tub. We lined up a fairly large number of customers, including the college itself, bought an old model-T truck, and pursued our trade on Wednesday afternoons and Saturday mornings. I don't

John Nieuwdorp and Henry, with Model T truck

remember how well we fared financially, but I'm sure we didn't operate at a loss. In any case, we profited physically: lifting large tubs of ashes out of deep basements, tossing the tub's contents into a truck-bed ringed by high boards, and disposing of the cargo by shovelfuls at the dump must surely have hardened our muscles. At year's end we abandoned the business and sold our truck to Ed Bierma and John De Bie.

Student life at college, particularly at a co-ed institution, is normally spiced with outings and parties, and I engaged in a fair number of these. In the process I dated a number of girls but formed no attachment to any of them. What I quite vividly remember in this connection, however, is seeing an auburn-haired young lady walking with queenly grace through the library when I was sitting there, and thinking that this was someone I should like to meet some day. It chanced that at year's end I did meet her — under circumstances not particularly auspicious. The girls who made up the KKQ club were holding a farewell party at a beach house near Holland, and I was present as a guest of Ruth G. Sometime during the early evening I tired of the goings-on within and wandered off alone onto the beach and sat down on a bench at water's edge. To my surprise and considerable delight, two young women who happened to be nearby approached me and

105

began to engage me in conversation. One of them was the girl I had seen in the library. I learned that her name was Hilda De Graaf, that she was a graduate of Grand Rapids Junior College, had subsequently worked as a nurse's aid at Blodgett Hospital, and had enrolled in Calvin College that year as a junior. Our conversation was short-lived, for I dared not be too long absent from the party. But the meeting was momentous, because five years later this wonderful girl became my dear wife and after fifty-eight years of happy marriage, thank God, she still is.

Before the school year drew to a close, we noted that Prof. Louis Berkhof had been appointed as the first president of Calvin Theological Seminary; that Mr. Harry Wassink had been appointed instructor in physics at the college; that Professors Ralph Stob and Henry Ryskamp had acquired their Ph.D. degrees; and that Miss Vertregt had been married and was being replaced in the library by Miss Josephine Baker. We also noted that, with the Depression deepening and the school's deficit mounting, the members of the faculty had taken a sizable reduction in their salaries, and that the Christian Labor Association, with headquarters in Grand Rapids, had just been given birth.

In the summer of 1931, I lived with my parents in Cicero and worked for three months in Thomas S. Smith's wholesale produce market.

*　　*　　*　　*　　*

I began my senior year of college in September 1931. In the academic year 1931-32 the college employed nineteen full-time teachers. Fourteen professors formed the core of the staff, and these, with the president, constituted the actual and operative faculty. Three instructors and two assistants stood at their side, but they attended no faculty meetings and took no part in policy formation.

The student body had decreased in size. Enrollment now stood at 355, of which fifty-three were seniors. Gone from the scene were many of my friends: George Stob had graduated as early as 1930; missing since June of 1931 were Peter De Vries, John Hamersma, Jack Lamberts, John Nieuwdorp, Casey Plantinga, Clarence Pott, Bill Spoelhof, Sam Steen, Don Stuurman, and John Timmerman. Most of these had gone off to graduate school in pursuit of advanced degrees — Hamersma and Steen in law, Lamberts and Timmerman in English, Plantinga

106

Hilda De Graaf

and Stuurman in philosophy, Pott in German, and Nieuwdorp in medicine. Spoelhof and De Vries traveled other roads: Bill took a teaching job at Kalamazoo Christian High School; Peter returned to Chicago, where, before joining the staff of *Poetry* magazine, he did odd jobs to keep bread on his table. The absence of these stalwarts diminished me, but there was one consolation: Henry Zylstra was still aboard. Although Hank was of the class of '31, he had received a one-year appointment at the college as assistant in English and German and as coach of the debating team. This kept him on campus and enabled us to continue our close association and to establish even more securely our already firm friendship.

After living one year in a family home and two years in the dorm, I was ready for a change of residence. Before the previous school year had

Leroy Vogel ("Bird"), Martin, and Henry

come to a close, my friend Leroy Vogel — we called him "Bird" — and I had decided to room together in some off-campus apartment. We found a place to our liking at 1213 South Butler Street in southeast Grand Rapids: an aged Dutch lady lived at that address with an unmarried middle-aged daughter, and we discovered that the upper floor of their small house was for rent. After inspecting the premises, we promptly engaged the furnished rooms and moved in a few days before the opening of school. We found the accommodations well suited to our purpose: we had at our disposal a pantried kitchen equipped with stove, pans, and dishes, a good-sized bedroom furnished with twin beds, and a large front room which, after we had brought in our desks, chairs, and bookcases, we were able to convert into a pleasant study area. There was no phone in our apartment, but we were permitted to use the one in the downstairs hall for free when making local calls. Heat and light were furnished, and for our total accommodations we paid twelve dollars a month rent, six dollars apiece.

The Butler Street house stood just south of Hall Street, so we dubbed our place "Butler Hall," and a hall it soon become, for our friends repeatedly visited us there, making it a meeting place for banter, fellowship, and intramural education. Hank Zylstra was a frequent visitor, and the three of us often engaged in a serious discussion of matters relating to our studies. I remember one evening we were talking about literature. We wondered whether one form of it was better fitted to express the Christian vision than another. We canvassed the merits of the ode, the lyric, the sonnet, the epic, the novel, the drama, and the like, and we had not finished our survey when, looking up, I shouted in amazement, "Hank, there is the sun." Bird had retired at midnight, but Hank and I, quite unconscious of the passage of time, had been overtaken in our conversation by the dawn.

When two people live together, they must work out a certain division of labor. Bird and I agreed that we would make our own beds and cooperate in the washing and drying of dishes; Bird volunteered to prepare the meals if I would undertake to keep the premises clean. I readily consented to this arrangement, since I possessed no culinary skills but was, on the contrary, an experienced janitor and had mastered the art of dusting and mopping. Moreover, I was loath to see our premises fall victim to Bird's slovenly household habits. His desk was a mess: piled high with papers, pipes, unwashed sox, apple cores, empty coffee cups, and sundry other items, it resembled a dump, and I sometimes chided him about this sorry state of affairs. I myself am a clean-desk man, and I have often wondered how people of the opposite sort could ever recover an article they sought. But that year I learned that a man with a cluttered desk has hidden powers. Bird, I found, was often able to finger a misplaced paper in the twinkling of an eye, while I, with all my organizational apparatus, was sometimes at a loss to locate a properly filed item that I wished to retrieve.

Bird and I got along famously. We were both seniors, we were both headed for the seminary, we had known each other since freshman days, we were both "Friggers," and we had a similar outlook on life. We argued, but we never quarreled. When we argued, it was about matters of substance, except when, as in the case of the bread, we argued for argument's sake and in order to sharpen our wits. Toward the end of a meal Bird would sometimes take a half slice of bread and announce that he could eat no more. "Nonsense," I said, "if you can eat a half slice you can eat a whole." Bird attempted a rejoinder but, cutting him short, I added, "Moreover, replacing the half slice destroys the symmetry of the loaf." This objection seemed not to weigh heavily with him, whereupon I attempted to show that there were physiological, psychological, philosophical, theological, and even economical reasons why his detested practice should be abandoned. He adduced counterarguments but I discredited them all, and this play and interplay continued for months until we tired of it and declared a truce. In later years, amidst running laughter, we fondly recalled our unresolved debate.

I think Bird was a fair cook, but I don't remember how our eating comported with accepted dietary rules. We purchased most of our food supplies from the Korfker grocery store on the corner of Butler and Hall, and these foods must have served us well, for we maintained both our appetite and our health. Prices were low: I remember buying two pounds of choice pork chops for twenty-five cents, and I know that the ground beef we normally fed on was regularly available at ten cents a pound, or three pounds for a quarter. We did not patronize restaurants, even though as late as 1935 one could visit the Bierstube and dine on pig hocks and sauerkraut, hot German potato salad, a vegetable of the day, and several slices of pumpernickel for $.60, or buy a fried perch dinner for $.35. The cigarettes we sometimes bought were priced at fifteen cents a pack or two packs for a quarter; but we normally contented ourselves with buying a sack of Bull Durham tobacco and a packet of papers and rolling our own. We were, after all, in the midst of the Depression, and we had no money to waste.

We had gone to church regularly in former years, but we tended to "shop around," and we formed no attachment to any single congregation. In that year, however, we lived within a stone's throw of the Oakdale Park Christian Reformed Church, and it was here that we regularly attended Sunday services. Rev. Zeeuw was then the pastor of the church, and we enjoyed his preaching. We were saddened, however, when Rev. Zeeuw was found guilty of window-peeping and deprived of his pulpit. What happened to him afterward I do not know; I trust that he found forgiveness and restoration.

It is only fair to report that our studies and bull sessions were interlaced with occasional visits to the movies. There was a theater on Madison Avenue at Hall, and, when an afternoon's work had exhausted us, we would sometimes seek relief in the dark confines of that establishment. We had to pass through a cemetery to get there and through what is now a hostile neighborhood; but in those days we could walk unafraid and unmolested on the darkest of nights and arrive home unscathed. President Kuiper once saw us entering this church-outlawed establishment, but he evidently made nothing of it, for we were never summoned to his office or in any way reprimanded.

The college was about three quarters of a mile away and we reached it by foot in all kinds of weather. To save time and effort we usually cut diagonally through Franklin Park, though on our way home we sometimes paused to watch the games that were being played there.

Class elections were held at the beginning of the school year, and when the seniors met to cast their ballots, they elected me class president. By virtue of this election, I took a seat on the student council for the third successive year and was appointed council president at the first meeting of that eight-member body. Serving with me were Ann Geerdes, Florence Stuart, Gus Frankena, Enno Wolthuis, Gelmer Van Noord, Carl Kass, and John Daling.

I had something to do with John Daling's presence on the council. It was believed in the early thirties that freshmen were not in a position to elect class officers, for they were unacquainted with each other and could therefore not make informed choices. The president of the senior class was therefore given the power of appointment, and I exercised that power. After consulting with the dean and the registrar, I named as freshman class president a person whose high school record indicated that he was a man of parts — John Daling. Having been named president, he was given his designated seat on the council, and he served it well. John, who was a few years older than I, soon became one of my friends and we later served together on the college faculty. He has since passed out of this life, but I am much indebted to him for many things, in part for his early solicitude concerning our food supply and eating habits. In that year and the one following he expressed his friendship and concern by often coming to Butler Hall bearing fruits and vegetables from his father's farm and canned meats from his mother's kitchen.

Through the ratification of a revised constitution, the student council was enabled that year to exercise complete jurisdiction over all school activities and to monitor the activities of the various relatively independent student boards. Numbered among the council's accomplishments that year was the creation of an official Calvin seal, the inauguration of

111

The Plato Club, 1931-32
Standing: Enno Wolthuis, Ed Bierma, Elco Oostendorp, Tunis Van
Kooten, Gus Frankena, Menko Ouwinga, Peter Van Tuinen, Leo Peters.
Seated: Rein Harkema, Ed Borst, Prof. Jellema, Henry Stob, Henry Zylstra

a new kind of "Soup Bowl," and the enforcement of an act forbidding the payment of monies for work done on all school student staffs.

I remained a member of the Pierian and Knickerbocker Clubs in 1931-32, but I did not engage much in their activities. My attention was focused rather on the Plato Club. I had joined this philosophical organization at the beginning of the previous year and was happy now to continue my membership in it. At a meeting held in September 1931, twelve of us gathered under Prof. Jellema's sponsorship to elect the season's officers. When the ballots were counted, I chanced to emerge as the group's choice for president, and I continued to chair our meetings throughout the year. The club membership included Enno Wolthuis, Ed Bierma, Elco Oostendorp, Leo Peters, Rein Harkema, Ed Borst, Henry Zylstra, and myself. Prof. Jellema was, of course, our guide and mentor, and under his direction we studied with great profit *The Republic* of Plato. We met biweekly in various places, mostly in the rooms of the participating members. On November 16,

1931, we met at Butler Hall, and on that occasion I read a paper entitled "What is Goodness?" It was only when the clock struck one that the group disbanded that evening. Our meetings were like that: in smoke-filled rooms, along tortuous paths, with minds stretched out, we pursued the elusive Plato. But, despite our best efforts, we never quite caught up with him. Yet we enjoyed the chase and doubtless were made better by it.

The Calvin College *Chimes* was ably edited that year by Peter De Visser, a gifted fellow who in later years became book editor at the William B. Eerdmans Publishing House and also the managing editor of the *The Reformed Journal*. I retained the position on Peter's staff that I had earlier occupied, and, as one of the three associate editors, I wrote a fair share of the editorials that appeared in print that year.

It was noted in the *Chimes* and announced in chapel that a J. C. Geenen prize in psychology would be awarded that year to a Calvin student who submitted a winning paper on a topic in that developing field. Challenged by the offer, I prepared over the course of some months a lengthy dissertation on "the Soul" and submitted it to the judges for evaluation. I was pleased to learn at year's end that my entry had been approved and had been deemed worthy of first prize, a sum of money in an amount I cannot now recall.

When spring came and all nature had burst into life, I was suddenly cast into sorrow by a piece of news from home. A phone call from my brother Tom informed me that Father had been taken seriously ill and was now near death's door. Responding quickly to the call, I summoned Bird and Hank Zylstra to my side, and these good friends offered at once to drive me home — and without delay. When I came into the house, I found my older brothers huddled around the sickbed and ministering as best they could to Father's needs. His temperature had risen to 105 degrees, but I was able to hold his hand, plant a kiss on his cheek, and express to him my love and deep respect. He squeezed my hand, fastened a kind and reassuring eye on me, and fell into a fitful sleep from which he did not awaken. Father died early the next morning from what the doctor said was lobar pneumonia and pleurisy. The date was April 23, 1932. Father had lived on this earth for sixty-nine years, five months, and twelve days, and now he had been taken up to be forever with his Lord.

I still have a letter that he wrote on April 17, a short week before he died. He was well then, had gone to church twice that day, and

Mother and Father

wrote how pleasant it was that the minister had preached on one of his favorite texts — "My flesh and my heart may fail, but God is the strength of my heart and my portion forever" (Ps. 73:26). Mother told me that in the five days that he lay sick he often repeated those words, as well as others so dear to him: "I am always with you; you hold me by my hand. You guide me with your counsel, and afterward you will take me into glory." That these words were on his dying lips I can well believe, for he lived close to God and served him faithfully all his days.

Father died early on Saturday morning, and the funeral service was held on Tuesday afternoon, April 26, 1932, in the Second Christian Reformed Church of Cicero. The service was conducted jointly by the Reverends P. A. Hoekstra and J. J. Weersing. Interment was in Mount Auburn cemetery, where a small stone slab still marks his grave.

When Father died, a part of me died with him. Nearly half a century separated us in age, but no gulf yawned between our spirits, and there was nothing to cut our shared sentiments asunder. We children deeply mourned the passing of our father, but when we laid his body in the grave we took comfort in the fact that his life was Christ and his death gain — a sure entrance into the inheritance of the saints. And when the earth closed in upon him, we realized that to keep him in sacred memory we could do no better than to exhibit in our own lives the beauty and godly power of his.

Mother, after forty-four years of marriage, was now a widow at 65. A scant two years earlier she had lost a son in the bloom of life, and now her dear husband had been wrenched from her side. We consoled her as best we could, and Mart and the married children did everything they could to help her through the period of mourning. But her faith matched that of Father, she bore up courageously in the ensuing days and months, and came at last to live her independent life with grace.

When the funeral was over, I went back to school and took up the studies that I had temporarily put aside. My senior course work and class schedule did not differ greatly from that of previous years. I took four hours of New Testament Greek with Prof. Stob, three hours of Roman culture with Prof. Rooks, six hours of intermediate German with Miss Timmer (my very first female instructor), three hours of Prussian history with Prof. Hoekstra, six hours of philosophy (ethics and metaphysics) with Prof. Jellema, six hours of sociology with Prof. Ryskamp, and six hours of organic science (the "frog" course) with Prof. Van Haitsma.

I was now very close to completing the pre-seminary course, and about to receive the AB degree. I had in the course of four years received seventy-nine hours of instruction in various languages and had acquired some proficiency in Greek, Latin, Dutch, German, and English. I had taken twenty-four hours of philosophy — all the college had to offer — and had developed an abiding interest in the subject. With fifteen hours of instruction in history and eight in Bible, I had acquired some insight into these subjects; but the six hours each in sociology and the six hours of biology left me without a thorough grounding in these disciplines. Yet, in spite of its top-heaviness in languages, my education had equipped me to pursue the subjects that were of special interest to me with some hope of success — philosophy and theology — and for the tutoring I received at Calvin I shall always be grateful.

It is hazardous to comment on the merits and demerits of one's teachers. I thought most of mine were scholarly, industrious, and dedicated men. Stob, Vanden Bosch, Hoekstra, and Jellema were, I think, outstanding. I learned much from them, and they have in various ways left their imprint on me.

I did not as a college student — nor at any time thereafter — involve myself in the largely subterranean and clandestine discussion that went on in board and faculty circles concerning Prof. Jellema's alleged bent toward philosophical Idealism. There were those who missed in him a distinctively Christian approach to philosophical reflection, and there were those who regarded him as the very embodiment of the Christian thinker. The truth lay, I think, somewhere between those two opinions. Jellema was certainly out to articulate and impart to his students a Christian understanding of the universe and to bring faith and reason into accord. But the method he followed and the tools of instruction he employed were not always suited to his purpose. His Socratic method was well adapted to rid the student of inherited prejudices and unexamined biases; but it was not equally suited to establish a foundation on which a student could securely stand.

Moreover, it can hardly be denied that the philosophical air we breathed was redolent with Idealism, for that school of thought was in the ascendancy throughout the English-speaking world. Jellema himself had studied at the University of Michigan under the Anglo-Hegelean Dr. Wenley, and he had written his dissertation on Josiah Royce, America's foremost advocate of Idealistic tenets. I am unable to say to what extent Jellema was influenced by these distinguished philosophers. I can only say that most of the tools of instruction put at our disposal bore an Idealistic imprint; for the history of philosophy we read Windelband, Ueberweg, and Thilley; we were encouraged to read John and Edward Caird, to consider Green and Wallace, and, if we had a stomach for it, to dip into Bosanquet and Bradley. Among the textbooks we used in class were Mary Calkins' *Persistent Problems of Philosophy* and Andrew Seth's *Ethics*. None of this as such made Prof. Jellema an Idealist, for it leaves out of account the corrective judgments he made, as well as the independently constructed lectures he gave. But it does, in my view, absolve his critics of the charge that their doubts and misgivings arose out of malice and that their concerns were fabrications woven from whole cloth.

It is difficult to describe, and harder to assess, the development I had undergone while in college. I had been exposed in philosophy, history, and literature to some of the best that had been thought and said in the Western world. In my logic course I had been shown how sound thinking is conducted, and in student discussions I had learned a bit about how persuasive arguments are to be framed and corrupting fallacies avoided. Through the extracurricular activities I had engaged in, I had acquired some experience in the management of affairs and had, perhaps, grown in an awareness of the dynamics governing social relations. I dare say that my Christian faith had remained intact, even though it had taken on new dimensions and had been cleansed of its more parochial excrescences. I had acquired a deeper awareness of the antithesis and of Christ's lordship over all of culture; but I had also grown in my appreciation of the Greek mind and indeed of much that pagan and secular thinkers had contributed toward the formation of civilization and the establishment of a humane society. I had almost no training in the natural sciences and was unable to judge of the truth or falsity of Darwin's theories, but I did not see in any supposed evolutionary development a threat to the biblical doctrine of creation, since creation and evolution are answers to quite different questions and need not come into conflict. The Bible remained for me an authoritative book, but I no longer read it without discrimination and I did not take all its pronouncements literally. I became, I suppose, more tolerant of divergent opinions, less prone to judge prematurely, and more disposed than formerly to take the middle road when disputes raged.

Calvin's graduation exercises took place on May 31, 1932, in the Welsh Auditorium in downtown Grand Rapids. Seventy-nine college students received their diplomas that evening, and I, like all the others who had taken the four-year course, was awarded the AB degree — in my case with a major in philosophy and a minor in Greek. I did not speak at graduation, but as president of the graduating class, I had earlier published in the annual a farewell message (again entitled "Vale") and in it thanked the board and the faculty for the substantial education they had provided all of us.

I had not gone on many dates my senior year, but I did occasionally see Hilda De Graaf. We once attended a roast together at Tunnel Park in Holland. I visited her at her sister's house on several occasions, and on the evening of our graduation I escorted her home and promised to write her during the summer.

With diploma in hand, I was eligible for admission to the theological school — but not quite. All applicants for admission had to get medical clearance, and the school doctor, the same Dr. Geenen who had put up the prize money for the essay on psychology that I had won — declared

117

me unfit, if not for further study, then at least for service in the active ministry. He said that I had a leaky heart, a defective thyroid gland, and some other ailment whose name I have forgotten; and he refused to give me a clean bill of health. When I got home, however, I visited Dr. Jonker, then medical director of the Nathaniel Institute, and he found me in perfect health and without any constitutional defects or ailments. Thereupon, with admirable promptness, he forwarded to the seminary a certificate attesting his findings. Dr. Jonker was no doubt right about me, for though Dr. Geenen forbade me to drink coffee and alcoholic beverages and said that I was never again to smoke, I have for sixty years since then engaged in all of these activities and am now, by the grace of God, still able to jot down these musings.

In the academic year 1931-32, many things, of course, were happening in the outside world. In 1931 the Japanese seized Manchuria; the Chicago gangster Jack ("Legs") Diamond was gunned down by members of the mob; and the people in New York witnessed both the completion of the Empire State Building and the opening of the George Washington Bridge. In 1932 the economy reached bottom, the vast Insull enterprises went into receivership, and an army of veterans marched into the national capitol demanding immediate payment of their bonuses. In that year, too, the infant son of Charles Lindbergh was kidnapped for ransom and brutally murdered; and in Germany the Nazis became the strongest party in the government by capturing 230 Reichstag seats. Closer to home, the Calvin Board of Trustees adopted the "hand-heart" design as the official seal of the college and seminary, authorized the seminary to introduce a postgraduate course leading to the Th.M. degree, and appointed Mr. and Mrs. Kett to "take charge" of the dormitory at a salary of $1,000 a year.

On the first or second day of June 1932, I returned to Cicero and took up residence with my mother and my brother Mart. Mother had been keeping the house but was now thinking of living with one or another of her married children, all of whom were urging her to sell the house and come live with them. Mart was currently unemployed. Several others in our large family, though still employed, were working only two or three days a week, and all of them in different ways were suffering under the conditions of the times. The Depression lay heavy on everyone, but I was fortunately able to return to my job at Smith's and, without a decrease in pay, to work there for the full three months I had at my disposal. On June 24 I celebrated my 24th birthday.

6

SEMINARY DAYS
(1932-1935)

I began my first (or junior) year at the Calvin Theological Seminary in September 1932. There were fourteen members in my class, all except one of whom had graduated from Calvin College the previous June. My cousin George Stob was the exception: he had graduated from Calvin in 1930. Originally headed for the seminary, he had undergone a change in sentiment on graduation from college and, while residing with his parents in Englewood, had spent the past two years in a number of jobs in the business world. I visited him often during this period and noticed in him a growing desire to return to his first love; and in the summer of 1932, with a renewed sense of calling to the ministry, he decided to enter the seminary. I rejoiced in his decision, and, after conferring with Leroy Vogel, I invited him to join us at Butler Hall, an invitation that he readily accepted.

The seminary building had been erected in 1930 on the southwest corner of the college campus (at Franklin Street and Benjamin Avenue), and we entered that new building when the fall classes convened. There were six professors offering instruction in various fields. The president of the seminary, Louis Berkhof, B.D., was the professor of systematic theology. Fifty-nine years old at the time, he had joined the staff in 1906 as professor of exegetical theology, had since 1914 been professor of New Testament studies, and had in 1926 assumed the chair in systematics. Samuel Volbeda, Th.D., was the

George and Henry

fifty-one-year-old professor of practical theology. He had joined the faculty in 1914 as professor of church history but had since 1926 been teaching practical theology. Clarence Bouma, Th.D., had joined the faculty in 1924 as professor of systematic theology but had in 1926 chosen to assume the newly established chair of ethics and apologetics, a circumstance that permitted Prof. Berkhof to undertake the teaching of systematics. Martin Wyngaarden, Ph.D., was professor of Old Testament studies and, like Bouma, had joined the faculty in 1924; both of these men were forty-one years old at the time of my enrollment. Henry Schultze, B.D., at thirty-nine the youngest of the group, was professor of New Testament studies, having been appointed to this post in 1926. Dietrich Kromminga, B.D., fifty-three years old at the time, was the professor of historical theology. He had joined the faculty in 1928, the year I came to college.

Four of these professors were foreign born — Berkhof, Volbeda, and Bouma being Netherlanders by birth, and Kromminga being a native of Oostfriesland in Germany; Schultze and Wyngaarden were Midwesterners, born in Iowa and Wisconsin respectively. Although only three of the six professors had acquired advanced degrees, all had engaged in graduate studies at various institutions of learning. Together they constituted a creditable body of scholars, teachers, and preachers.

In the academic year 1932-33, I took six hours of Hebrew with Dr. Wyngaarden; three hours of New Testament introduction, three hours of New Testament history, two hours of hermeneutics, and two hours of public speaking with Prof. Schultze; three hours of ancient church history with Prof. Kromminga; three hours of history of doctrine and two hours of introduction to dogmatics with Prof. Berkhof; three hours of theological encyclopedia with Dr. Bouma; and one hour of homiletics, one hour of liturgics, and two hours of practice preaching with Dr. Volbeda — thirty-one hours of instruction in all.

The seminary levied no matriculation fee, and no student paid more than fifty dollars a year for tuition. Students from outlying districts paid only twenty-five dollars, and those coming from the far south and west paid no tuition at all. Classes were held only in the morning. Each of the professors had his own classroom, and in each of these rooms there was a small "office" that was seldom used. Out-of-class contact between faculty and students rarely occurred; pleasantries passed between them in the halls and after mid-morning chapel, but when classes were dismissed, all went their several ways. Counseling programs did not exist then, and I dare say none felt in need of them.

The students were organized into a group known as "Corps"; but, except for an early group meeting to elect a "praetor," the student body tended to dissolve into little more than a friendly aggregate of individuals, though some formed the kind of association that George, Bird, and I enjoyed. There were among the students two or three who had entered college late in life and had come to seminary already married, but the vast majority of students were unmarried. It was the rule in those days that no one entered into matrimony until his studies were completed and he was ready to enter the active ministry. Engagements were embarked on with the utmost seriousness and were not lightly broken. It happened once that a student broke his engagement to a young woman and escaped expulsion only by expressing his deep regret to the faculty and entering a tearful plea for clemency.

The three of us at Butler Hall formed a congenial group. We moved a bed and a desk in for George; but the rent remained the same, which meant that each of us paid only four dollars a month for our accommodations. George proved to be an expert cook, and it was he who was now charged with preparing the grocery list and with cooking the noon meal. We ate cereals in the morning, more often than not spaghetti with canned tomatoes and meatballs at noon, and for the evening meal we traipsed to Mrs. Stadt's boarding house, where we feasted on potatoes, vegetables, and meats in the company of several other students. I don't remember what we paid for this evening repast, but it could not have been more than fifty cents. In those Depression days one could eat at the Cody Hotel cafeteria in downtown Grand Rapids for less than that. Sunday specials there featured roast young turkey with dressing for thirty cents and fricassee of chicken with tea biscuits for twenty-five cents. The coffee we bought for use in our apartment cost nineteen cents a pound, and we consumed heroic amounts of it. Bird and I washed and dried the dishes, and I continued to sweep and dust the premises.

We entertained many visitors. Henry Zylstra, Rod Youngs, John Daling, and fellow seminarians came regularly to our door; when their studies at the university permitted, Clarence Pott and Tunis Prins would also drop in. And on occasion Hilda De Graaf and her friend Hermine Weeber would stop by. But we did not neglect our studies, and all three of us managed to earn acceptable grades. At year's end I was fortunate enough to be awarded the Manhattan Junior prize, given annually to a beginning student selected by the faculty. The award yielded the princely sum of five dollars.

Our group was saddened during that year when George's mother fell ill and soon thereafter passed away. When the news came that she was stricken, we managed to get George aboard the Pere Marquette train just as it was pulling out of the station. After the funeral, George considered suspending his studies in order to be with his sorrowing and inconsolable father; but we dissuaded him from adopting such a course, and he was later glad he had heeded our advice. My own widowed mother sold her house in the fall of 1932 and lived first with my sister Gert and her husband, and then with my brother Tom and his wife. Mart, meanwhile, took up residence with my brother George and his wife and managed to get a government-supported job hauling refuse out of Cicero alleys with a large horse-drawn wagon.

The event of the year was, of course, the election of Franklin D. Roosevelt to the Presidency of the United States in November 1932. Herbert Hoover left office on March 4, 1933, and soon after his inauguration Roosevelt put into place a political and economic "New Deal." Already on March 5 a bank holiday was declared, and thereafter the government passed one resolution after another calculated to restore the economy, increase jobs, and secure savings and investments. To provide employment, Congress established the Civilian Conservation Corps (CCC), the Public Works Administration (PWA), and the National Recovery Administration (NRA). The Emergency Banking Relief Act and the Federal Securities Act were passed, and the Federal Deposit Insurance Corporation was established to forestall any future stock market crash. To aid the impoverished, Congress established the Federal Emergency Relief Administration (FERA) and passed the Agricultural Adjustment Act (AAA). By the end of June 1933, all these programs were in place and the people took heart, even though 30 percent of the work force was still unemployed and dust storms had begun to erode the farmlands of Oklahoma and Arkansas. In another sense, "spirits" were lifted throughout the land, for on January 1, 1933, the twenty-first amendment, which repealed national prohibition, went into effect, legalizing the manufacture, distribution, and sale of alcoholic beverages. For many it was a day of celebration.

A long month before President Roosevelt assumed office, a national leader of quite a different sort seized power on the European continent. On January 30, 1933, Adolph Hitler was appointed Chancellor of Germany by President Von Hindenburg. He soon thereafter claimed dictatorial privileges and became "Führer of the Reich."

Things were also happening on the local scene. In June 1933, Rev. R. B. Kuiper, having been appointed professor of practical theology at Westminster Seminary, relinquished the presidency of Calvin College and was replaced in that office by Dr. Ralph Stob, who would serve as president for the next six years. To fill the gap created by Prof. Stob's departure from the classroom, William Radius was appointed assistant in Greek at a yearly salary of $1,700. In late August, Henry

Zylstra left Grand Rapids in order to begin teaching at the Western Academy in Hull, Iowa.

When the school term ended, I returned to Cicero and lived all summer with my brother Bill and his wife Tillie, who provided me with room, board, and companionship at no cost, a circumstance that permitted me once again to devote the monies I earned at Smith's produce market to my own needs.

I came home furnished with a preaching license, and I delivered my first sermons on two Sundays in June 1933 — once at the Cicero I Christian Reformed Church and once at the Roseland II Christian Reformed Church.

* * * * *

I had a good but uneventful summer. I went out very little. I didn't even attend Chicago's World Fair, which, among other things, featured the fan dancer Sally Rand. After working all day, I spent a good deal of time with my mother, with Mart, and with my other brothers and sisters. From the newspapers I read during that summer, I learned that a sixty-six-nation economic conference was held in London; that H. L. Mencken had laid down the editorship of the *American Mercury;* that the United States was about to give formal recognition to the Soviet Union; and that construction was beginning on the Grand Coulee Dam on the Columbia River. I believe it was also during that summer that Anton Cermak, the mayor of Chicago, was killed in Miami by an assassin's bullet meant for President Roosevelt.

When fall came, I was off to begin my second (middler) year at the seminary and about to put into operation a plan we had hatched during the summer. Why, we had said to each other, shouldn't Mother and I live together in Grand Rapids? She had no fixed home, and I, free to live where I wished within reach of school, would much enjoy and greatly profit from her presence and care. And so it was decided. Informing Bird and George of our plan, and receiving their well wishes, I retrieved my belongings from Butler Hall and moved into a pleasant upper apartment I had rented at 904 Kalamazoo Avenue in southeast Grand Rapids. Mother arrived just as school was about to begin.

Mart had accompanied her on the train, and, heeding Mother's wishes that he remain close to her, he began to look for a job in Grand Rapids. Practiced in the butcher trade, he did in fact find employment

124

after a few days' search, and the three of us happily shared our new apartment. Mart, however, was engaged to a fine young lady in Cicero, and he now proposed that they get married and live in Grand Rapids. So it happened that on October 15, 1933, Martin J. Stob and Therese Vander Molen were married in a Cicero church at a Sunday evening service. Mother and I were, of course, at the wedding, at which I served as Mart's best man. Mart and Therese moved promptly to Grand Rapids and established themselves in a house located near the apartment Mother and I occupied.

I thoroughly enjoyed the year with Mother. She furnished the flat with items she had brought from Cicero, gave the whole establishment the appearance of home, prepared the meals, farmed out the laundry, and made life in every way pleasant for me. I did the shopping, took her to church, helped with the dishes, and involved her in my works and ways. It was a blessed time, and I have ever since been happy that we were able to spend our life together during that period.

It was also during that year that I began to court with greater regularity the girl of whom I was growing steadily fonder. I did not see Hilda often, but we did have several Sunday evening dates. I was introduced to the members of her family, and I took her once to meet my mother. In this way the prospects of our eventual union grew slowly brighter.

My studies at the seminary followed the prescribed pattern: with Prof. Wyngaarden I took one hour of advanced instruction in Hebrew, three hours of introduction to the Old Testament, three hours of Old Testament history, and two hours of Old Testament exegesis; I also took two hours of New Testament exegesis with Prof. Schultze, six hours of church history (medieval and modern) with Prof. Kromminga, six hours of systematics (theology, anthropology, and Christology) with Prof. Berkhof, three hours of Christian theism and three hours of Christian ethics with Prof. Bouma, and two hours of practice preaching with Prof. Volbeda.

Being licensed to "exhort," I conducted Sunday services on nine occasions in various churches during the year, receiving for each of the eighteen "sermons" a five-dollar honorarium. In those days one did not travel to outlying districts on Sunday. This meant that we students would leave on Saturday to fulfill our preaching assignments, lodge with a member of the church, and remain until Monday morning. If the distance we had to travel was not too great, we might be

125

Mother

permitted to leave for home on Sunday night a minute after midnight, but no earlier: one was allowed under no circumstances to desecrate the sabbath by traveling on it. I was once assigned to preach in the local West Leonard church and suffered a rebuke when an elder of the church saw me alight from the streetcar I had taken to reach my destination. He expected me, I suppose, to use the legs the Lord had given me. The meals we were offered by our Sunday hosts were

126

Hilda and Henry

generally good, but one Sunday I preached in a rural community where
the lady of the house apparently objected to cooking on the sabbath
and placed on our plates a bowl of cold soup. I still recall with what
distaste I broke through the crusted fat in order to reach the congealed
substance that lay beneath the surface.

There were no student clubs at the seminary, which left us free to
pursue our studies and prepare the sermons we were called on to preach.
However, I was engaged in another extracurricular activity that year: I
had been elected national president of the League of Evangelical Students, and this involved me in regular correspondence with other officers
and in a number of group meetings. As part of my duties, I undertook
to prepare for publication and distribution by the league a pamphlet on
"The Doctrine of God." The pamphlet, with my four chapters and an

additional one by my successor, appeared a few years later. It also happened that, after submitting relevant essays, George Stob and I were fortunate enough to be awarded proportional shares of the fifty-dollar Bethany Muskegon Mission Prize at the end of the year.

Things were happening outside seminary as well. In the Christian Reformed Church the Psalter Hymnal made its appearance, freeing congregations to use hymns in public worship, provided the psalms be not neglected. The Dutch language remained alive in the church, but in the course of that year Synod decided to publish its Acts in the English language only. The church was saddened by the death on November 9, 1933, of Prof. Emeritus William Heyns and on March 21, 1934, of Prof. Emeritus Foppe Ten Hoor, but it rejoiced with Prof. Albert Rooks for his having reached his fortieth-year milestone in his teaching career at the college.

In Germany the Hitler regime was fastening its tentacles on the church, but the establishment of the Confessional Synod ("Bekenntnis Kirche") and the publication of the "Barmen Declaration" in May 1934 brought hope and encouragement to the steadfast Christians of the land. The evil strength of Nazism was manifested, however, by the Hitler-inspired murder of Ernst Röhm, the head of the *Stürmabteilung* (SA), and by the replacement of the SA with the SS *(Schutzstaffeln)* under Heinrich Himmler.

In 1934, the Dionne quintuplets were born in Canada. In the same year, the United States Congress passed a bill granting Philippine Independence after a ten-year period of economic and political tutelage. In the Midwest the farmers continued to suffer as drought and dust storms devastated the land.

As the 1933-34 school year was drawing to a close, Mother and I had to make plans for the summer. I was committed to return to my job on Chicago's South Water Market. Mother could remain in the Grand Rapids apartment and be looked after by Mart and Therese; but she chose — wisely, I think — not to do so, but to spend the summer in the company of her daughter, my sister Jen. Jen and Hank (Vander Molen) had just lost their eleven-year-old son James, and Jen was now in the last stages of a pregnancy and could profit from Mother's presence and services. About the first of June 1934, Mother and I moved to Cicero, I to live with Bill and Till, and Mother with Hank and Jen. Saddened by Jamie's death, we rejoiced when Jen gave birth to a daughter, Betty Ann, in July 1934.

Wishing to preserve our lease on the Kalamazoo Avenue apartment, we offered in school notices to sublease it for the summer, and we were pleased when Prof. and Mrs. R. B. Kuiper decided to accept our offer. They occupied the premises for the full three summer months.

Besides working at Thomas S. Smith's, I also engaged in some preaching: I conducted Sunday services in seven different Chicagoland churches. I was also happy in midsummer to escort Hilda De Graaf on a tour of Chicago's World Fair.

*   *   *   *   *

I began my senior year at Calvin Seminary in September 1934. Sometime before classes convened, Mother and I re-established ourselves in our Kalamazoo Avenue apartment and settled down for another year of life together. During that academic year I took two hours of Old Testament biblical theology and two hours of Old Testament exegesis with Prof. Wyngaarden; two hours of New Testament biblical theology and one hour of New Testament exegesis with Prof. Schultze; two hours of American church history and one hour of Christian Reformed church history with Prof. Kromminga; six hours of systematics (soteriology, ecclesiology, and eschatology) with Prof. Berkhof; two hours of applied Christian ethics with Prof. Bouma; and three hours of church polity, one hour of catechetics, one hour of pastoral theology, and two hours of practice preaching with Prof. Volbeda.

All these courses, as well as those I had taken in the previous years, were prescribed. The curriculum provided room for only one elective, open only to seniors, and I chose to conduct a study of German Idealism under the guidance of Prof. Bouma. I was the only student involved in the study, and during the semester I plowed through Helmut Groos's massive volume *Idealismus und Christentum* and regularly presented typed summaries of the text, with commentary, to Prof. Bouma when we met for our weekly consultation. The 500 pages of involuted German taxed my powers of understanding and interpretation, but in the process of reading I learned a good deal about continental philosophy and markedly improved my grasp of the German language.

It is not easy properly to assess the education we received at the seminary. At the heart of the curriculum stood systematic theology: we received seventeen hours of instruction in prolegomena, the history of doctrine, and the six classical loci from a kindly man whose orderly mind construed biblical truth in strict conformity to the Reformed Confessions, particularly to the Canons of Dort. Already in those days I had problems with an eternal decree of reprobation and with the doctrine of limited atonement; but Prof. Berkhof held that these and related doctrines were not only firmly grounded in the Bible but were also in no way offensive to sound reason. Thus he usually met my inquiries concerning these things with the benign but bland reply "I see no problem there." I respected Prof. Berkhof and benefited from his instruction and friendship; but he was not, in spite of his considerable attainments, a theologian who grounded us in the classics or engaged us in dialogue with modern and contemporary thinkers. We read neither Augustine nor Aquinas; we were neither required nor encouraged to read Luther and Calvin; and we heard nothing of Schleiermacher and Ritschl except that they were "subjectivists" undeserving of our attention. Barth, likewise, tended to be dismissed as yet another "liberal" whose critical view of Scripture disqualified him as a mentor. This does not mean that we were left without guidance. Basing his teaching on Kuyper, Bavinck, Hodge, Warfield, and Shedd, Prof. Berkhof constructed a theology that incorporated important elements of Dutch and Scottish Calvinism and which, while breaking no new ground, did present in an orderly and comprehensive fashion the substance and flavor of Reformed orthodoxy.

Our training in practical theology was sound but by current standards minimal. We had three hours of instruction in church polity, and six hours were devoted to practice preaching; but in the course of three years we received only one hour of instruction in each of the several other practical disciplines — homiletics, liturgics, catechesis, and pastoral theology. There were no courses in counseling, church administration, or hymnology, and field work was entirely absent. I did not engage in catechism or Sunday School teaching, in the activities of young people's societies, in mission work, or in any other ecclesiastical endeavor. We were licensed to exhort and we did engage in "preaching"; but there was no monitoring of our performance, and we were in no way held accountable for these exercises. And, of course, our summers were unburdened: we were free to spend them as we pleased.

Yet I enjoyed Professor Volbeda's classes. He was not strong on "practice" and gave few methodological hints or prescriptions, but he laid bare the theological grounds of preaching, pastoring, and worshiping, and this stood everybody in good stead. He delivered his lectures in a latinized English freighted with polysyllabic words, and he seldom got beyond the prolegomenon of any subject he taught; but his eloquence and spiritual fervor lent grace to his utterances, and he was gladly heard. Of lasting value, I think, was his prescription for exegeting a text and for settling a sermon on it. Discover, he said, the single theme of the text, phrase it aptly, and then, apprehending from an analysis of the text the three or four angles from which its theme may be viewed, state in precise language how you propose to illumine it. We attempted to do this in practice preaching, but we seldom did it to his satisfaction. His suggestions would then follow, such as: *The Success of Importunate Prayer Guaranteed:* "(1) Its express authority, (2) Its significant iteration, (3) Its universal range" (Luke 11:9-10). Or, *The Patriarch's Faith Surviving in Death:* "(1) The object of faith called for it, (2) The vision of faith facilitated it, (3) The confession of faith pledged it, (4) The life of faith betokened it" (Heb. 11:13-15). Or, *The Resplendence of Moses' Countenance:* "(1) Its miraculous origin, (2) Its mediatorial purpose, (3) Its intermittent manifestation" (Exod. 34:29-35). I suspect that sermons so fashioned are rare these days, but his did actually unfold the text.

Prof. Kromminga taught church history with competence and Germanic thoroughness; but he was somewhat impatient with questions of philosophical import, and I was sometimes taken aback by his curt responses to my inquiries. However, he was in great favor with most students, and he doubtless lent substance to the faculty.

I tended to be closest to Prof. Bouma, whose interest in philosophical theology had been nourished at Harvard. Although he was staunchly "orthodox," he addressed contemporary issues in ethics and apologetics with understanding and empathy and with considerable powers of mind and spirit, and I profited from his lectures. He was an early ecumenist, and through the *Calvin Forum*, which he founded and edited, he sought to reach out to the worldwide Reformed community as well as to the secular world around him. Unfortunately, he was not on the best of terms with Prof. Jellema, and this displeased me; I was not able fully to allay his suspicions even though I did seek to moderate his judgments concerning his colleague.

Professors Wyngaarden and Schultze were there to teach us exegesis and biblical theology, and they did so with varying degrees of success.

Prof. Schultze was a popular preacher and an able exegete, but he was not a notable New Testament scholar and made no claim to be. In the classroom he addressed his subject with a certain competence, but also with a loose informality that at times bordered on the lackadaisical. He was, however, honest in his approach to biblical texts, open to critical insights, and indisposed to reconcile the varying gospel accounts of Jesus' life, words, and deeds. Unlike others in his generation, he regarded the "Synoptic Problem" beyond resolving. All in all, most of us appreciated his unpretentious presence and academic candor. Prof. Wyngaarden was generally held in less esteem and left most of us with a truncated view of the Old Testament and a less than adequate grasp of Hebrew. Since he was the successor to the deposed Prof. Janssen, perhaps his fear of stumbling led him to avoid critical confrontations and instead to seek refuge in a staid orthodoxy and the advocacy of a completely inerrant Bible.

Hilda De Graaf and I had for some time now been "going steady." I courted her on Friday and Sunday evenings, traveling to and from her home by streetcar. Because the cars stopped running at the stroke of midnight, on some evenings I had to return home on foot — and that through several dark and lonely miles. Hilda and I did not often indulge in outings and excursions, and we were infrequently seen in public places. We spent most evenings in her living room in the presence of her parents, although when weather permitted we retired for privacy to the porch swing and there consumed the cocoa and cookies that Hilda generously provided. At other times we would go for long walks or simply amble to the corner drugstore for a soda or an ice cream cone. Hilda would normally accompany me when I preached on Sunday evenings, and when I was free of such assignments I would attend the worship services at Coldbrook Church with her. We were both poor. Hilda was working then at Steketee's department store as an interior decorator and earning thirteen dollars and fifty cents a week. Out of this sum she bought her daily lunch, paid her mother three dollars for room and board, and set aside a tenth for charity.

One of our dates stands out vividly in my memory. On March 15, 1935, I took Hilda to the *Dies Natalis* banquet at the seminary, and later that evening I asked for her hand in marriage. She happily

The Seminary Class of 1935 with Faculty
Front row: Prof. Schultze, Prof. Bouma, Prof. Berkhof, Prof. Volbeda,
Prof. Wyngaarden, Prof. Kromminga.
2nd row: Nicholas Wassenaar, George Wieber, Elco Oostendorp, Edward
Visser, John Schuring, William Reinsma, Charles Greenfield.
3rd row: Roderick Youngs, Bernard Visscher, Leroy Vogel, Henry Stob,
George Vander Kooi, Henry Evenhouse. Back: George Stob

accepted my proposal, and we sealed our compact with a kiss. Some days later I sought and received her parents' approval of our engagement, whereupon I went to Engbers jewelry store on Seymour Square and bought a diamond ring to symbolize our commitment. Newspaper ads in 1935 advertised wedding rings for two dollars, and diamond rings at $8.50, but the one I bought cost the princely sum of thirty-five dollars. The purchase depleted my resources, but I rejoiced in the expenditure and looked forward with eager anticipation to an eventual union with the girl I loved.

During that academic year I "preached" in sixteen different churches and on seven occasions delivered sermons in Dutch.

The senior students were now nearing graduation, and almost all were looking forward to candidacy and an eventual call to ministry in a church. I had, however, fallen in love with theology, particularly on its philosophical side, and began contemplating graduate study. My mentors encouraged me to move in that direction, and I applied to four schools. I was happy when in April and May the divinity schools at Harvard, Princeton, Chicago, and Hartford offered me graduate scholarships of differing amounts. None of the stipends was large by the standards that later prevailed, but they fit the temper of the times and were sufficient unto the day. Princeton offered a scholarship of $100, Chicago one of $250, Harvard one of $350, and Hartford offered me a Jacobus Fellowship yielding $500. I was at first inclined to go to Harvard, and I sent several letters of inquiry to Dean Sperry. But I understood that Prof. Farmer was teaching systematics at Hartford and that the retired Prof. Mackenzie was still active there; and this, together with the prospect of receiving $500, moved me to decide in favor of Hartford. So, on May 23, 1935, I wrote a letter of acceptance and thanks to Dean Rockwell Potter and informed him that I would be in Hartford when school convened in the fall.

On April 1, I passed the oral examination leading to the Th.B. degree; in May the Board of Trustees took note of the fact that I was not standing for candidacy and voted to extend my preaching license; and on June 4, 1935, fourteen of us received our diplomas at the commencement exercises held in the Welsh Auditorium. The graduating class consisted of Henry Evenhouse, Charles Greenfield, Elco Oostendorp, William Reinsma, John Schuring, George Stob, Henry Stob, George Vander Kooi, Bernard Visscher, Edward Visser, Leroy Vogel, Nicholas Wassenaar, George Wieber, and Roderick Youngs.

The end of the school year involved the end of my apartment sharing with Mother; we vacated the apartment in late May and moved in with Mart and Therese at 936 Watkins Street. Mother continued to live with her children there until the spring of 1936, but I stayed only a few days after commencement. I then returned to Cicero in order to take up residence with Bill and Tillie and resume working at Thomas S. Smith's.

As usual, things were happening outside the seminary classrooms and halls. In 1935 the United States Congress established the Rural

Electrification Administration (REA), the Works Progress Administration (WPA), the National Youth Administration (NYA), and the National Labor Relations Board (NLRB). Congress also passed the Neutrality Act, which authorized the President to forbid the sale or transport of arms to any belligerent. Of special interest was the passage of the Social Security Act, which stipulated that payroll taxes were to be levied beginning in 1937, and that pension eligibility was to begin in 1940. During that year, Huey ("Kingfish") Long, the senator from Louisiana, was assassinated in the streets, and the CIO under John L. Lewis separated from the AFL.

In Europe there were wars, military expansions, and dictatorial restraints. The Italians under Mussolini conquered Ethiopia. Adolph Hitler introduced compulsory military service in Germany, and under Nazi pressure Karl Barth transferred from Bonn to the University of Basel.

Things were happening at Calvin too. Sometime during the year, Clarence Bouma launched the monthly magazine *Calvin Forum*. In May 1935 the Calvin Board of Trustees required every student to sign a card pledging obedience to the college rules forbidding participation in worldly amusements (movie attendance, dancing, and card playing). In the face of unfavorable communications from the college faculty and the student council, the Board reappointed Ralph Stob as president for the regular period of four years, believing that "the present unrest in faculty and student body . . . can be settled if the Board stands firmly behind the President." At the May meeting the Board also appointed Albert Muyskens to be instructor in mathematics and physical education, and as coach of basketball, at an annual salary of $2,100.

Although Harry Jellema was greatly appreciated by most of his students and revered by some, he was in disfavor with some members of the faculty and board, and this presumably led him to consider transferring to another school. In any case, at its meeting in May 1935, the Board of Trustees was informed that Prof. Jellema had accepted an appointment in philosophy at Indiana University and would not be available when college classes resumed in the fall. The faculty proposed that Dr. Cornelius Van Til or Dr. Cecil De Boer be appointed in his place, but the board was not ready to act and decided "to postpone the matter of appointing a successor to Professor Jellema until next year." The executive committee and the faculty were meanwhile charged with "making arrangements for the teaching of philosophy during the coming year." Jesse De Boer, a 1934 college graduate who had spent a year at the University of Illinois in pursuit of a philosophy degree, was thereupon asked to fill the temporary vacancy, and he began teaching at the college in September 1935 at an annual salary of $1,600.

Leaving my fiancée in Grand Rapids was not pleasant, but I could ill afford to forfeit the money I could earn on the South Water Market. I tried to make up for my absence by accepting as many Michigan preaching appointments as I could. As it turned out, I preached in Grand Rapids and environs on nine different Sundays and was thus able to spend many weekends with Hilda and my mother. On six of these Sundays I preached in both English and Dutch.

Thomas S. Smith's Wholesale Produce establishment was now declining under the weight of the depression and would be put up for sale the following year. I was thus informed that at summer's end my employment would be terminated. The news did not bother me, since my student days were drawing to an end and the Hartford Fellowship would see me through the next academic year. I had been employed at Smith's every summer for a period of ten years, and when it came time to leave, I expressed to Mr. Smith my heartfelt thanks for his willingness to take me on and bade him and my associates a fond farewell.

In late August I said goodbye to my kinfolk in Cicero, stopped in Grand Rapids to visit with Hilda, Mother, and Mart and Therese, and in early September 1935 boarded a train for Hartford, Connecticut, and a two-semester stay in historic New England. I was now twenty-seven years old.

7

HARTFORD AND WEDLOCK

(1935-1936)

Entering Hartford Theological Seminary in early September 1935, I was treated kindly by the dean and registrar and received with courtesy by the students I met upon arrival. The campus impressed me. The granite buildings rising in Gothic splendor, the green lawns, and the tree-shaded courtyards betokened serenity and peace as well as opulence and refinement. I was assigned to a private, well-furnished room in Hosmer Hall, from which I could look out on the campus and in which I soon made myself at home. I have entirely forgotten what I paid for room, board, and tuition. I only know that the money from the fellowship left me without financial worries and enabled me to devote myself without care to my various studies.

I was disappointed to learn that Prof. Farmer had left Hartford for Oxford, and I found that his replacement, Dr. Johanson, was hardly a match for his predecessor, nor indeed for Prof. Berkhof. But Johanson now occupied the chair of systematic theology, and I took two courses under him during the first semester. One of these, predominantly a lecture course, was on "the Modern Development of Religious Thought." In it the professor gave expression to the vapid theological liberalism that, I soon realized, reflected the dominant spirit of the school. I had grown skeptical of some features of the Reformed faith

With Wilhelm Vauth

while at Calvin, but the shallowness of the "modernist" alternative as expounded here turned me around and deepened my appreciation of my orthodox heritage. Nor did I hesitate to give expression to it in class discussions. I was happy, though, to be introduced during that semester to such theologians as Paul Tillich, Reinhold Niebuhr, Rudolf Otto, William Pauck, and others, and I spent a considerable time reading them.

The other course I took with Prof. Johanson was a "Tutorial in Systematic Theology," in which I was free to conduct my own researches and obliged only to periodically present papers embodying the results of my investigations. It was here that I fell upon Karl Barth.

There was a German exchange student at the school by the name of Wilhelm Vauth, and we soon became fast friends. It was he who put into my hands a copy of *Theologische Existenz Heute*, the magazine Barth published in collaboration with Brunner, Thurneysen, and others. When I read what Barth had to say, my spirits rose. I sensed that here was a man who, affirming a transcendent God and a veritable supernatural revelation, expressed my own deepest sentiments and afforded me a contemporary reference point from which to engage my mentors and fellow students in relevant discussion. During that year I went on to read in Barth's *Römerbrief* and in his *Dogmatics*, and also in Schleiermacher's *Christian Faith*. Before the semester ended, I presented to Prof. Johanson a lengthy paper entitled "The Doctrine of Revelation in Barthian Theology." I can fairly say that it was Karl Barth who, even in his Kierkegaardian existentialist phase, helped to establish me more firmly in the Reformed faith.

In addition to my work with Prof. Johanson, I took a course on "The Inner Life of Jesus" with Dr. Purdy, the professor of New Testament. I wrote a paper for him on "Jesus' Messianic Consciousness" and another titled "Why Jesus Had To Be Baptized." Prof. Purdy was a scholarly and mild-mannered man who held the biblical witness in deep respect and who, I'm happy to say, found my presentation suited to his own opinions.

That semester I was also privileged to take a seminar in Spinoza with the redoubtable Prof. Mackenzie, the retired professor of systematic theology. A small group of us met in his house weekly, and because I was thought to be somewhat schooled in philosophy, I was asked to prepare a disproportionate number of papers for class discussion. We did not get far into the Spinozan text, but under Mackenzie's tutelage the outlines of the philosopher's thought were laid bare, and this was a gain.

It was not all study during this semester, of course. I wrote Hilda at least twice a week; I corresponded regularly with family and friends; and I played Ping-Pong frequently. There were also bull sessions in the dorm and informative meetings with Wilhelm Vauth about German theology, particularly about Bonhoeffer, Althaus, and Barth. Food was served with grace in the elegantly appointed dining room, where we sat in intimate groups around small tables and were served by student waiters and waitresses under the watchful eye of the dining room matron. After dinner there was dancing in the foyer, and I was induced at last to join in the festivities; but my heart was not in it, and I never really acquired either the art or the habit of dancing.

During the Christmas break I returned to Grand Rapids, and, since Wilhelm was alone in a strange country, I persuaded him to accompany me home. We stayed at Mart and Therese's, where Mother also resided, and we spent a leisurely two weeks exploring the town. We even made a trip to Chicago, where Wilhelm met several members of my family. Naturally, I saw Hilda often, and the three of us went out frequently. During this vacation period I preached one English and one Dutch sermon at Coldbrook, Hilda's home church.

When we returned to school at the beginning of the second semester, I addressed myself with vigor to the task of writing my dissertation. I had earlier decided to write on "The Christian Idea of Revelation," and room was provided for this undertaking in my schedule because I was required to take only one additional course. I chose to study church history with Prof. E. E. S. Johnson, and for him I wrote a long essay on Albertus Van Raalte and another one entitled "The Life and Religion of Thomas Paine."

Nothing interrupted my labors that semester except the flood that inundated midtown Hartford in the spring of 1936. Several of us seminary students were recruited to help in the relief work, and quite a number of us spent several days helping refugees flee from the rising waters. During that rescue operation three or four of us were put up by a wealthy resident in his palatial home and treated royally with sumptuous dinners, soft beds, and maid service.

Another thing I remember is winning the table tennis tournament near school's end. This led to my learning a bit about Oriental culture. A finalist in the tournament was a student from China. On the day following our match, he presented me with a gift that I greatly admired for its beauty and antiquity. Some days later, however, a knowledgeable person informed me that I had been given an heirloom; I was not really expected to keep it, and in all courtesy I should return it to the giver. With appropriate apologies, I promptly did that, to the evident satisfaction of the donor.

Although I had indicated to Dean Sperry of Harvard that I would consider coming to Cambridge after my year at Hartford, I really had no fixed ideas about my future course of action. I had prepared for the active ministry, and I seriously considered standing for candidacy and accepting whatever call to parish service might come my way. But

Providence intervened. In a letter to me dated January 25, 1936, Hartford's President Barstow wrote, "I am happy to inform you that, on the basis of your splendid record during this year of graduate work, the Faculty of Hartford Theological Seminary has by a unanimous vote designated you as one of our German exchange students for the year 1936-37."

This came as a complete surprise. I had not applied for the fellowship, but there it was, placed unsolicited in my lap, and I saw in it God's leading. Dr. Barstow's letter went on to say: "I hope very much that you will be able to take advantage of this opportunity." I hoped so too, for I was greatly pleased with the prospect of studying abroad; but I had no disposition to leave the country without Hilda, and could make no decision on it before conferring with her. I was therefore quick to apprise Hilda of what I had been offered, but we left things in limbo for the nonce. In any case, a decision at the moment was premature, for the Hartford appointment needed confirmation from other agencies. The confirmation arrived when, on May 26, 1936, the director of the Institute of International Education wrote from New York: "We are happy to inform you that upon recommendation of Hartford Theological Seminary, our Committee on Selection has awarded you an American German Student Exchange Fellowship for graduate study in Germany during the year 1936-37. The Fellowship which you have been awarded covers board, lodging, and tuition for the period of the academic year from November 1, 1936, to June 30, 1937."

With Hilda's approval and with the Institute's assurance that she could accompany me, I accepted the appointment sometime in early June. I was informed on June 10 that the German authorities had honored my request and were assigning me to the University of Göttingen, my first choice. I had selected Göttingen because it was the only German university with an established chair in Reformed Theology, the chair Karl Barth had held before he left for Bonn and Basel.

Under the circumstances, Hilda and I laid plans early on for a summer or fall wedding. Already on June 27, I forwarded Hilda's health certificate to the foreign authorities and sent to the New York Institute a money order in payment of the premium on our two health insurance policies. We did not then know whether we could live on the cash stipend I would be receiving, but we determined to proceed nevertheless. We reasoned that we could borrow funds from friends or relatives if we needed additional monies.

I brought my 150-page dissertation entitled "The Christian Idea of Revelation" to a close before the school term ended, and at the graduation exercises held on May 27, 1936, I was granted a master's degree in theology. Thus ended my stay at Hartford.

*   *   *   *   *

During my stay in Hartford, the world continued, of course, to move on. In 1935, Hitler added twelve 250-ton vessels to his submarine fleet; and he banned weddings between Jews and Aryans. In the spring of 1936 he occupied the Rhineland, and threw his weight in support of Franco in the then-erupting Spanish Civil War. At about the same time, President Thomas Masaryk of Czechoslovakia went into retirement and was succeeded by Eduard Benes; Ethiopia's Haile Selassie was driven into exile; and in England the death of King George V led to the enthronement of the hapless and ill-fated Edward VIII. Of less consequence in 1935 was the retirement of Babe Ruth and the death in a plane crash of Will Rogers.

Things were happening closer to home as well. In March 1936, George Stob, my cousin, classmate, and close friend, was ordained to the gospel ministry in Sumas, Washington, and my buddy Leroy Vogel was finishing his studies at Princeton Seminary and contemplating going to Heidelberg. At the May 1936 meeting of Calvin's Board of Trustees, Dr. Cornelius Van Til was appointed professor of philosophy to fill the vacancy left by the departure of Dr. Jellema; but early in June, Van Til wired the board "that [he] could not see his way clear to accept the appointment tendered [him]." The board thereupon decided "to reappoint Mr. Jesse De Boer for another year" and to postpone making a permanent appointment until the next annual meeting. At its June meeting the Synod of the Christian Reformed Church issued a warning against birth control; and on June 11, 1936, the Presbyterian Church of America (later the Orthodox Presbyterian Church) came into being.

*   *   *   *   *

After attending the graduation exercises at the First Methodist Episcopal Church in Hartford in late May, I returned to Grand Rapids about the first of June for a visit with Hilda. We discussed the future, laid plans for the summer, and decided on a September wedding date. We determined that Hilda should continue working at Steketee's and that I would return to Chicago to be near my mother and to find remunerative employment. Mother had spent the winter with Mart and Therese; but she had moved back to Cicero in the spring and now lived in a rented apartment at 1443 South 59th Court. The apartment was too small to accommodate the two of us, so I took up residence with Bill and Til as I had done in the past. Through the good offices of relatives, I found a job at Western Electric Company: I was paid eighteen dollars a week for breaking up old telephones with a hammer and casting their various metal parts into the several barrels that surrounded me. It did not escape my attention that at the age of fifteen I had earned the same pay at a less menial job.

I did not see Hilda during the rest of June, but she did come to Chicago in early July, and she was introduced to my many relatives when she attended the Stob family picnic that was held on Independence Day. I had preached on three successive June Sundays in the Chicago area, but I determined thereafter to come to Grand Rapids and environs as often as I could. Fortunately, I was able to preach in English and Dutch at Beaverdam on July 12, in English at West Leonard and in Dutch at Eastern Avenue on July 19, and in Dutch at Coldbrook on July 26. On these occasions I was put up at Hilda's house; but I had to leave on the midnight train in order to be back at work on Monday morning.

In August I was able to travel to Grand Rapids only twice. I preached at Fulton, Illinois, on the second and at Cicero II on the ninth; but on August 16 I preached at LaGrave, and on August 30 at Allendale and Rusk.

On August 21, an announcement of our forthcoming marriage, accompanied by a large photo of Hilda, appeared on the society page of the *Grand Rapids Press,* and on subsequent days a number of wedding showers for Hilda were given by Flora Ryskamp, Marie De Graaf, Hermine Weeber, and Nell Krombeen.

I quit my job at Western Electric on September 4, 1936, preached at Roseland II in English and at Chicago I in Dutch on September 6, and, taking the midnight train, I arrived at Hilda's house in Grand Rapids early on Monday morning, the seventh. The next four days were busy ones. Hilda had made a great start in gathering together the things we were to take with us abroad; but these and hitherto

Bride and Bridegroom

unthought of things had to be put in trunks and boxes and shipped by freight to the port of New York. These tasks occupied almost all of our time.

When, on September 11, the day of our wedding dawned, our spirits were high, and I looked forward with joy to a perpetual union with the woman I loved. Hilda was engaged with her own preparations during the day, and I went to the neighborhood barber for a haircut and a shave. This was the first time I had been shaved by a barber, and it proved to be the last. I have never since been shaved by another.

The wedding was held at 8:00 p.m. on Friday, September 11, 1936, in the East Leonard Christian Reformed Church, which was only a short distance from Hilda's Leonard Street home. The congregation had been invited to witness the ceremony, and the church was packed. My mother and all my brothers and sisters with their spouses were, of course, in attendance, as were all of Hilda's family and her many friends. Unfortunately, the weather that evening was not fair: a heavy rain fell as we entered the church, and the downpour remained unabated through most of the night. Hermine Weeber attended Hilda as her bridesmaid, and my good friend Henry Zylstra was my best man. John Daling and Hilda's brother Andy served as ushers.

When Hilda and her attendants were gathered in a side room for the adjustment of her gown and for other preparations, Hank Zylstra arrived with a briefcase in his hand. When asked what he carried, he inquired in return whether there was a men's room in the building. When I said there indeed was such a room, we repaired thither, and he withdrew from his case a clothes brush for my grooming and then a pint of whisky, saying, "I thought we needed this." I readily concurred, whereupon we toasted each other and went upstairs.

Prof. Louis Berkhof had agreed to perform the wedding ceremony at a full-fledged worship service. There were the usual prayers and songs of praise, and also a sermon, whose text and contents I have forgotten. William Westberg was the soloist that evening. When Prof. Berkhof left the pulpit and came down to unite us in marriage, Hilda (as she later told me) wondered whether he had had a nip, but when we kissed, the secret was out. It should be said, though, that I suffered no reproach.

A reception was held in the basement of the church for members of the family and about seventy invited guests. There was a program of sorts. Prof. Henry Ryskamp, my newly acquired brother-in-law, and his wife Flora, Hilda's sister, were the master and mistress of ceremonies. There were toasts, a few speeches, and a child's recitation by Ruth De Graaf, now Mrs. Lamont Dirkse. There was also much hugging and kissing between us and the family members we would soon be leaving. There were also gifts, of course, some money that we pocketed, and some household goods that we stored in the back room of Mr. De Graaf's grocery store.

When the festivities were drawing to a close, Hilda and I left in a borrowed car for Holland, Michigan. Hilda's brother Clarence and his wife Marie had vacated their house on Black Lake for the night and made it available to us. I was twenty-eight years old at the time, and Hilda had just turned twenty-seven.

*   *   *   *   *

We returned to Grand Rapids the very next day, Saturday, the twelfth, and re-established ourselves in Hilda's parental home. On Sunday, the thirteenth, I preached twice in LaGrave Avenue Church. On Monday and Tuesday we packed our bags for the journey, and at noon on Wednesday, September 16, 1936, we entrained for the east coast.

I should point out that the German Exchange Fellowship I had received did not cover our travel expenses. Just how we managed to pay for our boat and train tickets I do not remember. I know that Hilda had saved a hundred dollars out of her meager earnings, and that I had laid aside a slightly larger sum; but additional funds must have come to us from other sources. It is probable that my brother Tom paid for most or all of our boat fare. To finance our stay in Europe, we also borrowed five hundred dollars from Hilda's uncle, David De Boer, at 5 percent interest; but this we kept in reserve under the management of Henry Ryskamp. In any case, when we left Grand Rapids we had our train and boat tickets in hand, and we carried in our wallets one hundred dollars in traveler's checks, one hundred and fifty German marks (the equivalent of thirty-seven U. S. dollars), and $26.50 in cash. This, we judged, would hold us until the first German fellowship check arrived on the first of November.

Considering the state of our finances, we did what then seemed expedient and prudent but was in fact a most unromantic and regretful thing: on this our first real honeymoon excursion, instead of taking a Pullman sleeper, we booked coach seats on the train and sat up the

146

*John and Helen
Hamersma
see us off*

whole of an almost sleepless night. This was a mode of travel obviously unsuited to a new and beautiful bride. The train fare was $28.50. We stopped enroute and had breakfast in Allentown, Pennsylvania, with Prof. E. E. S. Johnson of Hartford, who had expressed a desire to see us before we embarked. He wished, it turned out, to give us last-minute instructions about Göttingen, and to bid us Godspeed.

We arrived in New York City at 12:30 p.m. on Thursday, September 17, and went directly to the Hotel Pennsylvania, where a room had been reserved for us. While Hilda was resting, I procured a visa at the German consulate, and toward evening we ate dinner in a neighborhood restaurant; the bill was eighty-five cents. We went to bed early that night, for we were exhausted, and at mid-morning on the eighteenth we checked out of the hotel. The night's lodging cost us the virtual king's ransom of $5.75.

My friend John Hamersma lived with his parents in nearby Ridgewood, New Jersey, and he had earlier invited us to spend the night at his house and be escorted by him the next morning to the Hoboken docks. We accepted his gracious invitation, boarded a bus on Friday afternoon, and arrived in Ridgewood in time to sit down to a hearty dinner. John and his fiancée Helen took us out on the town that evening, and on the next day they drove us to the docks.

We had booked passage on the *Veendam*, a Holland-American Line vessel, and the four of us boarded it about a half hour before it sailed. We had time to inspect our cabin, drink a toast to one another's health and welfare, and express our fond farewells before all guests were ordered ashore and anchors were weighed.

We broke from our moorings at 12:30 p.m. on Saturday, September 19, 1936, sailed past the Statue of Liberty, and moved out to sea on a voyage that would bring us eventually to Rotterdam — and to a new life on the continent of Europe.

The *Veendam* was a very large ship, but on this sailing the passengers were few. There were only sixty of them aboard — thirty-three in first class, fifteen in tourist class, and twelve in third class. Hilda and I were third-class passengers, but in spite of our low estate, we found the accommodations to our liking. Our cabin adequately met our needs, the food was excellent, and our fellow passengers were congenial even though not quite our type. During the voyage we socialized very little: we were on our honeymoon and we relished our freedom and privacy. Life aboard ship was leisurely. We sat quietly on deck, played daily at Ping-Pong and shuffleboard, and read a good deal. We attended no festivities, visited no ballroom, and saw no movies. It was a time of rest and peace, yet spiced with anticipation and enticing prospects.

Our expenditures aboard ship were slight. Modern travelers would find it hard to believe that after renting deck chairs, paying the orchestra assessment, and tipping the porter as well as the cabin, dining room, and deck stewards, and making purchases in the bar and commissary, our total expenditures came to $9.25. The round-trip boat tickets had cost $329.50.

After nine days of sailing, the ship anchored in Plymouth Harbor, and on the next day, at 5:00 p.m. on September 29, 1936, we came to rest at Rotterdam. For us the academic year 1935-36 had come to an end, and an unknown future beckoned us.

8

AT THE UNIVERSITY OF GÖTTINGEN
(1936-1938)

When we had made our travel arrangements, we knew that we were scheduled to arrive in Europe a full month before school started. Our course of action was deliberate: we wished to acclimatize ourselves before settling down, and the opportunity to do so had been provided by my German friend Wilhelm Vauth. He had invited us to spend a month at his parental home in the farming community of Rusbend, near the town of Bückeburg, in the beautiful Weser Valley of Schaumburg-Lippe, and to it we directed our steps. First, however, we had to pass through the Rotterdam customs offices, to set our feet on Dutch soil, and to survey a portion of the Lowlands where our parents first saw the light of day.

Our coming ashore at Rotterdam was made pleasant by the reception we received. Greeting us at dockside were distant relatives of Hilda who had earlier been apprised of our coming. Oom Hannes and Tante Grietje, as we called them, along with their adult daughter Adriana, welcomed us to The Netherlands, conducted us to their modest home, and prepared for us an ample supper. For want of space, however, they were unable to put us up for the night. Thus, after spending a pleasant evening in conversation, we rented a room in a nearby Salvation Army hostel where, amid primitive conditions, we slept the sleep of the innocent. The night's lodging cost us $1.15.

Adriana and her boyfriend, Henry Roelofs, called on us early the next morning and took us on a full day's tour of the city and its busy harbor. Oom Hannes and Tante Grietje were no less hospitable: in order to provide us with sleeping accommodations that night, they, despite our protests, vacated their bedroom and slept in the bunk-lined cabin of their tugboat, which was moored nearby. Living in the house at the time was Tante Grietje's aged mother, a sister of Hilda's paternal grandmother. She was keenly alert, and it was a delight to hear her speak in Dutch of things long past. Her sleeping quarters, we noticed, consisted of a space built into a wall, and this intrigued us.

On the following day, the first of October, we headed by train for Amsterdam, stopping en route for a look at The Hague. We slept that night in an Amsterdam hotel and spent nearly the whole of the next day in an exploration of the city and its prestigious Ryksmuseum. At 6:00 p.m. that evening we entrained for Appeldoorn, where we were met by Hilda's uncle, Harry Veldsma, who put us up that night in his comfortable home.

On the next day, the third of October, we took a train to the border town of Bentheim, where, after passing through customs, we transferred to a German train bound for Bückeburg. Wilhelm met us upon our arrival there, and after we dined on sauerkraut and bratwurst at a local Gasthaus, he drove us in a borrowed car to his home in Rusbend.

*   *   *   *   *

The house we entered was set on a "farm" of ten or fifteen acres on which, between stints of outside employment, Vater Vauth raised corn and garden produce. One came up to the house from an unpaved road and entered it after traversing a patio fitted for outdoor relaxation. I do not remember how the inside rooms were arranged, but I know that there was a large kitchen, a larger dining and sitting room where we ate and socialized, and a parlor furnished with, among other things, a foot-pumped organ that Hilda sometimes played. We reached our upstairs sleeping quarters by ascending a steep staircase, and the bed we occupied was spread with a thick feather quilt. What to us was unusual about the house was the fact that the barn, which stabled two cows and several pigs, was attached to the house and was in a sense

Mr. Vauth and Henry harvesting corn

one with it. It was at the far end of the barn that the two-seater non-flushable toilet stood, and the journey to it led past the penned animals, who by their grunting and mooing gave Hilda some uncomfortable moments, especially when the journey had to be made at night by the light of a lantern.

Living in the house besides Vater and Mutter Vauth, who appeared to be in their early or middle fifties, was a twentyish daughter named Enna, a teen-ager named Sophie, and two much younger children, whose names matched our own, which is why during the month of October and (we were told) for a considerable time thereafter they were known to the world as "Kleine Heine" and "Kleine Hilda." Wilhelm also lived at home, but he was undergoing instruction preparatory to ordination and this involved his periodic absence from the scene.

Hilda knew no German, so her first days with the Vauths were quite difficult; but she soon learned to communicate reasonably well, and

Hilda in traditional German dress, with Hilda and Heinie

this stood her in good stead when we arrived in Göttingen. She and I were generally at leisure and had time for our own pursuits, but Hilda assisted with the house work and I helped Vater Vauth harvest the corn and do the daily chores. Kleine Heine was in the process of mastering the intricacies of German script, and since I was setting myself to the same task, the two of us could often be found at the table absorbed in our joint endeavor.

I was not helpful in easing Hilda's transition to life on a German farm. On the very evening that we arrived in Rusbend, Wilhelm proposed that he and I attend a Hitler rally that was to be held the next day in a field near Hameln, a town famed for its fabled Rattenfänger. Unmindful of the fact that this would leave Hilda amid virtual strangers whose language she did not understand, I readily — even eagerly — agreed to the proposal. We set out on bikes the following morning and arrived at the distant scene in time to hear Hitler address a vast crowd of awed and admiring citizens. It was here that I first heard the "Heil Hitler" chant and saw arms outstretched in the Nazi salute, and the performance had a chilling effect on me. When the rally ended, we set out for home; but before we had gone very far, I, being unused to riding a bike, grew faint from exhaustion. Wilhelm escorted me to a nearby inn where, upon retiring, I fell into a deep sleep that lasted all night. Wilhelm meanwhile continued on his way home and informed a distraught Hilda of my indisposition and unintended absence. After receiving directions from the proprietor of the Gasthaus in Krückeberg, I found my way back to Rusbend on the following day, and was greeted by Hilda with what may fairly be described as mixed emotions.

Early on we had placed an ad in the *Göttingen Tageblad* inquiring about apartments for rent and, when we had received a number of replies, Wilhelm and I set out for Göttingen. On October 14 we boarded a train at Kirchhorsten and proceeded via Hannover to Hildesheim, where, after touring that picturesque town, we spent the night. The next morning in Göttingen we engaged furnished rooms at No. 4 Obere Masch Strasse, and arranged to have our trunks shipped from Rotterdam to this address. As soon as our work was completed, we left Göttingen and, via the train and our bikes, returned to Rusbend toward noon on the sixteenth.

Hilda, meanwhile, was not confined to the house. The two of us sometimes sat in privacy on the bank of the canal that flowed past the house; we took walks along the road, stopping sometimes at the nearby inn for a stein of beer; and we made joint trips to Bückeburg, Vehlen, and Stadthagen. It was during this time, too, that Hilda accompanied Enna on a trip to Porta Westfalica.

We were nonpaying guests at the Vauths during our four-week stay in Rusbend, and we deeply appreciated the family's Christian kindness and hospitality. We sought to express our appreciation by providing occasional treats, and before our departure for Göttingen we placed in each family member's hand a gift representing our gratitude.

We bade farewell to the Vauths on October 31 and boarded a train for Hannover. We surveyed the city that day and lodged there that night. On the evening of the next day, November 1, 1936, we took up residence in our newly acquired, two-room, mid-town apartment.

Before we settled down for an academic year of work, we took notice of the fact that a black American by the name of Jesse Owens had embarrassed Hitler by winning three gold medals in the Berlin Olympic games in August. We also learned — this time to our own embarrassment — that the American Ezra Pound was broadcasting for Mussolini and that his fellow countryman, Fred Kaltenbach, was doing the same for Hitler. It was not long before we also heard that Franklin Roosevelt had handily defeated Alf Landon in the race for the Presidency of the United States.

*　　*　　*　　*　　*

Frau Klempt was our landlady at the Obere Masch address, and we paid her fifty-five Marks (about $13.50) a month for the two rooms we occupied in her second-floor residence. The medium-sized bedroom was furnished with twin beds, a loose-standing wardrobe, and a small chest of drawers on which stood the porcelain wash basin and water pitcher with which we performed our daily ablutions. A door at the corner of this room led onto a balcony, which we seldom used but from which we could survey the whole of the short block on which we lived. The living room-study area contained a desk set at a window, a bookcase, a small settee, a round table with chairs, and a coal-burning stove. The single door that led into our rooms opened on a hall; on the other side of it was the toilet room as well as the living quarters of Frau Klempt and her two teen-aged children, Ilsa and Herbert. The Klempt kitchen stove was placed at our disposal; but after a trial period, Hilda found it expedient to exercise her independence and prepare meals in our own apartment. To this end we bought a *Spiritus Apparat*, a small kerosene stove with one burner on which food could be heated when patience and caution were exercised. Of course, we had to buy the kerosene, coal, and kindling wood we used, and to pay the electric bill and radio assessment; but since we had no phone, telecommunications cost us nothing. We had no icebox or refrigerator either, and this required us to shop daily for groceries. Early on, Hilda assumed the shopping duties, and her German vocabulary in the food category soon outstripped my own. She was able to buy everything we needed, except that the baker would

154

Göttingen city street, Johanniskirche in background

sell her only day-old bread and then but half a loaf, and that Herr Schlimpen would allow her to buy only two eggs at a time, preferably such as had a crack in them. The house we lived in was one of a solid block of lawless houses that ranged along the cobblestoned street and abutted the narrow sidewalk. It was just a few blocks from the railroad station, and just off the tree-lined Goethe Allee by which one could easily reach the commercial establishments on Weenderstrasse as well as the beer *Keller* in the ancient *Rathaus.*

Göttingen was not a large town: its population did not exceed perhaps thirty or forty thousand; but it was an old town with many reminders of its medieval origin. Located in the province of Hannover, it lay in a valley surrounded by forested hills, one of which, the Nikolausberg, lay within walking distance and attracted many hikers, including ourselves. Just when the site was settled is not certain, but it is said that the deepest foundation underlying the Albanikirche dates from the days of Charlemagne. What is known is that the city's Rathaus dates from the fourteenth century and that the once fortified and still standing wall that outlines the inner city, was in place before the Rathaus was built. The wide wall, now severed in spots by crossing thoroughfares, was shaded by lofty trees and much used by strollers when we were there. Hilda and I often walked it on Sunday afternoons. Still gracing it is the small stone house that Bismarck built and lived in when he was a student at the university.

Dominating the skyline were the city's churches: visible for miles were the twin towers of the Johanniskirche and the lofty spire of the Jakobikirche. These churches and the less imposing Mariankirche were unheated in winter, and on cold days the worshipers, we among them, sat huddled in overcoats and gloves during the entire service. The town was famous for the ancient Gasthaus on Kurzenstrasse called the "Schwarzen Bären" and also the sculptured fountain known as the "Gänselieselbrunnen," which stood on the Rathaus square. On market days the square was full of vendors offering tempting fruits, vegetables, and flowers to the householders who each week were attracted to the place.

The university was clearly the most prominent and influential institution in the city, but its true name was not widely known outside officialdom. Just as the town derived its fame from the university, so the university tended to derive its identity from the town: thus it came to be known to the public as Göttingen's university or the University of Göttingen. But this was not its real name. Founded in 1737 by the prime minister of provincial Hannover, Gerlach Adolph Von Münchhausen, the school was by its charter called the Georgia Augusta University, and that name it still retains, although hardly anyone now thinks of calling it that. The university had an auspicious beginning, and, though comparatively young as European seats of learning go, it has had a memorable career. It drew its earliest students from the ranks of German nobles and landed gentry, and its distinguished faculty has throughout the years attracted students from around the globe. I am unqualified to judge its stature during my residence there, and I suspect that, like other German schools, it suffered under the restrictions imposed by the Nazis and the purges effected by Hitler; but I have no cause to question the competence of my teachers or to complain of their attitudes and behavior. In 1936 the university's buildings were spread across town, though there was a campus of sorts where a number of the constituent schools and colleges were clustered. Instruction in mathematics and the natural sciences perhaps took on a different form, but in theology and philosophy — and in the humanities as a whole — instruction proceeded by the lecture method. Except in seminars and tutorials, where discussion and dialogue could take place, the typical student could fairly be described as a "hearer" who sat respectfully in an auditorium and listened without comment or rejoinder to the reading of a manuscript by the professor, who in all likelihood would reconstitute it as a chapter in his next book. That mode of instruction and learning had its disadvantages, but it could also lead the student to pursue his own inquiries, and this quite often happened. In my own case, the lectures I heard served largely as stimuli that moved me to read around the subject on which the professor was discoursing.

*   *   *   *   *

When I was enrolled as a graduate student in theology on November 7, 1936, Hilda also entered the university: in the company of a number of her newfound friends she joined a class in "German for foreign students." The instruction she received not only improved her hold on the language but also introduced her to significant aspects of Teutonic culture.

I began my studies under three instructors. Committing myself to

The Vehlen Cyclist

nine hours of course work, I took a four-hour course in "Dogmatik, I Teil" (on the foundations of dogmatics) with Prof. Otto Weber; a two-hour course in the "Grundzüge der Theologie Calvins" (on the principles of Calvin's theology) with the same Prof. Weber; a two-hour course in "Leidensgeschichte" (on the passion of Christ) with Prof. Joachim Jeremias; and a one-hour course in "das Historische Bewusstsein" (on historical consciousness) with Prof. Nohl. These were all lecture courses, and at the outset I attended the scheduled lectures with exemplary regularity. However, this was not the custom of my German counterparts, and in due time I learned to moderate my zeal and be selective. I had some difficulty at first in following the lecturers' rapid discourse, but I soon became sufficiently proficient in German both to understand what was being said and to respond in kind.

I decided early on that I should work toward an advanced degree

*Henry the
Heidelberg
Swordsman*

and, receiving Prof. Weber's consent to be my sponsor and promoter, I proposed that I write a dissertation on "Jonathan Edwards: A Study in Puritan Ethics." This subject proved acceptable to Dr. Weber, and securing a set of Edwards' complete works, I began already in January 1937 to read regularly in these volumes and to take relevant notes. Although broken up by a nearly month-long Christmas recess, the first semester extended from the tenth of November to the middle of March, and during that time I addressed myself as best I could to my studies. But, of course, other things were going on in the meantime.

The Thanksgiving season was brightened by the appearance in Göttingen of our friend Leroy Vogel, who had come from Heidelberg to spend a week with us. On Thanksgiving Day we dined together in the "Schwartzer Bären" and expressed our gratitude to God for the many blessings we had received. On subsequent days we took Bird up Nikolausberg and showed him the sights not only in Göttingen but also in Hannoverischmünden. Before year's end, Hilda and I made other brief excursions into the countryside and visited Lippoldsberg, Bodenfelde, and Witzenhausen. Our social life was not extensive, but the English-speaking students at the university formed a kind of loose fraternity, a number of us got together on occasion for lunch or supper, and almost all of us were present at a Christmas party held in the Ratskeller on December 18.

Although we noticed with mounting interest the preparations made by those in Göttingen who would in piety or indifference observe the anniversary of Christ's birth, we ourselves did not spend Christmas Day on German soil. We spent it in the company of our relatives in Holland. In the village of Uithuizen, the birthplace of my mother, her only living sister, my "Tante Grietje," still lived with her husband, "Oom Wiebrand" Bultema, and they had invited us to join them and their children during the Christmas recess. We eagerly accepted the invitation, both for the opportunity it gave us to see the very locale where my parents were born and raised and for the pleasure of meeting for the first time a set of close relatives whom we had not known about until recently. An unmarried daughter of Tante Grietje, my cousin Tena, lived in Nieuwschans, where she practiced nursing, and it was she who met us at the railroad station when we arrived at that border town on December 23. Tena greeted us with the hugs and kisses befitting a near kin, conducted us to her home, prepared for us a sumptuous dinner, and put us up for the night. The three of us took a train the next morning to the city of Groningen, and we went on from there to Uithuizen, where we were most affectionately received by Oom and Tante, and in subsequent days treated with extraordinary hospitality. Christmas fell on Friday in 1936, and on that day we worshipped in the old Hervormde Kerk that my mother attended when she was a child. On Saturday ("De tweede Kerstdag") we went to church in Oudezijl, and on Sunday we attended services in Roodeschool, where Tjaard Van Ellen, the husband of my cousin Coba Bultema, taught school.

Since I had expressed a desire to see my father's birthplace in Broek in the "Gemeente" Eenrum, Tjaard proposed that we begin our quest for it on Monday morning. We started out on bike in the direction

Mr. and Mrs. Cornelius Stob

of Usguert, saw the place where my mother was born, stopped at the "Boerderij Klooster" in Usguert, where my mother had worked as a maid, then went on through Warffum and Baflo to Eenrum. Our inquiries at the "Gemeente Huis" yielded no information about the exact location of my father's birthplace, but we were told that an elderly pair by the name of Stob lived in Hornhuizen. We took to our bikes and went over Wehe, Kloosterburen, Molenrij, and Kruisweg to Hornhuizen, where we were able to call on an eighty-three-year-old Cornelius Stob, who proved to be a cousin of my father, and who with his wife seemed delighted to meet a namesake from America. After a short visit with our genial hosts we returned to Uithuizen. We must

161

have ridden 80 kilometers that day and I was completely exhausted, but I was glad to have made the trip and to have passed through the scenes of my parents' childhood.

On the following days we visited Oldenzijl, Sandeweer, and Oudeschip and spent a night with Tjaard and Coba in Roodeschool. When the time came for us to leave Uithuizen, we bade our hosts a tearful farewell, expressed our deep gratitude, and proceeded to Groningen, where we spent a day with my cousin Jan Bultema and his wife. Jan, a police officer, had the day off, and he conducted us on an informative tour of the city. We spent New Year's Day with Tena in Nieuwschans and entrained the next morning for Göttingen and home.

Classes at the university soon reconvened, and my studies during the rest of the first semester continued apace, although the presence of Wilhelm Vauth in early January did not enhance my concentration. Wilhelm was spending ten January days in Göttingen for the purpose of completing his examinations, and he was a frequent guest in our house during his whole stay. Soon after his departure, Hilda and I began taking our warm meal in the student "Mensa." What we usually had for dinner was a bowl of "Linsen Suppe," sometimes garnished with a piece of wurst. It was also in January that I bought a bike; the purchase took twenty-three Marks ($6.00) out of our treasury.

In early February, Hilda and I hiked to Rosdorf and made a trip to Kassel. It was no doubt a sign of my growing Germanness that in this month I bought a suit with knicker pants at a cost of thirty Marks; the outfit went well with the walking stick that I had earlier bought for seventy Pfenning. On the seventeenth of February we English-speaking students got together for a "Costüm Fest" sponsored by the German Austaushdienst, and a week later the group gave a farewell party for Herr Lautenbach, who, in behalf of the German government, had directed our faltering feet during the period of our orientation.

The month of March was memorable in a number of ways. On the eleventh we celebrated our semi-anniversary. On the twenty-third, Wilhelm Vauth was ordained to the gospel ministry and became pastor of the Lutheran church in Vehlen, near Bückeburg. We sent him a copy of Heim's *Versöhnung* as an ordination gift. In mid-March the first semester ground to a halt, and in the interval between terms I engaged in some sober reflection: I began to have second thoughts about pursuing the theological course of study. I had enjoyed my acquaintance with Jeremias and Weber, and I no doubt profited from their lectures, but I found that what they contributed to my already existing store of theological knowledge was hardly enough to justify my continuing to plow familiar ground. Moreover, the allure of philosophy had fastened upon me. Therefore, I determined to change course, and on March 25, 1937, at the beginning of the second (or summer) semester, I transferred to the school of philosophy and enrolled in several courses there. During this three-month semester (April through June) I took a three-hour course in "Philosophie der Geschichte" (philosophy of history) with Prof. Heyse; a two-hour course in "Philosophie der Gegenwart" (contemporary philosophy) with Prof. Bollnow; and a two-hour course in "Die Geschichte der englischen Philosophie" (history of English philosophy) with Prof. Baumgarten. To avoid too abrupt a break with the school of theology, I also took a four-hour course in ethics with Prof. Friedrich Gogarten, joined Prof. Weber's two-hour seminar on Reformed thought, and attended Prof. Jeremias's weekly lecture on Galatians. Hilda meanwhile continued her studies by taking a university course in English literature taught in the German language.

During that semester I continued my independent study of Jonathan Edwards. Knowing that Edwards was a critical student of Locke and an eminent philosopher himself, I believed that a dissertation on his system of thought would be acceptable to the philosophical faculty, and I at once conferred with Prof. Heyse about this. Although he was the head of the department, he was noncommittal on the subject and referred me to his associate, Dr. Baumgarten, who, it turned out, had already been appointed my sponsor in case I chose to pursue a doctorate in philosophy. Baumgarten was undecided and needed time to reflect; but he reminded me that in any case I would need at least another year to complete a dissertation. He suggested that I ask the people in Hartford to renew the fellowship, and he promised to write a letter in support of my request. I followed his good advice, and already on April 9, 1937, I received a favorable reply from Hartford's Dr. Johnson: "The faculty has voted the reappointment of you as an Exchange Fellow to Germany for the year 1937-38." I was, of course, elated with the news and was doubly gratified when on June 3 the secretary of the Institute of International Education in New York wrote: "Our Committee on Selection has granted you a renewal of your fellowship." I was now assured of another year's stipend and had gotten a new lease on life. But the precise subject of the projected dissertation remained for the moment undetermined; when at the end of June the semester came to a close, the issue was still unresolved and I had no alternative but to spend the summer in pursuit of Edwards.

In April, I visited Bursfelde with Professor Carl Stange, the honorary "Abt" of the ancient monastery there, and Hilda and I attended a picnic hosted by Herr and Frau Stumer. On the first of May we were present at a local fair and we later visited Mariensprings and Heiligenstadt. But the event of the month was our going off in different directions for diversion and relaxation. Sometime in May the exchange students from various German universities were invited to be the guests of the government on a ten-day Rhine and Midland Tour funded by the Carl Schurz Foundation. The invitation, unfortunately, did not extend to student spouses, and I considered not joining the tour until our friend, Hans Kropatchek, a fellow student at the university, invited Hilda to spend the entire period of the "Reise" in the company of himself and his wife at his mother's home in Ilfeld, deep in the Harz mountains. When Hilda sacrificially — and with some trepidation — accepted the invitation, I joined the group of travelers with a somewhat troubled conscience. I saw Hilda off for Ilfeld on May 27, and I joined the bus caravan the next day. Hilda's stay with the Kropatcheks was pleasant enough but quite uneventful, and she was happy to return home when the period of my exile ended. Our group, meanwhile, was taken on a wide-ranging tour that was both pleasant and informative: we visited Münster, Kassel, the Wartburg, Bamberg, Nuremberg, Düsseldorf, Hameln, Goslar, Köln, and several other places, in each of which we were feted, wined, dined, and domiciled like princes of the realm. On June 7, after ten days of separation, Hilda and I were together again, and for several days thereafter we entertained each other with tales of our adventures.

With the coming of June, the end of the school year and the prospect of a long summer's recess were on the horizon. We had already determined where we were to spend the summer; only the details needed fixing. Wilhelm Vauth, still a bachelor, lived with his sister Enna in a large country parsonage in Vehlen, and he had proposed that we stay there during the summer and share household expenses. We enthusiastically endorsed the proposal, and on June 12 I set out on bike on the long journey to Vehlen to inspect the premises and to make final arrangements. It chanced that, as I rode, I met up with a gypsy caravan. As I approached the horse-drawn wagons, a female member of the group signaled for me to stop. When I did so, she asked me for a cigarette, which I promptly provided. She thereupon offered to tell my fortune, but I replied that I had neither time nor money for such frivolities and that, in any case, I put no stock in necromancy and divination. She restrained me for a moment, however, and in dulcet tones said simply that "a great change in the circumstances of your life is about to happen."

Proceeding on my way, I dismissed the pronouncement as an idle tale and gave it no further thought. Because the distance to Vehlen was great, I lodged overnight in a Gasthaus and arrived at Wilhelm's quite early on the morning of the thirteenth. I discussed with him our mutual plans for the summer, but made no reference to my encounter with the gypsy. I left Vehlen in late afternoon that same day and rode until nightfall. I slept in a Gasthaus that night and arrived home toward evening on the fourteenth. A visibly excited Hilda met me on the stairs. She held in her hand a letter that she urged me to read without delay, and, when I sat down, I read it with unbelief.

The letter was from my brother George, and in it he congratulated me on my appointment to the chair of philosophy at Calvin College. The news was incredible. I had received no word concerning an appointment from any official source, and the likelihood of such a thing coming at this time and under these circumstances had never entered my mind. Yet the startling news proved to be true, and the smoking gypsy stood wondrously vindicated.

A day or so later, a letter dated June 5, 1937, arrived at our house. It was sent from Fremont, Michigan, and was signed by Rev. L. J. Lamberts, secretary of Calvin's Board of Trustees. This is what it said:

Dear Mr. Stob:

The Board of Trustees of Calvin College and Seminary has granted you the extension of licensure. This body took further action that may surprise you. It appointed you to the chair that Dr. Wm. H. Jellema vacated two years ago. When giving you this appointment, it decided:

(1) To make this appointment for a period of two years;
(2) That in case you may see your way clear to accept, to ask you to devote at least one year to the study of philosophy;

(3) To accord you the rank of instructor and to set your salary at
$2000 per annum, with the understanding that you will begin
to receive this salary after you have entered upon your active
work.

You will understand, of course, that the Board does not intend to
limit your services to a period of two years, but that it is following
the time-honored procedure in the matter of appointments. I hope
you will send me a favorable reply before long.

Yours very truly,

L. J. Lamberts,
Secretary

The mail that brought Rev. Lambert's letter also brought letters
from President Ralph Stob, Prof. Henry Ryskamp, and Dr. Clarence
Bouma. From these informants I learned something about the circumstances surrounding the appointment. After Jellema had left, and
Cornelius Van Til had declined the offer to fill his position, the board
had appointed Jesse De Boer as a temporary replacement. Now, in
May 1937, the board was again in session and took under consideration two nominations the faculty had presented to it: Dr. Cecil De
Boer, professor of philosophy at the University of Nebraska, and Mr.
Jesse De Boer, the able incumbent of the chair during the two-year
vacancy. But wishing to add to the list of nominees a person with
philosophical aptitudes and schooling who was also versed in theology,
the board placed my name in nomination. After receiving from the
faculty's education policy committee a *nihil obstat* regarding the addition of my name, the board proceeded to vote. To the surprise of
many both inside and outside the academic community — and no
doubt to the consternation of some — I received a majority of the
votes and was consequently appointed to the chair Prof. Jellema had
graced with distinction and renown for fifteen years.

Honored by and grateful for the appointment, I was nevertheless
frightened by it. Sensitive to the demands and responsibilities of the
task I had been invited to undertake, I was equally aware of my own
limitations and deficiencies; and I wondered why at this early stage in
my career I had been brought to this *Stunde der Entscheidung*. Daunted

by the challenge I faced, I was initially uncertain what response I should make. Hilda and I naturally discussed the matter by day and night, and we consulted as best we could our friends and relatives. But the final decision was wrought out of our wrestlings with God. A week or so after being apprised of the appointment, I dispatched a letter of acceptance. Although I did this with some trepidation, I was convinced that my action had the Lord's concurrence.

Thus, with my work at the university still in progress, and with my twenty-ninth birthday still before me, I had committed myself to teaching philosophy in the college from which I had graduated a scant five years before. A heap of correspondence followed. Stob, Ryskamp, and Rouma continued to write, and kind letters arrived from Professors Broene, Vanden Bosch, and Van Andel; but it was with Rev. Lamberts that I was chiefly engaged in the ensuing weeks. It appeared that the executive committee of the board, with Rev. Lamberts as its spokesman, wanted me to work toward a theological degree and only when that was in hand to spend a year in the study of philosophy. I found it hard to understand the proposal and still harder to concur in it. I informed Rev. Lamberts that I had already enrolled in the school of philosophy in March and argued that the interests of all concerned would be best served if I stayed on course and pursued a doctorate in philosophy. I added that in so doing I should also be fulfilling the board's demand that I "devote at least one year to the study of philosophy." The committee eventually saw the wisdom of this proposal and acknowledged that in so proceeding I would be meeting all of the board's technical requirements.

But another issue was constantly being raised in the correspondence. The Professors Vollenhoven and Dooyeweerd of the Free University of Amsterdam were developing what was popularly regarded as a specifically Christian philosophy which in its cosmic sweep embodied the essential elements of Calvinism, and the committee hoped that I would stay in Europe long enough to pursue a course of study under them. Indeed, it earnestly advised and virtually requested me to spend a postdoctoral year at the Free University. This I was reluctant to do. I did not doubt that I could profit from another year of study and reflection; but the arrangements made to facilitate my stay in Amsterdam were hardly to my liking, and I sensed that the proposed venture could adversely affect the many ties that bound Hilda and me together. The financial support the board offered was in the form of a repayable loan and amounted to only five hundred dollars. I knew that Hilda and I could neither live a whole year on so small a sum nor afford to go further into debt. I feared that my stay in Amsterdam would in all probability entail Hilda's return to the States, and neither of us relished the prospect of a six- or seven-month separation.

On the other hand, I was a new appointee without much leverage, and Hilda joined me in thinking that I could not cavalierly brush aside the wishes of the board. So we at last capitulated. On January 23, 1938, after a half year's pondering, I wrote a letter to Rev. Lamberts. In it I said, among other things, "I cannot in good conscience leave the advice of the Board unheeded. Let this writing, therefore, serve as a formal acceptance of your plan and as an expression of my intention to study at the Free University next year." With that the mass of sometimes confusing correspondence came to a temporary end.

It was on May 28, 1937, that I was appointed instructor in philosophy at Calvin College, and on June 21 I accepted the assignment. On the twenty-third we attended a party given by the English-American "Kultur Kreis"; on the twenty-fourth we celebrated my twenty-ninth birthday; and on the twenty-fifth we went to the opera for a performance of *Scipio*. The school term was now drawing to a close, and a long summer stretched invitingly before us. On June 29 we shipped our belongings to Vehlen, and on the thirtieth we vacated our apartment and severed our connection with Frau Klempt, our not always agreeable landlady. We had no cause to worry about the following year's lodging, for it had earlier been determined that when classes resumed we would be living with Prof. and Mrs. Stange in their house on Hanssenstrasse.

Hilda had visited the towns and villages that nestled in the countryside outside Göttingen, and she had spent ten days with the Kropatchecks in distant Ilfeld; but, barred from joining the "Carl Schurz Reise," she had not visited the German Rhineland. So I proposed that, before settling down for the summer, we take a ten-day vacation and explore that scenic region. Leaving Göttingen on the first of July, we visited Köln, Andernach, Coblenz, Bonn, St. Goor, Mainz, Worms, Heidelberg, Speyer, Würzburg, Meiningen, Eisenach, and Erfurt. The trip, of course, included a boat ride up the Rhine and, quite naturally, a two-day stay in Heidelberg for a pleasant visit with Leroy Vogel. Arriving back in Göttingen on the ninth, we entrained at once for rural Vehlen, where we took up residence in Wilhelm Vauth's spacious parsonage.

* * * * *

The country "Pfarrhaus" that we settled in was flanked on one side by a small grove of apple and plum trees, whose fruit we plucked as soon as it ripened. Out back was a vegetable and flower garden that Enna tended, and all around us were small farms with cultivated fields and meadows where cows and horses grazed. The house was set in a pleasant and peaceful environment: the stone and steepled church stood nearby, as did the residence of the hamlet's only school teacher. Hilda and I occupied two sparsely furnished upstairs rooms in Wilhelm's house. A bed, a chair, and a stand supporting a washbowl and water pitcher stood in our sleeping quarters; the adjoining room became my "study": a small table served as my desk, and we fashioned a bookcase out of crates. Hilda purchased fabric and made curtains for the windows. We did not feel deprived; considering the state of our pocketbooks, we felt privileged to be living there.

Hilda assisted Enna with the housework and meal preparation. Wilhelm and I, though engaged in our own work, pitched in where we could. For example, I was frequently dispatched to purchase food and supplies from the only store that served the neighborhood. To this end I rode the trusty bike that I had shipped up from Göttingen. We spent our days pleasantly in the performance of our varied tasks, and on Sundays we worshiped in the church where Wilhelm preached the gospel with competence and élan. Wilhelm was a member of the "Bekenntniskirche," which had prepared the Barmen Declaration, and he had no sympathy at all for the "German Christians" who had endorsed Hitler's anti-Jewish laws and proscriptions. In his public utterances, however, he had to be circumspect and prudent, for the Gestapo had long ears. In addition, Wilhelm's older brother had been — to the dismay of his parents — for some time a brown-shirted member of the party's "Schutz Abteilung." A person of that sort would not hesitate to indict any deviant, even though he be a brother.

My correspondence with the people at Calvin continued during our stay in Vehlen, but soon after our arrival there I addressed myself to serious study. I continued reading in Jonathan Edwards, and by the middle of August I had finished writing two long chapters on Edwards' ethics. I continued to hope that the philosophical faculty would accept a dissertation on Edwards' moral philosophy; but, being unsure and desiring certainty, I went to Göttingen in late August to confer with Prof. Baumgarten, my appointed mentor. Baumgarten did not object to my proposal, but he suggested that I might do better by considering more modern thinkers, especially such German philosophers as Dilthey, Jaspers, Heidegger, Rickert, Neurath, and the like — or even Nietzsche. As we continued to talk, I began to be persuaded by his arguments. The discussion then turned to my interest in religion and theology, and he proposed that I consider Max Weber, who had written epoch-making works on the typology and sociology of religion. This appealed to me, for a treatment of Weber would involve me in a study of how an apparently value-free empirical method can be employed to uncover the rationale of valuative behavior.

Before we parted, we had tentatively agreed on a subject: "Die Leitenden Kategorian der Interpretation in Max Weber's Systematische Religionssoziologie." The subject would later be modified, but I returned to Vehlen resolved to suspend my work on Edwards and to fix my mind on contemporary German theories of concept formation. With the coming of September, I read as widely as I could in Nietzsche, Misch, and Dilthey, but lacking Weber's works, I had to postpone a study of the master himself until later.

During our stay at Wilhelm's we made short trips to Obenkirche, Stadthagen, Minden, and Porta Westfalica, but we could usually be found at home tending to our business. We hosted occasional guests, among them the Priestlys, whom we had met in Hartford, and in late July we entertained my Dutch cousins Tena Bultema and Tjaard Van Ellen for several days. During this time I also received word from Clarence Bouma that he had placed in the July and August editions of *Calvin Forum* an essay on "Graeco-Roman and Christian Ethics" that I had earlier prepared for his course in senior ethics at the seminary.

What particularly marked our stay in Vehlen was the tragedy of death and the heavy burden of sorrow that we were forced to bear. The blow fell most heavily on Hilda. Late in August or early in September we received word that her sister Therese had on August 22 died in childbirth at the age of thirty-three. "Ted," as we called her, was Hilda's favorite sister, and her premature death affected Hilda deeply. The weight of the loss was increased by the fact that distance prevented our attending Ted's funeral. When the news of her death reached us, her body had already lain for several days in a stone-marked grave.

We were still recoiling from the shock of Therese's death when word reached us that the seven-month-old son of Mart and Therese had been electrocuted when he touched a frayed lamp cord on the living room floor. This tragic death occurred on September 17, and our hearts went out in sympathy and love to our dear brother and sister. But there was more to come. Just as we were ready to leave Vehlen, we received the news that Hilda's father had died of a heart attack on September 30. We learned later that he had worked that day as usual but after supper had lain down on the sofa to relieve a faintness he felt. Some minutes later he lay dead. He was but sixty-five years old. Mr. De Graaf was a God-fearing man, an elder in the church, and in all his dealings with people a gracious and considerate gentleman. "Ted" likewise was a child of God and a fitting wife to her husband, Dr. Tom De Vries, professor of chemistry at Purdue University. The knowledge that these two dear ones were now with the Lord did assuage Hilda's grief, but it could not cancel her bereavement or wholly erase her sorrow. That we were nevertheless able to joyfully celebrate our first wedding anniversary on September 11 was no doubt due to the mitigating power of God's good grace. We dined that day in Bad Oeyenhausen, and we reviewed the year amazed at all that had occurred in it.

We left Vehlen on October 1, 1937, and, as we had planned, we spent the next two weeks in The Netherlands. We made our home during this period with Hilda's uncle Harry Veldsma, who lived in Appeldoorn with his wife Grietje. We spent pleasant days with our relatives there, but I varied the routine of everyday life by pedaling my bike as far north as Groningen and Uithuizen. My purpose was to gain further information about my ancestors, and I was able to gather a considerable number of relevant facts at various town halls. I visited Zwolle, Kampen, and Meppel en route, and from Uithuizen I rode to Ulrum, where I mounted the pulpit from which Rev. De Cock launched the "Afscheiding." Of course, I renewed acquaintance with Oom Wiebrand and Tante Grietje, as well as with Tjaard and Coba, and their hospitality proved to be as gracious as before. Hilda was well entertained in Appeldoorn, and I had ventured forth with her encouragement and blessing. We ended our stay in Holland on the fifteenth of October and were back in Göttingen on the sixteenth and ensconsed in our new quarters at 10 Hanssenstrasse.

*　　*　　*　　*　　*

Prof. Stange and his wife occupied the two lower floors of the large mansion-like, turreted stone house in which we now resided. A gate in the six-foot-high steel fence that enclosed the grounds provided access to the house, and an enormous key unlocked the front door. We occupied two large rooms on the third floor. A window in our bedroom afforded a view of the street, and another in our living-study room looked out on a lawn in the rear of the house. Our rent came to fifty Reichsmarks (about $12.50) a month, which included maid service as well as all utilities. We ate breakfast and supper in our rooms but took our noon meal with a nearby caterer who ministered to the appetites of students. I still remember with delight the fresh crisp "Brötchens" that the baker delivered each morning to our door. We were very pleased with our accommodations and happy to be well placed a full two weeks before the school year began.

During the thirteen months we had spent in Europe the world had not stood still, and certain happenings had not escaped our notice. In 1937, Franklin Roosevelt began his second term as President of the United States; Neville Chamberlain succeeded Baldwin as Prime Minister of England; Edward, Duke of Windsor, married Wallis Simpson after the coronation of his brother George VI; Japan attacked China and occupied its coastal regions; Dietrich Bonhoeffer's seminary at Finkenwalde was disbanded by order of Heinrich Himmler; Martin Niemöller was imprisoned by the Nazis, first in Sachsenhausen and later in Dachau; and the formation of the Rome-Berlin-Tokyo axis, which portended no good, shook up the somnolent statesmen of the West.

In The Netherlands, the "Wysbegeerte der Wetsidee" being promulgated by Dooyeweerd and Vollenhoven came under attack with the publication of Prof. Hepp's *Dreigende Deformatie* and Rev. Steen's *Philophia Deformata*. In that year, too, the Zeppelin *Hindenburg* was destroyed by fire at the naval airbase in Lakehurst, New Jersey, with the loss of many lives; Amelia Earhart was lost in an attempt to circumnavigate the globe by air; and John D. Rockefeller died at the age of ninety-seven.

172

*   *   *   *   *

The second school year began in early November 1937, and I addressed myself with vigor to my studies. In the winter semester I enrolled in three two-hour seminars, each of which entailed writing critical papers, and all three of which were taught by Prof. Heyse, dean of the philosophical faculty. One of these was on the "Grundfragen der Philosophie," another on "Kant's Prolegomena," and the third on "Hegel's Jugend-schriften." In addition, I attended three two-hour lecture courses, one with Prof. Baumgarten on "Englische Philosophie," another with him on "Hegel's Philosophie des Geistes," and a third with Prof. König on "Grundfragen der Zeitlehre." While engaged in these twelve hours of course work, I began to read assiduously in Max Weber and to a degree in William James, because for a time I contemplated writing a dissertation on "Die Wertung der Religion bei Max Weber und William James." But by the beginning of 1938 I sensed that I could not canvass all this literature in the time at my disposal, and I dropped consideration of James in order to concentrate on Weber.

During that semester there was very little opportunity for any leisurely engagement in nonacademic activities. I did accompany Prof. Stange to Bursfelde in late October and again in early January, and Hilda and I spent a weekend in Kassel in mid-December; but we could usually be found working on our respective assignments. Hilda maintained the apartment with the help of the maid, did the daily shopping on foot, conducted the necessary correspondence, kept me and my clothing in repair, and found time for reading and reflection. Our absences from each other were infrequent and never of long duration. I attended morning classes with some regularity and would read in the library between sessions; but I preferred to work at home, and it was at my desk there that I spent most of my time. However, one exercise in learning kept me from home one evening a week: a number of us students had formed an "Aristotle Club," and at our weekly meetings we studied the Greek text of Aristotle's *Physics*. Out of courtesy to a foreigner, my companions made me chairman of the group, but the pressure of work forced me to leave the club when the first semester came to a close.

We were, of course, not always working. Our accustomed regimen tended to be relieved by a perusal of the daily newspaper, an occasional trip to the movies, visits on selected evenings to the Rathskeller to drink a stein or two of beer and listen to German folk-songs, atten-

Henry at the Rathskeller

dance at church on Sunday mornings, and walks through the neighborhood or on the wall on Sunday afternoons. Nor were we without visitors, and conversations with the Stanges occasionally took place. But there was little room for fun and games.

At the end of the first semester, in mid-March, I had gone through almost all of Weber's writings, had assembled copious notes, and was ready to do my own writing; but there was still school to attend. During the second semester I took eight hours of course work: Prof. Heyse's seminar on "Ubingen in die Grundfrage der Wissenschaft," in which we touched on a variety of issues in science and philosophy, and his class on "Der jetszege Lage Europas," in which he praised the attempt of the Nazis to transform European culture along Aryan lines. I also heard lectures on Nietzsche by Prof. Baumgarten and on

German Idealism by Prof. Hirsch. But I put most of my energy into a mastery of Weber's thought and into a scrutiny of the empirico-rational method he employed. During April, May, and the first two weeks of June, I labored on my dissertation, with little time for sleep or recreation. Hilda endured my preoccupation with fortitude and patience, though not without lonesomeness and pain. I also suffered under frustrations, ineptitudes, and exhaustion; but I finished writing in early June and had a typewritten copy of my dissertation in the hands of the faculty on June 15. It was written entirely in German and bore the title: "Eine Untersuchung zu Max Weber's Religionssoziologie."

It happened that at that very time Hilda's widowed mother was en route to The Netherlands for a visit with her brother Harry Veldsma in Appeldoorn. Hilda had agreed to meet her at the port of Rotterdam, and she left for The Netherlands by train on June 16. During her ten-day absence I saw my dissertation through the press: a hundred printed copies flowed from the "Dieterichsche Universitäts-Buchdruckereî," a number of which were distributed to members of the faculty and the librarian. This private printing was in fulfillment of a university requirement and was done at the students' expense. Hilda returned to Göttingen on the 27th of June and reported how frightened she had been when she was removed from the train at the German border and interviewed in the station by an officer of the *SS*. It turned out, however, that she was guilty of nothing but a failure to renew her visa; and after she paid the standard fee, the officer sent her on her way with all her papers in order.

The oral examination (Mündlichen Prüfung) that I was required to undergo took place on June 30: from nine to twelve o'clock in the morning and from two to five in the afternoon, four members of the philosophical faculty and two members of the theological faculty questioned me on a whole range of issues in philosophy and theology. I entered the inquisition chambers with some trepidation, but I was soon put at ease, and I sensed at day's end that the Herr Professors were not displeased with my responses.

The faculty needed time to read and evaluate my dissertation, and in the interval between inspection and judgment Hilda and I made a trip to Berlin. On three mid-July days we explored the city and its environs and were favorably impressed with its sights and sounds. Shortly after we returned from Berlin and Potsdam, some student friends invited me to attend a farewell party. Six or seven of us gathered that evening in someone's small apartment, where there was food, a fair quantity of beer, and some champagne. We talked a great deal, ate a lot, and lifted glasses in "Brüderschaft." But I failed to notice that the clock was ticking the hours away, with the result that I arrived home in the company of Fritz Gebhardt a few hours after midnight. Needless to say, an anxious and sleepless Hilda had some unflattering things to say when I came into her loving presence.

On July 27, 1938, the university awarded me a doctorate in philosophy with the notation "Sehr Gut." With my degree in hand, and the diploma safely tucked away, my study at the University of Göttingen came to an end. In the next few days we bade goodbye to our friends and packed our bags, and on July 30 we left the scene of our many adventures. We boarded the train for The Netherlands, where new experiences, some painful to record, awaited us.

The busyness of the last several months had not disposed us to follow world affairs or observe events happening outside our closed circle. But I remember staying up late one night in June to hear on the radio that Joe Louis had bested Max Schmeling, the pride of Germany, in a boxing match that lasted but two minutes. This blow to German pride paled into insignificance, however, when compared to the national jubilation that attended Hitler's annexation of Austria on March 15, 1938, and his seizure of the "Sudetenland" from Czechoslovakia in May. The significance of these events did not escape our notice, and I remember telling Fritz Gebhardt that, though we were now good friends, it was not unlikely that in the not too distant future we would be locked in mortal combat.

*   *   *   *   *

Among the people in Göttingen with whom I had dealings, there are some whose names and faces I am unable to recall. But there are others whom I have not forgotten, and of whom I can give a fair account even though their identities are wrapped in the mists of fading recollections. Among these are a number of my instructors. I remember Prof. Otto Weber as a large and burly man who delivered animated lectures with an uncommon intensity. A member of the Reformed church, he was a "Barthian" of sorts, although he was not uncritical of the theology of crisis. When I knew him he was engaged in translating Calvin into German, and he later published an introduction to Barth's theology. I studied Calvin's doctrine of the church with him and regularly attended his lectures on the foundations of dogmatics. Those early lectures grew into a book, the first volume of which appeared in 1955; a second appeared in 1962, and both volumes were published in English translation by Eerdmans in 1981-83. Born in 1902, Weber was only six years older than I. Although we were relatively close in age and shared a common faith, our temperaments were diverse, and my appreciation of his competence and erudition was not attended by intimacy or fellowship. I sensed, however, that he regretted my move from theology to philosophy.

Prof. Joachim Jeremias was a mild-mannered, soft-spoken, gentle man whose kindliness and charity endeared him to all his students. He was a reputable scholar, versed in all the Mideastern languages and cultures and master of every critical apparatus and technique; yet he interpreted the New Testament along evangelical lines and in accordance with his own deep Christian faith. He was a member of the Lutheran "Bekenntniskirche" and shared in its hostility to the regnant anti-Jewish sentiments of the general populace. I took a number of courses with him and was a guest in his house several times.

I heard Prof. Friedrich Gogarten lecture on ethics. He was not an inspiring lecturer, nor were his presentations always lucid; but they had substance and quality even though they were not exactly to my taste. His "Barthian" contempt for metaphysics, his "Lutheran" contempt for good works, and his rejection of Calvin's *sensus divinitatis* did not speak to my condition. Gogarten appeared to be more or less a lone wolf, and there was something of tragedy in his bearing. An early associate of Karl Barth, he defected and joined ranks with the "German Christians," but I suspect he was too conservative to feel entirely at home with them. A student of Troeltsch, he went through an existentialist phase before meeting up with Barth, but he remained a traditional Lutheran in his ethics of fixed creational ordinances and of the opposition between law and gospel.

Emanuel Hirsch stood to the left of the above colleagues. Formerly a professor of church history, he was at my time a professor of systematics and the dean of the theological faculty. I attended a number of his lectures on the "Geschichte der evangelischen Theologie" and took a course with him on German Idealism, a subject in which he was an acknowledged authority. He was also a close student of Kierke-

gaard and published works on that seminal thinker. He was a friend
of Paul Tillich, and the two shared an affinity for an existentially tinged
philosophical idealism. A "liberal" Christian, he had no sympathy for
Barth and was an avowed "German Christian" with marked Nazi
loyalties. He was withal a most accomplished and erudite scholar who
handled facts and concepts with astounding facility, and his brilliant
lectures commanded a large following.

Of Hempel in Old Testament and Dörries in church history I can
say very little. I attended a few of Hempel's lectures but soon discovered that he evacuated Scripture of all supernatural revelation, and
I went elsewhere. But I did, at his suggestion, buy a copy of the
Septuagint, for I can still hear him say, "Meine Herren, haben sie eine
Septuagenta? Wenn sie keine haben, verkaufen sie alles was sie haben,
und kaufe eine." I took no courses with Dörries but had a number
of conversations with him and liked him very much. He was a wholesome Christian who publicly espoused the cause of a confessional
church loyal to Scripture.

My instructors in philosophy were of a different sort. Prof. Heyse,
director of the philosophical seminar, with whom I did most of my
work, was a staunch supporter of the Hitler regime and an open
apologist for cultural Aryanism. A Kantian of sorts, he was a student
of existentialism and was learned in the history of Western thought.
Like Rosenberg, he deplored what he regarded as the Semitic-Christian
overlay upon European culture. I would not have known this, or
known it as clearly, had I not read his book *Idee und Existenz,* because,
except in one course, he kept pretty close to abstract philosophy. In
this book, however, he attempted to show how Augustine had clothed
Greek thought in Christian garb, how the unholy alliance between
Athens and Jerusalem had polluted Occidental thought, and how
necessary it was to return to the Greek tragedies in order to give the
Teutonic peoples a charter and a future. Of course, I did not buy this
thesis, but I found Heyse personally attractive and ingratiating, and
he always stood ready to assist me in every way he could.

Prof. Baumgarten was of my generation and a likable fellow, but
he too was alienated from the church and indifferent to the faith. His
specialty was English philosophy, and his sentiments were Humean.
Like his mentor, he was an acute philosopher who tended toward
skepticism in metaphysics and reserve in ideology. It was this reserve,
perhaps, that moderated his adherence to Nazism. However that may

Professor Stange

be, in our many conversations he never expressed himself on political issues. He was my consultant and "Referent" as I wrote my dissertation, and I found him ever ready to assist and advise. We were far apart in our view of things, but we conducted our engagements in philosophical discussions in friendly fashion, and he found no fault with my critical assessment of Max Weber.

I took a few courses with Professors König and Bollnow but had almost no exchanges with them and did not really come to know them. I can only say that König's lectures on "Space-Time" opened new vistas formerly closed to me.

We lived, as I have said, in Prof. Stange's house, and this brought me into contact with that elderly, bearded gentleman. He had been professor of systematic theology in Göttingen, was now retired, and spent his time translating Italian poetry into German. Author of a textbook on dogmatics, of a volume on Luther's theology, of another on Kant's ethics, and of still another on Christian and philosophical worldviews, he enjoyed a considerable reputation in Germany but seems not to have been widely known elsewhere. Hilda and I were not on intimate terms with the family, but we often met one another on the stairs, and we were once invited to a formal dinner in the family dining room, where we met other guests from the academic community. I would sometimes visit Prof. Stange in his study to seek an answer to some question I had, and he always received me cordially; but I was not encouraged to prolong my visit, and from this I learned to practice prudence and restraint. I observed that the maid brought him a bottle of beer just before he retired for the night, and on a few occasions I was present when this occurred; but I was never proffered a libation, on the ground, no doubt, that young men needed no soporific agent to induce sleep. On rare occasions, Stange preached in Bursfelde, but he otherwise never went to church. I once inquired about this, and he replied that he had taught the local preachers all they knew about theology and considered it unnecessary to hear his own material regurgitated on Sunday mornings. I suggested that sermons were proclamations rather than inquiries and that worship was quite unlike an academic pursuit, but he was not overly attentive, and there the matter rested.

We did not establish many personal friendships during our stay in Germany, but there were a few persons to whom we were bound by relatively close ties. Chief among these was Wilhelm Vauth. We first met in Hartford, we lived together in Rusbend and Vehlen, and we remained in close touch with each other until the war clouds gathered overhead. Wilhelm was a dedicated Christian who served the Lord with competence and devotion. He was also an incisive thinker whose grasp on things was sure but whose humble spirit and lively sense of humor kept him from falling into theological assertiveness and ideological partisanship. Hilda and I thoroughly enjoyed his company and often profited from his counsel. But the war separated us from each other. It was not merely that we were on opposite sides in the conflict; that could not have destroyed our friendship. It was Wilhelm's premature death that broke the bond between us. Subject to the draft in spite of his ministerial status, he was inducted into the German army early on and sent to do battle on the Russian front. It was there that he was felled by enemy bullets in August 1941 and sent to a military hospital. It is one of life's tragedies that this good man died on July 21, 1942, from the effects of the massive wounds he suffered in defense of a cause he loathed.

Less close to us were two other friends, one a young campus minister and the other a budding theologian. Adolf Wischman was the Lutheran "Studentenpfarrer" on the university campus, and we often conferred together about things ecclesiastical and theological. It was he who, upon my request, allowed us to partake of communion in the Lutheran church even though this ran counter to established rules. Adolf survived the war and later became president of the "Aussenamt der evangelischen Kirche in Deutschland." Hans Kropatchek was a fellow student at the university, and his wife became a close friend of Hilda's. Hans, whose company I always enjoyed, was studying theology at the time and earned a degree in 1943 on the submission of a dissertation entitled "Das Problem theologischen Anthropologie."

A person with whom we associated closely throughout the second year of our stay, and who proved to be a faithful friend, was Fritz Gebhardt. He had completed his studies in philosophy, but had not yet written a dissertation, and was currently employed as a functionary in the "Philosophische Seminar." He was an almost constant visitor at our house, and he and Hilda got along splendidly. Unfortunately, he was not a practicing Christian and did not go to church; but he was a kind, thoughtful, and most pleasant companion. We first met in the "Aristotle Club," and afterward we did many things together. We even got him to attend church with us on one or two occasions. He ate a fair amount of our food, and when we left Göttingen Hilda gave him all of our dishes and kitchen ware, which he presumably put to good use in his bachelor apartment. While I was riveted to my desk, he would often entertain Hilda with stories or read to her from our copy of Grimm's "Märchen," and when he met Hilda on the street during one of her shopping trips he would invariably invite her to join him for coffee in the nearest coffee house. When I was writing the last chapter of my dissertation, and when the deadline for its submission was drawing near, he stood ready every morning to bring my penciled manuscript to the typist for transcription; for two weeks on end he and his trusty bike stood at attention to perform this most helpful act. For this and other services I owed him a great deal, and in my published dissertation I included his name among those to whom I expressed my heartfelt thanks.

*   *   *   *   *

"For Jews No Admittance!"

Were we to depend solely on what we saw with our eyes and heard with our ears, there would not be much to tell about Hitler's Germany of the middle thirties, for our direct experience of German life was limited by time, and our observations were curtailed and overshadowed by our academic pursuits. What we did notice were various surface phenomena. We saw soldiers parading in the streets, and we once participated in an air-raid drill. The swastika was displayed everywhere, and when we were addressed in the shops or on the streets it was never with a "guten Tag" or an "Aufwiedersehen," but always with a "Heil Hitler," accompanied by a stiff-armed salute. Hitler himself was often to be heard over the airways, and what he invariably counseled was strength, pride, determination, and fortitude. Brownshirted members of the *SA* and black-uniformed officers of the *SS* were everywhere, and it seemed that every boy of a certain age was enrolled in some cadre of the "Hitler Jugend."

We knew about the Jewish question, particularly as it affected church policies; but no anti-Semitic sentiments were uttered in our presence, and we neither witnessed nor heard about any arrest, imprisonment, or deportation of a Jew. We once saw a sign on a public bathing house that read "Für Juden zutritt verboten," but we gave it no special heed since similar signs were well known to blacks living in our own southern states. When we lived on Obere Masch Strasse, the Jewish tobacconist whom I patronized did business without apparent molestation; but when we returned from our summer stay in Vehlen we noticed that his shop was closed. Whether the closing was due to lack of patronage or to sinister action by government agents we could not determine. We did not discuss with our German friends and acquaintances the various occurrences around us, for we were prohibited by the terms of the Fellowship to involve ourselves in politics. Furthermore, the natives were either Nazi sympathizers who were disinclined to share their secrets with strangers or critics who, for fear of reprisals, were careful to keep their sentiments to themselves.

Had it not been for the literature available to me, I should not have known what was really afoot in Germany. Heyse's volume *Idee und Existenz* was an eye-opener, and it led me to pick up Hitler's *Mein Kampf* and to go from there to readings in Moeller Vanden Bruck's *Das Dritte Reich* and Alfred Rosenberg's *Der Mythus des 20 Jahrhunderts*. From these and other writings it became evident that the National Socialist movement envisioned not merely the resurgence of a dishonored, bankrupt, and divided people, but nothing less than the transformation of Western culture. Hitler's proximate goal was to restore to the German people a place in the sun. To this end he repudiated the Versailles treaty, occupied the Rhineland, mobilized the industrial complex in the interest of arms production, built up the army, navy, and air force, and by personal charisma and strong-arm tactics enlisted the real or feigned loyalty of the people to a one-party system and to a "Führer" endowed with unlimited powers. Hitler's intermediate goal was to consolidate the Teutonic peoples and provide them with "Lebensraum," which is why he seized the Sudetenland and forced the annexation of Austria.

But his ultimate goal was grander. He aimed to produce a third "Reich," which, supplanting the Holy Roman Empire, would rid Europe of its Semitic-Christian overlay and restore to life the nascent genius of the warlike northern tribes who worshipped at the shrine of Wotan. He envisioned an Aryan civilization based on "Blut" and "Bodem," in which the "slave morality" of the Judaeo-Christian tradition would be finally discredited and the influence of international Jewry completely banned. The Nazi hatred of the Jews stemmed partly

183

from the aggrandizing role they were thought to have played in the disastrous period following World War I; but it arose fundamentally from the conviction that Israelitish culture had for ages suppressed the Teutonic spirit and ruthlessly slain its gods. In the opinion of many, it was this alleged sacrilege that now needed to be avenged. The Holocaust that took place when Germany was fighting for its life during World War II was meant to be a reprisal for deeply felt injuries, as well as an effective means of insuring both the continuance of a pure-blooded "Volkstum" and the demise of the despised Jewish race.

The church struggle centered on two issues. The first, addressed in the Barmen Declaration, concerned the relationship between church and state. At issue here was whether the church may surrender its autonomy, be compelled to endorse a political program and ideology, and be forced to compromise its loyalty to Christ and the gospel. The second concerned the relationship between the races. At issue here was whether it is biblically warranted to exclude Christian Jews from membership in the church, and whether the church may be restrained from solemnizing marriages between Jews and Gentiles. My friends in the "Bekenntniskirche" opposed the government and the "German Christians" on both of these issues, and not a few of their associates were imprisoned for their noncompliance with government pressures and regulations.

9

THE NETHERLANDS
AND HOME
(1938-1939)

With our German experience behind us, Hilda and I left Göttingen for the Netherlands on July 30, 1938, and arrived in Appeldoorn on the evening of that day. We made our home with Hilda's uncle and aunt, Harry and Grietje Veldsma, with whom Hilda's mother was also staying. We paid a short visit to my relatives in Groningen and Uithuizen, but I cannot recall how the rest of our days were spent. I'm sure we read books and newspapers, wrote letters, made shopping trips into town, and conversed a good deal; but nothing particularly memorable occurred during the whole of the long month of August, except that we notably improved our ability to speak Dutch.

Around the first of September the three of us removed to Amsterdam. Quartered in a hotel there, we explored the city and made train and bus trips to outlying towns and villages. But our travels and amusements did little to alleviate the pain Hilda and I felt when we contemplated the ocean-wide gulf that would soon come between us and leave us stranded on separate islands of loneliness and longing. The fact was that, at the request of Calvin's Board of Trustees, I had reluctantly consented to study on at the Free University of Amsterdam, even though funds for the support of both of us were not forthcoming. Under the circumstances, Hilda had sacrificially agreed to return to the States with her mother, both to be a companion to her in her widowhood and to find gainful employment. The arrangement was satisfactory to neither of us, and should have been vetoed; but we had given our word to the board and at the time no alternative seemed to present itself. Fortunately, no lasting damage was done, but it should never have come about.

On the ninth or tenth of September we traveled to Rotterdam and spent some days with Oom Hannes and Tante Grietje Vander Graaf, the same good people who had greeted us on our arrival in 1936. On September 12, 1938, Mother De Graaf and Hilda set sail for New York on the S.S. *Vollendam*. Friends and relatives had gathered at the docks to bid the passengers farewell, but for Hilda and me the occasion was all but joyous. After tearful embraces we let each other go, but the parting was heart-rending. What made it bearable at all was our shared assurance that we remained in the custody of the Lord, and that we would be reunited when the winter of our discontent had passed and spring had come.

Hilda and her mother traveled third class. Their cabin, Hilda said later, was small and equipped with stacked bunks; she lay on the upper one with her head close to the ceiling. The passengers were mostly German Jews who had managed to escape to Holland and were now seeking refuge in the land of the free. The weather was stormy, but neither Hilda nor Mother became seasick, and Hilda was fortunate to be often in the company of Prof. Hoekstra, who taught philosophy at Wayne State University and was now returning from a vacation spent abroad. The ship arrived in New York on September 19. Clarence and Marie De Graaf were at dockside to greet the disembarking passengers and to drive them to Grand Rapids. A period of reorientation followed Hilda's return to Leonard Street, but around the first of October she was rehired by Steketee's and assigned to work in her old department. She was paid a mere twenty-three cents an hour — on top of which she had to outlive the suspicion that her marriage had broken up and that divorce was imminent.

Uncle Harry Veldsma had been in Rotterdam to see his relatives off, and, when the *Vollendam* weighed anchor and moved out of sight, I accompanied him home to Appeldoorn. From there I made several trips to Amsterdam, and on one of these trips was able, through the good offices of Prof. Vollenhoven, to secure lodgings with the Byleveld family. I took up residence there on September 21, 1938, and five

With Mrs. and Mr. Byleveld

days later was enrolled as a postdoctoral graduate student in the Free University of Amsterdam.

*   *   *   *   *

I was most fortunate in being able to live with the Bylevelds. The head of the family, Mr. Hendrick Byleveld, was a tall and distinguished looking gentleman who had made a name for himself in Dutch society and was about fifty-two years old when I came to live there. His wife, of the well-situated Dake family, had several paintings to her credit, and was gentle, kind, and motherly. There were nine children in the family, five boys and four girls ranging in age from twenty-six to eight. I came to know the two oldest children only slightly. Greet, the eldest, lived with her husband, Rev. Albert Brink, in the north of Holland, and Heleen was married to H. A. Van Kerkhof not long after I arrived on the scene. The rest of the children lived at home, and their company afforded me great pleasure. Henk (23), Hannie (22), Tonnie (20), and Walter (19) were students at the university; Jan (17) and Wim

187

(16) were students in the *gymnasium;* and Hettie (8) attended grade school. Under the circumstances, conversation at the table tended to be lively and informed.

Mr. Byleveld could be said to be the living embodiment of prewar Dutch Calvinism, a paradigm of sophisticated Kuyperianism. A native of Amsterdam, he obtained a law degree at the Free University toward the end of World War I, and soon thereafter put his considerable talents into the service of the Christian Anti-Revolutionary political party. In 1919-1920 he served as secretary of the navy in the cabinet of Prime Minister Ruis de Beerenbrouck, and when the government fell, he became administrator of the Federal Department of Trade and Commerce, advisor to the Queen, and chairman of the Council on Grants and Patents. From 1925 to 1929 he was a member of the lower house of the Dutch Parliament. When I came to know him, he was chairman of the board of directors of the National Insurance Agency, chairman of the program committee of the Reformed Radio Broadcasting System, member of the Anti-Revolutionary Party's central committee, member of the Free University's Board of Directors, and elder in the Reformed Church (Gereformeerd) of Amsterdam-South. Had it not been for the information supplied by others, I would not have known much of the above biography, for Mr. Byleveld, though amply expressive on matters of public concern, was reticent in the extreme when it came to his own career and accomplishments.

Mr. and Mrs. Byleveld were like a father and mother to me, and I soon joined the children in addressing and referring to them as Vader and Moeder. They in turn treated me as a son, and the care and concern they lavished on me did much to make my separation from Hilda less burdensome than it would otherwise have been.

The Bylevelds lived in a three-story house at 72 Schuberstraat in Amsterdam-Zuid, and a room with bed, desk, and bookcase was provided for me on the second floor. I took three meals a day with the family and was charged for room and board a mere sixty-five *gulden* a month. Although all of us had our own agenda, we met frequently for conversation, games, and occasional parties and outings; and when I had the opportunity, I regularly accompanied the family to church. On Sunday afternoons we normally played chess, and before I left for home I had acquired a fair mastery of the game.

*   *   *   *   *

188

The Free (Reformed) University of Amsterdam

The Begijnhof

The Free University of Amsterdam, with which I was now associated, was founded in 1880 by Abraham Kuyper and his associates. It was a Christian institution based on the principle that Christ's sovereignty extends over the whole of life, and it was designed to articulate through instruction and research a Reformed world-and-life view. Its beginnings were small. When its doors opened on October 21, 1880, there were five students and five professors in three faculties: Dr. Abraham Kuyper, Dr. F. L. Rutgers, and Dr. P. J. Hoedemaker taught theology; Dr. D. P. D. Fabius taught law; and Dr. F. W. Dilloo taught courses in language and literature. Kuyper was honored with the first rectorship, and it was in this capacity that he delivered his famous lecture "Souvereiniteit in Eigen Kring."

That reality is constituted of several distinct spheres, each of which is governed by laws peculiar to itself, was the central thesis of Kuyper's address, and it was this idea that gave rise to the term "free," which was used from the beginning to characterize the university's status. In its founders' view, church, state, and school were to be sharply distinguished. It was believed that the university could answer to its own

190

genius and fulfill its own functions only if it remained independent of church and state and free of foreign entanglements. Freedom, however, was not to be construed as lawlessness. Free from alien institutional bonds, the school was nevertheless to be bound by the laws of God and the principles of divine revelation.

Although the university was already fifty-eight years old when I was in residence, it was still comparatively small. Twenty-six professors and three lectors constituted the faculty; the student body numbered no more than six hundred, and of that number only forty were women. There was no campus; instruction was given in remodeled dwellings located on Keizersgracht.

I was enrolled on September 26, 1938, and during the fall term I faithfully attended the lectures and seminars delivered and conducted by Professors Vollenhoven and Dooyeweerd. But I was not particularly happy with the program on which I had embarked. The lectures were not always germane or suited to my purposes, the seminars were often a futile attempt to fit a philosopher into a preconceived slot, the students were ten years younger than myself, and I grew weary of class attendance. By the end of the calendar year, I had determined that I could be better employed by simply reading what my appointed mentors had set down in their books, articles, and mimeographed "dictaten." I did, however, become a member of the philosophical society sponsored by Dooyeweerd and Vollenhoven, and at one of the meetings of the "Amsterdam Kring" I presented a paper on American philosophy.

I associated very little with the Dutch students and formed no friendships among them, but Henry and Sis Van Til and Lubbertus and Evelyn Oostendorp were pursuing graduate studies at the time, and with these friends from home I enjoyed considerable fellowship.

*   *   *   *   *

In Amsterdam there is an ancient courtyard surrounded by quaint buildings, to which one gains access by entering a gate off the Kalverstraat or off the Spui. The court is called the "Begijnenhof" because it once housed a sisterhood named after St. Begga; in about the year 1400 the nuns of this order built a chapel on the grounds. The chapel passed into the hands of the Dutch Reformed Church in 1578, and in 1607 it was assigned as a place of worship "for the English people dwelling in Amstelredamme in Holland." The first pastor of the church was Rev. John Paget, a Puritan refugee from England. The Pilgrim fathers who arrived from Scrooby in 1608 worshiped in this church until they left for Plymouth in 1620.

Now known as the English Reformed Church, the building has retained its original shape and size, although its interior has been refurbished and enriched over the years. A brass lectern with emblem and royal monogram was presented to the church early on by King William III, and the panels on the raised pulpit were exquisitely carved at the time of the accession of Queen Wilhelmina. The handsome silver communion set and baptismal basin date from 1781.

The church was without a pastor during my stay in Amsterdam, and, hearing of my presence in the city, the consistory invited me to minister to the congregation during the vacancy. I gladly accepted the invitation and delivered my first sermon during the worship service held on Sunday, October 9, 1938. I preached on Psalm 73:1 that day, and I occupied the pulpit every Sunday thereafter until I left for home. Worship services were held only in the morning, which left me free to attend the Dutch church in the evening. My main responsibility was preaching. The elders — chief among whom were Mr. Kreyen-broek and Dr. Vander Bend — took upon themselves the burden of pastoral work; but I was sometimes asked to counsel troubled souls, which I willingly did, with some trepidation. On one occasion I conducted a funeral, for which I had to borrow from an obliging Dutch clergyman a Prince Albert coat and a black top hat.

I was paid one hundred and fifty gulden a month for my services, a sum of money that, with my Calvin stipend, left me without financial worries. This unexpected windfall made me regret, however, that I countenanced Hilda's premature return to the States. I suspect we could have managed to stay together in Holland with the funds now at our disposal. On the other hand, with Hilda present I might have given more heed than I did to the consistory's request that I extend my stay and consider the formal call they wished to extend to me.

*   *   *   *   *

Hardly a day passed that I did not write Hilda. This and other correspondence combined with my sermon making and my readings in philosophy kept me tolerably busy, but ample time remained for a variety of other activities. I read newspapers and magazines, went on shopping trips, explored the city, searched the museums, attended concerts, observed the people and their habits, smoked Ritmeester cigars, savored spots of Dutch jenever, and did other things besides.

My bike was my steed and I rode it everywhere. There were few autos on the streets in those days. In the rush hours swarms of cyclists, often riding eight or ten abreast, their whirling wheels abutting those of their neighbors both fore and aft, poured down the streets like an avalanche. A novice entering that wild stampede put himself at no small risk, but the natives who had mastered the flow went merrily on their way and seldom suffered a mishap.

In September 1938 portentous things were also happening in the public arena. On September 29, Hitler, Mussolini, Daladier, and Chamberlain met in Munich in an effort to ease mounting tensions in Europe. On the next day, the four leaders sealed the fate of Czechoslovakia by signing a pact validating Germany's claim to the Sudetenland. Not realizing that his capitulation to Hitler's outrageous demands had further threatened the existing order, Chamberlain returned to Britain proclaiming "peace in our time." But Churchill, with prophetic insight, denounced the pact as dishonorable, cowardly, and conducive to no good.

In October I played host to Wilhelm Vauth, who had come from Germany for a visit, and in November I composed a long letter about Amsterdam for publication in the *Calvin Forum*. On the twenty-fourth I celebrated Thanksgiving Day in the company of the Van Tils and the Oostendorps. What riveted my attention, however, was what had happened in Berlin and other German cities on the ninth. On the evening of that day, gangs of anti-Semitic vandals, aided and abetted by Hitler's storm troopers, burned Jewish synagogues, smashed Jewish shop windows, and bloodied as many hapless Jews as they could lay their hands on. Because of the broken glass that lay around everywhere, that infamous night is remembered as "Kristallnacht," and it was viewed by the citizens of Holland as a public and dramatic sign that Hitler and Himmler were determined to decimate the Jews or to exterminate them altogether.

In December, I joined the Bylevelds in giving St. Nicholas Day gifts; entertained cousin Tena Bultema on her visit to Amsterdam; wrote an article on the Free University for placement in the *Calvin Forum;* enjoyed a violin concert by Nathan Milstein; viewed from a discreet distance the licensed bordellos in the "Jordaan" with Mrs.

Byleveld; attended a closed meeting with Karl Barth in the lounge of an Amsterdam hotel; celebrated the birth of Christ on Christmas day; and for four late December days played host to Fritz Gebhardt.

I don't remember how we celebrated the arrival of the new year, but I know that I appeared as Uncle Sam at a family "Kostum Feest" on January 2, 1939, and that I was a guest at the wedding of Heleen Byleveld on the twelfth. It was also during January that I attended a concert by Jo Vincent and paid a visit to Rotterdam.

A highlight of the month of February was a visit I paid to the home of former Prime Minister Hendrick Colyn in The Hague. Mr. Byleveld had arranged the meeting, and he and I spent an hour or two with Colyn discussing the state of affairs in the world and smoking his big black cigars. On one evening later in February, I took part in the "Societeits Feest" put on by the student fraternity. I was somewhat surprised to see that a bar had been set up in one of the rooms and that both students and professors freely engaged in drinking beer and hard liquors. I distinctly remember how on this occasion Prof. Vollenhoven and I, each with a stein of beer in hand and with arms entwined, cemented our friendship by drinking "Brüderschaft." I should point out that the drinking of alcoholic beverages on festive occasions was almost universal among the Dutch Calvinists. No party was complete without a glass of wine or a jigger of gin; even churches were licensed to dispense wine and jenever at wedding receptions and similar events, and a bar set-up was a feature of every synodical meeting.

In March 1939 things were not rosy in Europe, or for that matter in Asia. Japan was fighting in China, and Shanghai would soon fall into its hands. Closer to home, the Spanish civil war was winding down, but Hitler was on the move, and the governments of England and France were apprehensive and ill at ease. What had long been feared occurred in March: Hitler invaded Czechoslovakia, seized Prague, and divided the country into two German satellite states. During the same month he wrested the Baltic port of Memel from Lithuania. Britain and France responded to these moves by promising Poland and Romania protection against aggression; but to most observers this meant that armed conflict was in the offing, for Berlin's unrestrained Führer was evidently bent on further conquests. Mussolini meanwhile had his eye on Albania and had dispatched his troops to acquire it.

Under the circumstances, I was advised by the American consulate in Amsterdam to consider cutting short my stay in Holland; heeding

194

this advice, I determined to leave for home in April. The remaining days of March were still at my disposal, and I decided to make the most of them and to get in as much travel as I could. I made trips to Marken and Vollendam and, on the recommendation of the Bylevelds, I traveled to France and spent six very pleasant and instructive days in Paris, exploring the city and making daily visits to the Louvre.

I devoted most of April to loosening my ties to Holland. I made a day's trip into the countryside with an elder of the church; I visited Haarlem and Scheveningen, and in mid-April I visited my relatives in Appeldoorn and Uithuizen, not forgetting to leave with them some token of my appreciation of their hospitality and kindness. I bade farewell to my professors at the Free University and promised to become a contributor to the philosophical journal they published. And I gave gifts to the good people who had harbored me these many months and had become very dear to me.

I preached the last of my twenty-two sermons in the English church on April 16, and the church took the occasion to present me with an inscribed copy of a colorful painting depicting the church building as seen from the Kalverstraat. On the evening of the twentieth there was a farewell party at the Bylevelds, and I was given not only an album of the family members in various poses but also a beautiful painting by Mrs. Byleveld, and, above all, an illuminated scroll, etched in medieval Latin, attesting to my adoption as the family's eldest son and brother.

I entrained for Rotterdam on April 21, boarded the *Nieuw Amsterdam* at seven in the evening, and at five minutes after midnight on Saturday, April 22, 1939, the huge ship weighed anchor and headed for New York via Boulogne-sur-Mer and Southhampton. I traveled third class, but I don't recall how I spent the hours during the seven long days it took to cross the ocean. I only know that I waited impatiently for the ship to arrive in port and bring me at last within reach of my dear wife. John and Helen Hamersma were at the docks to greet me when the ship slid into its berth on April 29, and after boarding the first train west, I came to rest in Hilda's arms the next day. After seven long months I had come home.

*   *   *   *   *

The satisfaction I took in being with Hilda knew no bounds, but joy was tempered by the consideration that Providence had dealt unequally with us. While I, in comparative ease, had been exposed to a foreign culture and had made contact with interesting persons of various backgrounds, Hilda had in customary surroundings been working long hours at an uninspiring job for meager pay. This inequity bothered me, but it could no longer be undone; and I did not know how to express my sorrow and regret that it was with my complicity that this injustice had occurred.

There was another factor in the equation. Hilda and I had been in almost daily correspondence during our forced separation, and for this reason there was not much to tell about what had transpired on the surface of our lives. But for over half a year we had not spoken to each other face to face, nor plumbed the depths of each other's psyche. We had traveled separate roads, had appropriated dissimilar experiences, and had been buffeted and upborne by winds blowing from different quarters. A segment of our life together had gone unshared, and this could not but affect our restored togetherness; under the circumstances, some adjustment and reorientation was called for. It is to Hilda's credit that this occurred without stress or strain. What again became evident to both of us was that love has drawing powers and is unsurpassed at building and restoring bridges.

Hilda lived with her mother at 776 East Leonard Street, and we made our home there for two or three weeks after my return. Mother De Graaf invited us to take up permanent residence with her, but Hilda wanted a home of her own, as did I. So sometime in May 1939 we moved into a house owned by Hilda's uncle, Thomas Veldsma: located at 204 Benjamin Avenue, SE, the two-story, three-bedroom house was well suited to our purposes, and the monthly rent of $35 appeared to be within our means. Of course, we had to supply the furniture and this put us to some expense. Fortunately, Hilda was able to send on to our new home her bedroom set, sofa, and piano, and we were able to retrieve from storage the dinette set, day bed, and utensils we had received as wedding gifts. But more was needed. Hilda selected the three upholstered chairs we bought from Huisingh's, as well as the rugs, drapes, and curtains we bought from Steketee's. I had appropriated the front bedroom upstairs as my study, and to furnish it I bought a glass-topped desk and three sectional bookcases from the house's former tenant. I paid fifty dollars for the lot.

Hilda had taken a three- or four-day vacation on my arrival home but had thereafter gone back to work, and she continued to be employed at Steketee's until the end of August. This was unfortunate, but it seemed dictated by necessity or at least by prudence. Current expenses were mounting, we were in debt to a number of persons and institutions, and I would not be able to make any significant contribution to our treasury until school opened in September. Thus Hilda became the provider, and the burden was not light, for alongside her daily work at Steketee's she had numerous household cares and responsibilities that I could only minimally share.

Just what schedule I observed during those summer months I do not recall, but I know that the prospect of teaching in the fall both frightened me and drove me to my books. In Hilda's daily absence I did, of course, tidy up the house, do the shopping, and perform minor household chores; but I was usually at my desk, both to prepare for the opening of school and to meet other responsibilities that were coming my way. Word of my return had made the rounds, and I was often asked to preach. In May, I preached at Coldbrook and Moline, and in June at LaGrave. I was interviewed by the Calvin Board of Trustees on June 2, a full two years after my appointment. In response to their questions, I spoke at some length of my commitment to the faith and to the ideals of the school; and though I expressed reservations about the "moral" restrictions imposed upon faculty and students, I promised to observe the rules prohibiting movie attendance, card playing, and dancing. The trustees now knew something of the person to whom they had entrusted the chair of philosophy, and they seemed satisfied.

My brother Mart lived with us for two weeks in June because one of his children was suffering from a communicable disease and the family house was under quarantine. On nine successive Sundays in July and August, I preached in various churches, near and far, and on August 8 and 9 I was billed as the main speaker at the annual convention of the National Union of Christian Schools in Paterson, New Jersey. I delivered two lectures on "the Antithesis" and tried to show its relevance both to education and to life.

Things were also happening in those days in and around Calvin College. Jesse De Boer, who had been the interim instructor of philosophy for four years, relinquished his chair and applied for admission to the seminary (though he seems later to have opted for graduate work in philosophy). Of greater consequence was the storm that had gathered around the presidency of Dr. Ralph Stob: although his term of office had expired, he was eligible for reappointment and evidently desired to stay on; but he was under pressure by faculty and student body to resign. After considering the situation for several days in early June, the trustees declined to reappoint him and named Prof. Johannes Broene in his place. Since I had been absent from the scene, I was not privy to what had been going on and could form no judgment about the rightness or wrongness of the board's action; but I commiserated with my kinsman and offered him my condolences. He retained his tenured position as professor of Greek language and literature and resumed his classwork when school opened in September.

Other actions of the board bore some relation to my membership on the faculty. It added three new members to the staff in June — John De Vries in chemistry, Richard Drost in history, and Grace Pels as dean of women and assistant in English. Although I outranked those three in tenure, the four of us were in fact the new kids on the block; regarding ourselves as an unpracticed quartet in the faculty chorus, we determined for the nonce to sing in muted tones.

The board also decided to require all students to sign a pledge card promising to live by the existing rules pertaining to "worldliness." This decision was revealing of the times: students on other campuses were swallowing live goldfish, and new movies like *Gone with the Wind* and *The Wizard of Oz* were drawing patrons in droves throughout the country. In response to critics of the college, the board also took curricular action: it instructed the staff to prepare for submission and possible publication a syllabus showing how the instructional material in each course was integrated with the Reformed world-and-life view. The preparation of such a syllabus would perhaps be quite within the reach of those of us who worked in the humanities, but instructors in hard sciences such as mathematics and chemistry would doubtless find the going difficult.

The Synod of the Christian Reformed Church met in June 1939 and appointed Rev. John C. De Korne to succeed Dr. Beets as director of missions. It also adopted a declaration on war which, while giving expression to prevailing views, would be updated several times in subsequent years. What directly affected the members of the faculty was the appointment by Synod of a "committee of ten" charged with monitoring the moral and spiritual life of the college community. The appointment of this committee did not sit well with the faculty, and as it turned out, the "investigation" conducted by the committee did not always proceed with the tact and charity required.

While these and similar things were going on at home, war clouds were gathering over Europe. Hitler was still in search of "Lebensraum," and to forestall Russian resistance to his expansionist schemes, he entered into a nonaggression pact with Stalin on August 23, 1939. The storm anticipated by the ominous events preceding that agreement broke loose a week later. On September 1, 1939, Hitler's troops mounted a massive attack on Poland and reduced that country to servitude in a scant three weeks. England and France could do nothing to stop the German onslaught; but they had pledged their support to Poland, and to honor their commitment they declared war on Germany on September 3. With that, World War II was set in motion, and there was no telling how and when it would complete its course.

It was in the shadow of these events that I began my career as a teacher.

10

TEACHING AT CALVIN COLLEGE

(1939-1943)

I began teaching philosophy at Calvin College in September of 1939.
I was thirty-one years of age; I held the rank of Instructor, with
faculty status; and I was paid two thousand dollars a year for my
services.

The college had undergone very little change since I had left it in
1932. It occupied the same campus; it boasted no new buildings; and
almost all the professors who were present while I was in residence
were still at their posts. Harry Jellema was of course absent; I was his
replacement. And Johanna Timmer was just now in the process of
leaving; but all the rest of the stalwarts were still aboard. Johannes
Broene was there, but having been appointed acting president in June,
he would be chiefly engaged in administration. Albertus Rooks had
reached retirement age, but he had been asked to stay on as dean for
at least another year, and he remained an active member of the faculty.
And then there were the others from my student days: Albert Broene,
Harry Dekker, Lambert Flokstra, Peter Hoekstra, Henry Meeter,
Edwin Monsma, James Nieuwdorp, Henry Ryskamp, Ralph Stob,
Seymour Swets, Henry Van Andel, Jacob Vanden Bosch, John Van
Haitsma, and Henry Van Zyl — sixteen in all. After my graduation
three men had been added to the staff: William Radius in classical

languages, Harry Wassink in physics and engineering, and Albert Muyskens in mathematics and physical education. And now John De Vries in chemistry, Richard Drost in history, and I in philosophy were being inducted into the ranks of the faculty. This brought our corporate number to twenty-two. Grace Pels, though coming in as dean of women, was ranked as an assistant and had no formal faculty status. Josephine Baker was at her accustomed place in the library, and Mr. Vos still functioned as the keeper of the school's financial records.

The college and seminary was then, as now, under the supervision of a board of trustees, but in 1939 all of the curators (as they were then called) were clergymen each representing a classis; and their number did not exceed eighteen, this being the number of classes then existing in the Christian Reformed Church. When I began to teach, Rev. W. P. Van Wyk served the board as president, and J. J. Hiemenga, L. J. Lamberts, and Daniel Zwier completed the slate of officers. Indicative of the size and leanness of the college and seminary at that time was the board's budget for the academic year 1939-1940: it amounted to slightly more than one hundred and twenty-seven thousand dollars.

Although the board, under Synod, was the school's governing body, the internal affairs of the college were conducted by the teaching staff. The college of those days was in both theory and practice a faculty-run institution. The president had certain prerogatives and some special duties, but he was held to be no more than first among equals, and nothing went on at the school in which the faculty was not involved. There were committees to consider various matters, but they implemented nothing without the approval of the entire staff assembled in plenary session. The faculty established the curriculum, set the calendar, approved student grades, took notice of minor infractions, authorized suspensions and expulsions, granted scholarships, passed judgment on students applying for admission into the Seminary, and concerned itself with many other things — all in open debate and with meticulous attention to detail.

The faculty room was the scene of all this activity. It was located on the first floor of the administration building and, though unequipped with reclining chairs and other amenities, it served not only as a place of business but also as a sort of lounge where members met for relaxation and small talk in the intervals between classes. It was not much larger than the average classroom, but it matched the size

*Henry Affecting
a Thought*

of the faculty and adequately served its purposes. A long oblong table stood in the center of the room, and worn wooden armchairs were positioned along its sides; those chairs bore no names, but everyone knew who would occupy each one when the faculty met in monthly session, and trespassing was unheard of. A small toilet room and a cloak room furnished with mailboxes adjoined the larger meeting place, but no other facilities were available to the staff. There were no faculty offices, and secretarial help was not to be found. The business office did employ a stenographer — Miss Caroline Veen — but this young woman had all she could do to keep up with the work assigned to her by the president, dean, and registrar.

We newcomers were cordially greeted by President Broene when we attended our first faculty meeting, and the older members of the faculty both welcomed us with open arms and did everything they could to integrate us into their fellowship. For the rest, however, we were on our own and were permitted to conduct our classes and pursue our inquiries as we saw fit.

The curriculum required that every student in the school take a minimum number of courses in philosophy, and since I was the sole instructor in the department, this meant that in due course each

The Plato Club, 1939-40
Standing: Bernard Haan, Ralph Wildschut, Roger Heyns,
Paul Ouwinga, William Heynen. Seated: Gordon Buter,
Oliver Buus, Henry Stob, Clarence Boomsma, Arthur Baker

student at the college would come for a shorter or longer time under my tutelage. In the academic year 1939-1940 there were 475 students enrolled in the college, and 255 of them were enrolled in the seven different courses I was asked to teach. In the fall semester I taught six hours of introduction to philosophy in two sections to eighty-four students; three hours of logic to thirteen students; three hours of medieval philosophy to twenty students; and three hours of ethics to eight students. In the spring semester I taught six hours of ancient philosophy in two sections to fifty-two students; three hours of modern philosophy to twenty-nine students; three hours of logic to forty-six students; and three hours of metaphysics to three students in an afternoon seminar held in our home.

It would be disingenuous to say that I was sufficiently versed in all these disciplines to do them justice; but by employing relevant text-books and by dint of hard work, I was able to keep a step or two ahead of my students and able both to convey to them some sense of the philosophical enterprise and to elicit from them a rather favorable response to my offerings. The going, however, was tough. I was at my desk by six in the morning and seldom left it until an hour or two after midnight. Even so, I would sometimes fail to meet my own standards of preparation and would call in sick, the better to be ready for the morrow. Hilda could hardly take pleasure in this regimen, but she understood the pressure I was under and stood faithfully at my side.

In addition to the fifteen hours of weekly classwork, there was, of course, a plethora of papers, exercises, tests, and examinations to read and evaluate. I would not have been able to carry this load had I not had the assistance of a senior student to whom I have ever since had the strongest ties of friendship and collegiality. That student was Clarence Boomsma. I distinctly remember our first meeting: I was ascending the stairs on the first day of school and was greeted at the top by a pleasant young man who informed me that he was president of the Plato Club and wondered whether I would be willing to serve as its sponsor. I told him I would be delighted to do so, and after engaging in some other pleasantries, we parted company only to meet again in classrooms and halls during subsequent days.

I was much drawn to Clarence and, noting his competence, asked him whether he would be willing to assist me in assembling a bibliography and in correcting logic papers. He expressed a willingness to do so, and together we managed to have him paid out of the funds supplied by the National Youth Administration (NYA), which had been put in place by Franklin Roosevelt during his first term as President. Clarence often came to our house during that first year to deliver completed assignments, and we drank many a cup of coffee together with Hilda around our kitchen table. He was thus no stranger to our house by the second semester, when he sat in my study as one of the students enrolled in my seminar in metaphysics.

The Plato Club, which I came to sponsor, met regularly during the year. We held nine monthly meetings, usually in one of the dorm rooms, and we managed to investigate with some thoroughness the whole of Plato's *Republic*. Meeting in smoke-filled rooms, we studied the text from 7:45 to 10:00 in the evening, after which we retired to the dorm dining room, where we normally stayed until 11 p.m. Clarence Boomsma served as president of the group, and Oliver Buus functioned as secretary. There were twelve members in the club: the others were Arthur Baker, Gordon Buter, Edward Doezema, Bernard Haan, William Heynen, Roger Heyns, Paul Holtrop, Paul Ouwinga, John Visser, and Ralph Wildschut — a fine bunch of fellows, some of

205

whom distinguished themselves in the business and professional worlds after graduation. The last meeting of the year was held in our living room, and the evening reached a climax when Hilda served our guests a delicious and bountiful lunch.

Some of my time that year was taken up by work in two faculty committees of which I was a member: I served with Wassink and De Vries on the athletics committee, and with Muyskens, Meeter, and Monsma on the dormitory committee. My memory of what we did as committee members has grown dim, but I seem to recall that we were given a list of dorm residents to visit, and that we ordered the doors to the dormitory to be securely locked at midnight. The house rules we were charged with enforcing included the provision that no woman should be permitted to enter any part of the dormitory other than the dining hall, lobby, and reading room; that intoxicating liquors should not be brought into or consumed in the dormitory; that card playing was not permitted in the dormitory; that every dormitorian should refrain from theater attendance; and that every student, unless he was sick, was expected to attend divine services on Sunday morning and evening. As for athletics, it was decreed that every varsity player had to be enrolled in a sufficient number of courses to achieve graduation after four years of residence.

Among the things that concerned the faculty that year was the monthly presence on campus of the "committee of ten," which had been appointed by Synod to inquire into the spiritual and moral condition of the college. The board and the Synod had heard that some members of the faculty were not as adept in integrating their faith with their teaching as they might be, and that others were unduly tolerant of "worldly amusements." In its address to these matters, the committee members interviewed each of us separately and held one plenary session with the whole faculty during the course of a long afternoon. To satisfy the committee that we were seriously engaged in distinctively Christian education, each of us submitted a syllabus of our course material, and the syllabi seemed to meet with the favor of most committee members. It is interesting to observe that the committee proposed and the board adopted the following resolution:

To continue the excellent policy the Board followed in the case of Dr. Henry Stob who was encouraged to stay a year at the Free University of Amsterdam before he began his work at Calvin. Those who are appointed should receive the opportunity and be urged to prepare themselves at the Free University or take a theological course at our Seminary. The men who are to train our future leaders should have a good grasp of Reformed theology.

The Synod of 1940 endorsed the policy that the board followed in my case and urged its continuance whenever practicable. But being indisposed to lay down a general rule, and not willing to make theological training a condition for appointment, it simply declared that "Synod strongly stresses the fact that the men who are to train our future leaders should have a good understanding of our Calvinistic principles, especially in their particular field." Nobody on the faculty, of course, could object to that. We were one in holding that reason should function within the boundaries of religion and that science should be pursued in alliance with the truth revealed in Scripture and received in faith.

The faculty as a whole was less disposed to countenance the "moral" restraints the board had placed on students and staff — and which the Committee of Ten now urged us to endorse and implement. We did not like the pledge card the students were required to sign; we were reluctant to police behavior; and we knew of no way we could ensure compliance with the rules. Many of us, moreover, did not believe that playing bridge was necessarily evil or that occasional movie viewing was morally debilitating. The Committee of Ten, however, was adamant; and on receiving the committee's report, the board reaffirmed its erstwhile stand against "worldly amusements." It declared:

> We consider dancing a serious offense and advise that watchfulness on the part of authorities be enjoined; . . . we consider card playing a positive danger to the good morals of the students and feel that the faculty ought to take a strong stand against it; . . . and impressed with the danger that is involved in theater attendance the Board reiterates its determination to use all available means to combat this evil in our college.

In spite of this strong language, the board made one concession to the faculty: it withdrew the objectionable pledge card. In its place it ordered that the following generalized statement be inserted in the school's application forms: "The undersigned, having carefully read the Calvin College 'Informational Handbook,' hereby promises to regulate his conduct in harmony with the principles therein set forth."

The school's recruitment policy came likewise under consideration. The Synod of 1936 had instructed the faculty and board to "aim at a student body whose religious spirit moves in a positively Christian direction and whose moral standards of conduct are beyond reproach." The faculty did not quarrel with this demand, but it hazarded the opinion that students from a wide range of evangelical churches should be encouraged to attend the school. The Committee of Ten, however, believed that the atmosphere of the school should be homogeneous with that of the church which founded and now governed it. "Our people," it said, "send their sons and daughters in the expectations that here they will be among their own, in a body of young people that is definitely Christian Reformed." This, the faculty believed, was to erect too high a fence, and it was pleased when the board took a less restrictive stance and ordered "that only such students be admitted who are orthodox protestant in their religious convictions and can present a testimony from their consistory as to their Christian principles and conduct." The faculty could live with that; and with this its engagement with the Committee of Ten came to an end.

My teaching and the preparation for it, as well as my sponsorship of the Plato Club and my work on faculty committees, kept me busy and left me with little time or energy for extracurricular activities. But in the fall of 1939 I did accept an invitation to join "the Academians," a group of professors, ministers, and educated laymen that met periodically in the Pantlind Hotel for discussion and fellowship. On January 11, 1940, I read to the group a paper outlining the Christian philosophy being developed by Vollenhoven and Dooyeweerd. A week or so before that, I delivered an address entitled "Christ as Prophet" to a combined meeting of the churches of Grand Haven and Spring Lake; and in March 1940, I published an article on "God's Antithesis: The Ultimate Disjunction" in the *Calvin Forum*. Although it was not until May 28, 1940, that Classis Grand Rapids East granted me "permission to preach in the churches of the Classis," I had preached on eight different Sundays in various Grand Rapids churches in the months prior to that.

At home Hilda and I lived in straitened circumstances, but we were thankful for our good health and for the many new associations we were able to form. Money was in short supply, but Hilda was able to buy the necessary groceries on a budget of five dollars a week. I possessed only one suit, which I wore every day at school; but it underwent a renovation on Saturdays when Hilda brushed and pressed it and made it fit for church. We had no car, of course, and depended for transportation on the city buses. I myself walked to and from school in all sorts of weather. Near the beginning of the school year we joined the Dennis Avenue Christian Reformed Church; John Weidenaar was our minister, and we both enjoyed a pleasant association with him and his wife and found his sermons instructive and edifying. Our spirits rose early in 1940, when Hilda was told by her doctor (what she already surmised) that she was with child and that we could expect a son or daughter sometime in October. But the pregnancy itself taxed Hilda's strength and caused her to be frequently ill. During that time she was under the care of Dr. Dan De Vries, whom she visited often and who was ready on occasion to tend to her at home.

The school year ended in late May at about the time of the annual board meeting. Besides considering the report of the Committee of Ten and acting on it, the board in 1940 appointed Prof. Henry Schultze to succeed Johannes Broene as president of the college, and named Rev. J. J. Hiemenga as the assistant to the president. Prof. Schultze promptly accepted the appointment; but when Hiemenga declined, Rev. William Kok was appointed in his place. Prof. Vanden Bosch's forty years of service to the college and Prof. Van Andel's service of twenty-five years were commemorated by the board and thanks were expressed to Prof. Clarence Bouma for declining an invitation to teach at the Gordon School of Theology. One action of the board affected our family's financial situation: the minutes report that "in view of the fact that Dr. Henry Stob's salary for the first year is low, it was decided to cancel the first year's repayment of the five hundred dollars loaned to him, implying that one hundred dollars is considered paid."

The yearly Synod of the Christian Reformed Church was held in the college library in June of 1940. Synod readily ratified the appointment of Prof. Schultze and took other actions affecting the college. It ordered that "on the educational policy committee there shall be at least one member that has received theological training"; and it instructed the faculty "to deal in the spirit of love, yet also in view of the strong tide of worldliness which is threatening our churches, very firmly with all cases of misdemeanor and offensive conduct in the matter of amusements, particularly theater attendance, card playing, and dancing, and to discipline and finally expel all students who refuse to heed the admonition of the school authorities in this matter." Such was the temper of the times. A sidelight is cast upon it by another action that Synod took: in response to an overture from Classis Pella, Synod decreed that solos and other special musical numbers should be banished from future prayer services before Synod. Justifying this action, it declared that "since the Synod of 1930 discouraged choir singing, it is manifestly improper to introduce such or similar features at the prayer service for the meeting of Synod." In another action, Synod appointed a committee to effect a revision of the compendium used in catechetical instruction. I was appointed to that committee along with Martin Monsma and Gerrit Hoeksema. I was named secretary, and I would continue to be engaged in that committee's work for the next several years.

Although the academic year ended in May, I was not set free after commencement. In response to representations made by the superintendent of Grand Rapids Public Schools, the faculty had agreed to set up a summer school in which grade school and high school teachers could advance their education and careers. As it turned out, I was asked to teach in it. I accordingly taught a six-week course in introduction to philosophy to a group consisting of seven public school teachers and three college students. This employment cut deeply into the summer recess and left me with little time for rest and relaxation. I devoted what time I had to my studies and to sermon preparation. During June, July, and August, I preached once in the Chicago area and on nine successive Sundays in a variety of Grand Rapids churches — always in the same chalk-stained suit that Hilda regularly refurbished.

I should mention that in 1940 the "Back to God" radio broadcast was inaugurated with Prof. Henry Schultze as the preacher; the Reformed Bible Institute opened in Grand Rapids with Johanna Timmer as teacher; Rev. J. C. De Korne began his duties as director of missions; and Dr. Henry Beets was nearing the close of his long tenure as stated clerk of synod.

Of more immediate concern to the peoples of the world was, of course, the war that had erupted in Europe in September 1939.

Because there was little movement by the belligerents during the winter — the French and Germans being entrenched behind the Maginot and Siegfried lines — the conflict came to be called the "phony war," a designation that would change in the spring, when Hitler launched his first significant offensive. Russia was the first to move. In March 1940 it forced Finland to yield large chunks of territory, and in April it annexed Estonia, Latvia, and Lithuania. Hitler was not far behind. He invaded Denmark and Norway in April and overran Belgium and Holland in early May. The suddenness, efficiency, and success of these attacks and conquests confounded the world and dismayed the Allies — particularly the French, who seemed stricken with a loss of nerve. Sweeping around the Maginot line with powerful Panzer brigades, the Germans reached the Channel port of Dunkerque on May 21. The pinned-down English army stationed there managed a dramatic retreat by sea, but the weakened Allied forces proved impotent against the German advance, and on June 15 Paris fell into the hands of Hitler's troops. The French government sued for peace on June 16, 1940, and Hitler left southern France to be ruled from Vichy by the collaborators Petain and Laval. Italy, which had declared war on France on June 10, reaped the fruit of Hitler's conquests and could now deploy her troops in regions yet to be taken.

It is difficult to say how these events affected the life and mood of the American people. We were not in the war, and though we read the papers and listened to the radio with a mixture of excitement, sorrow, and apprehension, we tended to be absorbed in our daily tasks and taken up with our parochial concerns. But there was movement on this side of the ocean as well. In the fall of 1939, General George Marshall rose to become chief of staff of the United States military. In June 1940, President Roosevelt appointed a group of eminent civilian scientists to a National Defense Research Committee headed by Vannevar Bush, and in August he concluded a U.S.-Canada Mutual Defense Pact. This indicated that Washington was readying the nation for some contingency, even for entry into the war on the side of Britain. There were those, on the other hand, who made nonparticipation a principle and a program. Prominent among these was Charles Lindbergh whose America First Committee preached isolationism and pacifism. Amidst the ebb and flow of mood and sentiment, one thing was sure: the war was real and all our doings lay under its shadow.

SUMMONING UP REMEMBRANCE

*   *   *   *   *

When classes resumed in September 1940, the war was in full progress and the Battle of Britain had begun. The Germans occupied the channel ports of Western Europe and seemed able to mount an amphibious attack on the British Isles from these vantage points. This, however, did not occur; instead, Hitler called on his vaunted air force. German bombers rained death and destruction on English cities during the whole of that autumn, but the British fighter planes, the re-doubtable "Spitfires," rose to meet the enemy and gave such a good account of themselves as to give Goering pause. Winston Churchill, who replaced Neville Chamberlain as Prime Minister on May 11, 1940, became the man of the hour. Promising his people nothing but pain, sweat, and tears, he rallied them around the flag, stiffened their resolve, and inspired them to endure with fortitude their temporary misfortunes. America, meanwhile, was lending its support and inching toward involvement. On September 2, 1940, President Roosevelt withdrew fifty destroyers from our "mothball fleet" and transferred them to England, and on September 15, Congress legislated the first peacetime conscription in U.S. history.

But what was happening in Washington and across the ocean did not impinge on our lives as much as what was happening in our own home. Hilda was by this time well advanced in her pregnancy, and though she suffered from high blood pressure and accumulations of albumen, she and I eagerly looked forward to the birth of our baby. The doctor ordered Hilda into the hospital early on Saturday, October 19, and she labored in pain for nearly forty-eight hours before delivering a boy at 4:31 a.m. on Monday, October 21, 1940. We named our firstborn Henry James, and I handed out celebratory cigars to many of my friends. But our joy was short-lived. On the day following our boy's birth, the doctors and nurses informed us that the baby was suffering from respiratory problems and was in critical condition. However, we were able to see and hold the precious child before he died on October 24, after living on this earth for just three days. Time has eased the pain and sorrow we suffered in subsequent weeks and months, but nothing can erase the memory we cherish of our first child.

Hilda remained confined to her bed and could not attend the funeral. Only Mr. Zaagman, the funeral director, Rev. Weidenaar, our pastor, and I were present when Henry James was laid to rest in Woodlawn

Cemetery, where a stone marker still rests on his grave. Hilda stayed in the hospital for another week and was permitted to go home then only on condition that she remain in bed for another fortnight. To keep house and enable me to perform my outside duties, my mother stayed with us until Hilda was able to be up again and about her daily tasks.

Having spent an apprentice year in the classroom, I was now acclimated to teaching, and I went about the business of this second academic year chastened by death and loss yet resolved to carry on with God's help. I remained a member of the faculty committees of athletics and boarding houses, retained my membership in "The Academians," and continued to sponsor the Plato Club.

On the advice and with the assistance of Mrs. Pels, the dormitory committee established a cooperative residence for women students that year. We leased a house at 830 Bates Street, fitted it for occupancy, and charged the several girls who lived there five dollars a week for room and board. The athletics committee installed new lockers in the gym, gave Coach Muyskens permission to take his basketball team to Pella for a game with Central College, and named four women students to assist him in conducting physical education classes.

In Plato Club we made the acquaintance of several American philosophers. Clarence Boomsma served as the club president during the first semester, but later withdrew to devote himself to seminary studies. Remaining as members of that year's club were Henry Bajema, Philip Kroon, John Leitch, Paul Ouwinga, Robert Reitsma, Robert Van Dyken, Nicholas Van Til, Bernard Velzen, and Ralph Wildschut. We held eight monthly meetings and considered, in sequence, Jonathan Edwards, James McCosh, Josiah Royce, William James, Ralph Barton Perry, Roy Sellers, George Santayana, and Alfred North Whitehead.

The faculty was augmented by the addition of our new president, Prof. Henry Schultze, who performed the duties of his office with unostentatious efficiency. Not formally incorporated into our faculty ranks, but serving the college well, were a number of assistants with whom it was a pleasure to associate. Anthony Hoekema assisted in speech, Marian Schoolland in English, and Harold Dekker in debating. To complete the picture, I should add that Lena Bossenbroek came to join Caroline Veen in the office, and that Ruth Imanse took over the management of the bookstore.

During the course of this year, several members of the faculty expressed a desire to learn more about the "Wijsbegeerte der Wet-

The Baseball Team, 1940-41
Coach Stob, Veenema, Van Faasen, Broene, Berghuis, Westveer,
Boersma, Van Wieren, Buikstra, Hekman, Brower, Bierma, Steen

sidee," the new Christian philosophy being developed by the Dutch philosophers Vollenhoven and Dooyeweerd. Professors Van Andel and Monsma proposed the formation of a faculty philosophy club to pursue this objective, and I was asked to introduce the material, clarify points, and respond to questions. I gladly consented to do this. The first meeting of the group was held on April 2, 1941; two other meetings were held before the school year ended, and at each of the three meetings an average of eighteen faculty members attended.

During the 1940-41 school year the student enrollment rose to an even 500. Of that number, 212 were enrolled in my classes. In the fall semester I taught six hours of introduction to philosophy in two sections to sixty-four students; three hours of logic to nineteen students; three hours of medieval philosophy to seven students; and three hours of ethics to six students. In the spring semester I taught six hours of ancient philosophy in two sections to fifty-four students; three hours of logic to forty-one students; three hours of modern philosophy to twenty students; and three hours of metaphysics to two students. There is something in me that wishes to put down the names of those students — both men and women — who in that year and the previous one exhibited the marks of responsible scholarship and Christian discipleship in my classes; but such a naming, because selective, would be hazardous and perhaps unfitting. I cannot resist declaring, however, that there is imprinted in my mind the memory of not a few who by their intelligence and industry made our joint pursuit of learning a pleasure, and who by their courtesy and friendship smoothed out the rough and crooked places that appeared on our way.

Prof. Muyskens taught mathematics, coached basketball, conducted gym classes, and supervised athletics; but the students were also playing baseball, golf, and tennis, and he had no time to manage the teams engaged in those sports. So he looked for assistance to certain faculty members. Since I had played second base on Calvin's baseball team during my undergraduate days, I was asked to coach baseball. Baseball had become an official M.O.C.C. sport that year, and, dressed in newly acquired Calvin uniforms, our boys played home-and-away games with Ferris Institute, Lawrence Tech, Western State Teachers, and Grand Rapids Junior College. I had two good pitchers, Paul Westveer and Andrew De Kraker, and several fair batters, and that accounts for the fact that we won a majority of our games. Barney Steen, who later became athletic director at Calvin, did the catching. Among the other members of the team were Eugene Broene, Herman Van Faasen, Elmer Van Wieren, John Hekman, Don Van Beek, Edward Bierma, Ralph Veenema, and John Brower.

Our life at home continued apace. Hilda recovered her health, participated in the activities of the faculty women, and through frequent contacts came to know a considerable number of students. My extracurricular work did not cease. The synodical committee on the revision of the compendium met regularly, and that exacted time and thought; but the work was also a learning experience, and I did not find the assignment too burdensome. I was frequently called on to preach, and while school was in session I conducted worship services on ten different Sundays. I was also privileged to deliver the annual address at the March 15 *Dies Natalis* banquet put on by the faculty and students of the seminary. The March 1941 issue of the *Calvin Forum* contained an article of mine on "Peace," and in the August issue I published a review of A. A. Bowman's *A Sacramental Universe*.

We bought our first car in the spring of 1941: it was a second-hand

Plymouth that Verhage Motors sold to us for a sum that I assume was within our means, although I don't recall the amount.

The Board of Trustees met in late May and early June 1941. The budget for the year drawing to a close amounted to $138,000, and for the year 1941-42 the board adopted a budget of $146,000. It thanked Prof. Rooks for his many years of service, granted him honorable emeritation, and appointed Prof. Henry Ryskamp to succeed him as academic dean. My good friend Henry Zylstra had procured his doctorate from Harvard that year, and to my great delight he was appointed by the board to a two-year term as instructor of English. I myself was reappointed to a six-year term and elevated from the rank of instructor to that of associate professor. One item in the minutes of the board meeting casts an interesting light on the prevailing mores: "In reply to a question whether the Thespian Club, in their broadcast over station WLAV, might portray some biblical character, the executive committee answered negatively." The board endorsed this action.

Meanwhile, there was movement on the troubled world stage. At home Franklin Roosevelt defeated Wendell Wilkie in the November elections and began, with Vice President Henry Wallace, his third term as President on January 20, 1941. Japan was increasingly featured in the news. It had joined the Rome-Berlin axis, and in July 1941 it assumed a protectorate over the whole of Indochina. Washington could not — or did not — foresee how, when, and where the Japanese would strike again; but as early as November 1940 the United States imposed an embargo on Japan-bound supplies, and on July 26, 1941, Roosevelt both froze all Japanese assets in the United States and appointed General Douglas MacArthur commander of all army forces in the Far East.

England was holding Germany at bay, but the prospect of survival was not bright, and victory seemed even more remote. Yet Britain was not left without support: early in 1941, Congress passed the Lend-Lease Act; in May the Atlantic fleet took Greenland under its protection; and in July the U.S. Navy began to escort lend-lease shipments to Iceland. When an American merchantman was torpedoed and destroyed by a German submarine in May 1941, the United States stiffened in its attitude, closed Axis consulates, and froze all Axis assets.

Hitler, however, remained mobile and undaunted. Having occupied Yugoslavia and Greece, he declared war on Russia on Sunday, June

22, 1941, and began a deep penetration into that vast country. At summer's end the United States appeared to all the world to be committed to the Allied cause. When, on August 14, 1941, Roosevelt and Churchill drew up the Atlantic Charter on a warship off Newfoundland, there could be no mistaking where America stood regarding the raging conflict. But formally we were still at peace.

I spent the summer at my desk in preparation for the next school year.

* * * * *

As I began my third year of teaching in September 1941, my salary had increased from $2,100 to $2,200. Not all of that was take-home pay, however; there were the usual deductions for taxes and the medical and pension funds, and the demands of patriotism had to be met as well. Before the first semester of the academic year had come to a close, we were at war, and in response to a government appeal we all agreed to set aside part of our monthly paychecks to purchase defense bonds.

Our entry into the war was sudden and dramatic. Our relations with Japan had been tense and unsettled for some time, but there had been no break in diplomatic ties, and throughout November and into early December talks designed to avert open conflict were seriously carried on in Washington with emissaries from Emperor Hirohito. It was on Sunday, December 7, 1941, when Hilda and I were at dinner, that news reached us over the radio that Pearl Harbor had been subjected to a secret attack by Japanese bombers flying off mid-ocean carriers. Coming from the southeast, the Japanese flew over Diamond Head, destroyed the core of our Pacific fleet, and left in their wake 2,400 dead and 1,200 wounded American servicemen. President Roosevelt appeared on radio, called the day a "day of infamy," and summoned Congress to an emergency meeting. On the very next day, Monday, December 8, the United States, by a nearly unanimous vote of Congress, declared war on Japan. Only Jeannette Rankin, congresswoman from Montana, dissented. Germany and Italy responded on December 11 by declaring war on the United States. We now stood against the Axis powers in solidarity with the beleaguered British and Russians, and the immediate future promised little but disruption, sacrifice, pain, and death.

217

Henry Zylstra was now my colleague at Calvin, and we renewed our long-established friendship with great satisfaction. The student body numbered 504 men and women, and of this number 122 were enrolled in the four first-semester courses I undertook to teach. I continued serving on the two faculty committees to which I had been assigned, and also resumed conducting a discussion of Dooyeweerd's philosophy with the members of the faculty. We held meetings in September, October, and November, and then decided to disband the "club." At the last meeting I was presented with a desk lamp, which I have kept as a memento and which, after many years, still casts light on my scribblings.

In Plato Club we again took up a study of Plato's *Republic*. Nick Van Til served as president and Robert Reitsma as secretary; the other members of the club were Alexander De Jong, John De Kruyter, Richard De Ridder, John De Vries, Homer Hoeksema, Engbert Ubels, and Everett Van Reken. We met ten times during the year and ended the sessions at my home on April 27.

When the second semester began in January 1942, the country was at war, and male students were beginning to receive draft notices. This was unsettling to some, but most were ready to come to the defense of their country. Some even displayed an eagerness to take up arms and lay low the evil powers that were now ravaging the earth. Yet deferments were general, and for the moment the business of the school was carried on more or less as usual.

I taught the four second semester courses in philosophy that I was accustomed to teach — this time to an additional 104 students — and when spring came I coached a baseball team that engaged in eight contests with teams from Ferris, Aquinas, Western State, and Grand Rapids Junior College. It had become evident, however, that it would be difficult to assemble a team for the following year. Several of the best players were already classified 1-A, and I myself had been required to register for the draft. The prospects for the immediate future were not bright.

The college itself was asked to gear up for the war, and late in the academic year the faculty made a number of policy decisions affecting courses and credits. The ablest students were now allowed to take eighteen hours of course work each semester, and substantial credit was given for training in first aid and in physical education. To keep the church supplied with ministers, the college placed preseminary students on an accelerated course, and they were allowed to pre-enroll in seminary courses to help them retain their draft-exempt status.

That year I engaged in the usual extracurricular activities. I spoke early in the year to a gathering of local ministers on "What is Philosophy?"; I addressed the college Calvinism Club on "The Philosophy of Nazism"; and at the second American Calvinistic Conference held on campus in June, I delivered a lecture entitled "The Word of God and Philosophy," which was later published in a volume edited by Clarence Bouma. I preached only twice during the school year, but I conducted worship services on six different occasions during the summer.

The Board of Trustees met in late May and early June 1942. It had operated that year on a budget of close to $136,000. It took note of the fact that thirty-four of the students enrolled in the fall were now engaged in military service, that an additional eleven were employed in defense work, and that Harold Dekker, who had been assisting in the department of speech, had decided to enter the ministry with a view to a chaplaincy. The board also eased my personal financial burden. It adopted a recommendation of the executive committee absolving Hilda and me of the obligation to repay the five-hundred-dollar "loan" given us for my study in The Netherlands. The grounds for this decision were briefly stated: "Dr. Henry Stob had already received his appointment when he was asked to study another year. This puts him on a level with other members of the teaching staff who receive five hundred dollars if they want to be absent for a year to continue their studies." Our college debt was thus summarily canceled, and for this we were grateful.

The board also prepared for submission to the government a letter pleading for the deferment of Henry Zylstra and myself. This is how the letter read:

> The Board of Trustees of Calvin College and Seminary has taken note of the possibility that two of our professors, Dr. Henry Stob and Dr. Henry Zylstra, may in the near future be lost to our institution because they will be drafted for military service. The Board feels that all our professors and students should and will respond in the spirit of true loyalty and patriotism to the call of our country in the present emergency. However, the Board also is assured that the government desires to prevent as much as possible all unnecessary

219

serious disruption of the work of our educational institutions. Wherefore, the Board of Trustees of Calvin College and Seminary respectfully urges the proper authorities to give Dr. H. Stob and Dr. H. Zylstra a deferred status in the draft on the ground that their continued services at our institution are vitally necessary to the proper function of our educational activities, and that it would be exceedingly difficult to replace them, especially at this time.

This letter was endorsed by Synod, but there was no telling at the time how the local draft board would respond.

At its June meeting the Synod of the Christian Reformed Church gave Henry Schultze an indefinite appointment as president of the college; declared Harry Boer a candidate for the ministry and took notice of his intention to enter the military chaplaincy; honored Dr. Henry Beets upon his retirement as stated clerk; and appointed Rev. William Hendriksen as professor of New Testament in the seminary. The committee on compendium revision, of which I was a member, presented a first draft of its work to Synod and was given another year to complete its task.

Hitler's troops, meanwhile, were fighting on Russian soil and finding the going tough. Japanese forces, on the other hand, were steadily advancing in the east. The Philippines fell to the Japanese on April 8, 1942: American and Filipino troops on Bataan surrendered unconditionally, and on May 6, General Wainwright yielded up Corregidor. A month earlier, MacArthur had gone to Australia in order to direct the American response from there. Responses were not lacking. On April 18, Colonel Doolittle, flying from Admiral Halsey's carrier *The Hornet*, led an air assault on Tokyo, and on June 4 the United States navy destroyed four Japanese carriers in the Battle of Midway. But this did not arrest the progress of the enemy, and there was no telling when the tide would turn in our favor.

*   *   *   *   *

I entered my fourth year of teaching in September 1942. The previous year had seen some attrition in the student body, and I was thus surprised to learn that the enrollment now stood at 554. The number decreased, however, as the year progressed. At year's end only 400 students remained, and most of them — perhaps 65 percent

— were women. The all-male preseminary students had their own course to pursue; but noticeable among the other men was a shift in course selection. They tended, under the pressures of the times, to move from studies in the classics toward work in mathematics and the sciences.

In the first semester I taught courses in introduction, logic, ethics, and medieval philosophy to a total of seventy-six students. This number was low in comparison to previous enrollments, but this decline was to be expected, and it served to make the paperwork more manageable. I continued to be a member of the faculty committee on boarding places, but was transferred from the committee on athletics to the committee on religious and social activities, where I served with Meeter, Swets, Pels, and Van Andel. I was relieved of my coaching duties for the simple reason that no baseball team took the field that year. But Plato Club was alive and well, and we began meeting early in the year, this time with John De Kruyter as president and Rich De Ridder as secretary. We undertook a study of idealism, realism, and pragmatism, and the members managed to acquire a tolerable acquaintance with representatives of these philosophies. Besides De Kruyter and De Ridder, the club consisted of Alex De Jong, John De Vries, Jack Hasper, Bart Huizenga, Fred Klooster, Doug Paauw, Wes Smedes, and Walter Tolsma.

The synodical committee appointed to revise the compendium met several times during the fall, and we managed to complete our final draft in time for publication in the spring agenda. I had in September been given a seat on the Board of the Grand Rapids Christian High School, and I served that year with George Goris, Henry Hekman, Henry Holtvluwer, Jack Van't Hof, George Wieland, Louis De Korne, Bert Frieswyk, and one or two others.

While these things were going on in Grand Rapids, the war continued on its course. Hitler was meeting with resistance both on the eastern front and on his southern flank. In September 1942 the Russians held out against the Germans at Stalingrad, and in November they unleashed a counter-offensive from which the Germans never fully recovered. Meanwhile, in "Operation Torch," the Allies seized Oran, Algiers, and Casablanca, and by their presence posed an additional threat to Rommel's Africa corps, which had already been engaged by General Montgomery at El Alamain.

At home it was not all smooth sailing. The threat of the draft hung

Calvin's Contribution to the War: Henry Stob, Henry Zylstra

over me, and though I was not averse to serving my country in a war that I considered eminently justified, I realized that my induction into military service would entail another separation from Hilda, and this prospect was not pleasing to either of us. But there was something more disturbing. Hilda was again pregnant and feeling quite unwell. On November 26, 1942, she suffered a miscarriage that brought her low and required her hospitalization; she returned home in early December but had to keep to her bed in order to recover fully. Her mother stayed with us for a week to nurse her and keep house, and for this I was thankful; but it was some time before our sense of tragedy and loss was overcome and our hope of having children revived.

During the second semester the faculty noticed a certain restlessness among the students and asked President Schultze to address them at a school assembly. Men were now dropping out at regular intervals, and we devised ways of granting credit for abbreviated class attendance and for failure to take exams and meet other course requirements. The Board of Trustees was doing everything it could to keep Henry Zylstra and me from being drafted, but their efforts met with small success. In January of 1943 both of us were classified 1-A, which meant that we could be called up at any moment. But in response to the board's overtures, the authorities granted us

222

deferment until June 1. The length to which the executive committee was willing to go may be gathered from its report to the board in May. It declared in part: "In view of the fact that Dr. Stob had studied theology and very likely would have been an ordained minister today if the Board had not asked him to take the chair of philosophy, the Committee felt so concerned about this matter that it offered to take up the matter of his deferment with President Roosevelt, but Dr. Stob indicated that he wished this would not be done." And so, indeed, I did. With everyone else being called to the colors, I thought that that would be going a step too far. Moreover, although I appreciated the committee's helpfulness and concern, I sensed that, with a nation to govern and a war to win, the President had weightier matters on his mind than the status of some unknown teacher in a small Midwestern college.

On January 18, Henry Zylstra and I underwent a physical examination in the Grand Rapids armory and were declared fit for duty. On January 30 we made a personal appeal for a change in classification, but our appeal fell on deaf ears, and we knew then that we would soon have to exchange our academic robes for the garments and accoutrements of war. In early March 1943, Hank and I took steps to make our anticipated military service compatible with our age and training: we applied for a commission — I in the navy and Hank in the army.

Hank was the first to receive a response to his application, though it was not of the sort he had expected or now relished. He had indicated a desire (or willingness) to serve in military intelligence, and this led to his being sent a batch of cryptograms that he was asked to decode and return. He worked hard on these mystifying messages, and I assisted him as best I could. One batch followed upon another, and although Hank applied his very considerable talents to these assignments, there was always some puzzle that neither he nor I could solve or some code we could not break. This, of course, contributed neither to our self-esteem nor our equanimity. Moreover, during the whole time he addressed these assignments, no assurance came from Washington that a commission would follow upon their completion. Nor was I hearing anything from the navy. We therefore simply prayed and waited, while attending with divided attention to our duties at the college.

The school community responded to our situation with love and empathy. At the spring banquet put on by the Student Council, Hank and I were thrust forward as the honored guests. We were also featured in the May edition of the *Chimes* and given accolades beyond our deserving by both President Schultze and the student editor. When on May 18, 1943, I conducted the college chapel service, the exercise had a special poignancy for me, for there were many in the audience who were about to interrupt their studies and venture into an uncertain and precarious future. I noted in my brief address that world affairs were driving a wedge between us, drawing some into military camps, some into battle, and some perhaps even into death. But I bade my friends to go forward unafraid. I indicated that it is not what happens to us that counts, but how we stand up under what happens; it is not what we must bear but how we bear it that lends quality to our lives. As we part, to suffer and to endure we know not what, let us, I said, face life calmly and resolutely, not indeed in the proud confidence that we are impervious to fate, but in the sober assurance that no lasting evil can befall those who are called according to God's purpose. And let us, I added, pray for one another. Pray, not that we be taken out of our involvements with the world, but that in the world we may keep the faith. Pray, not that we be kept from battle, but that in the battle we quit ourselves like men. Pray, not that we save our life, but that if we must lose it, we may find in Christ a fuller life and more abundant.

At its yearly meeting in late May the Board of Trustees did a great many things, but of special interest to Henry Zylstra and me was a report it prepared for submission to Synod. It read:

> Last year we reported to your honorable body that Dr. Henry Stob and Dr. Henry Zylstra might possibly be called to the colors. This year we have to inform you to our regret that we shall lose the valuable services of both these men for the duration, since both have been drafted. All our efforts to have them reclassified proved fruitless. The draft board, however, out of courtesy deferred them 'til the end of the academic year. We hope and pray that the Lord may spare these men and may soon open the way for them to return to their respective chairs. The Board decided to keep open the chairs of both these men as long as they are in the armed service and to permit them to share in the promotions.

When Synod met, my thoughts were elsewhere. But I can report that Synod adopted the revised compendium that our committee had submitted after three years of hard labor; that it elected Dr. Cornelius Van Til to succeed Prof. Berkhof in the chair of systematic theology, while naming William Rutgers as his alternate; that it chose John De Haan to succeed Dr. Beets as stated clerk, while naming Ralph Danhof as alternate; and that it authorized the Calvin board to proceed with the erection of a science building as soon as conditions permitted and funds became available. Of special interest to Henry Zylstra and me was Synod's decision to hold our chairs open until our return, and to count our years of military service as service to the college. It was also gratifying that Clarence Boomsma was declared a candidate for the ministry at that year's Synod. He would soon be called to serve the church in Imlay City, Michigan, but before he left to take up his duties there, we spent a morning drinking coffee, renewing fellowship, and wishing each other Godspeed.

It was about the time when Synod was holding its first sessions that the mailman brought to our door a notice that would resolve the quandary we had long been in. It came not from the draft board but from the chief of naval personnel in Washington, and it informed me that I had been appointed as a lieutenant junior grade in the naval reserve. The letter was dated June 8, 1943, and accompanying it was a formal certificate signed by Frank Knox, the Secretary of the Navy, indicating that my commission was conferred on May 1, and that I was a bona fide naval officer. I accepted the appointment and took the oath of office on June 16, which was subscribed and sworn to by Henry Denkema, a notary public and friend of the family.

Henry Zylstra, to my great regret, was less fortunate. The commission he had applied for and labored so assiduously to secure was inexplicably not conferred. He was inducted into the army as a buck private and eventually sent to do battle on the eastern front. He suffered a great deal in the company of men who shared none of his interests and concerns, and who by their talk and behavior often offended his refined sensibilities. Later in the war, however, his talents and qualities of leadership were recognized. He was commissioned in the field, and in 1945 was mustered out as an officer with battle citations.

I should mention that, though Henry Zylstra and I were the only members of the faculty to be drawn into the service of our country, there were many of our friends and acquaintances who also left their posts to join the armed forces. More than twenty Christian Reformed ministers had by this time entered the military chaplaincy — among them Harry Boer and Harold Dekker. George Stob, too, had left his large church in Burton Heights, Grand Rapids, to serve as chaplain; and quite a few of my many nephews were now clad in blue and khaki. Lester De Koster, whom I had earlier come to know through the good offices of his then fiancée, Ruth De Vries, had also become a naval officer at about that time; and Bill Spoelhof also had entered the service and was deployed in the office of strategic services.

A most gratifying feature of my appointment was the permission it gave Hilda to accompany me on my first real assignment. After a brief period of indoctrination, I was ordered to report to the commanding officer of the Naval Reserve Midshipman School at Columbia University in New York, where I would undergo instruction in military government, and Hilda was allowed to join me there and enjoy the perquisites of our newly acquired status.

On June 18, I appeared for a physical examination in the Book Tower Building in Detroit and was found fit for duty; but I was given until July 28 to report to the training station in the Bronx. This gave us an additional forty days to settle our affairs. As I recall, we were given an allowance for the purchase of uniforms, but it didn't cover the expenses we incurred when we traveled to Chicago and were outfitted by the clothiers in Marshall Field's department store. We vacated our rented house on Benjamin Avenue the second week of July, moved our furniture to the back room of Father De Graaf's old grocery store, sold our aged Plymouth to Simon Heeres, and took up residence with Hilda's mother, whose two sons — Ed and Andy — had already gone off to war. Before leaving Grand Rapids, I tendered my resignation to the members of the high school board and thanked them for the kindness with which they had received their much younger colleague.

Hilda could not, of course, accompany me to the training school in Fort Schuyler, but I knew I would see her before long and had no doubt that she would put to good use the intervening days of waiting. At 11:35 p.m. on July 27, 1943, I boarded a train for New York and arrived in that city in time to report for duty as I had been commanded. I was required to travel in uniform, and this caused me some embarrassment because I was unfamiliar with military customs and procedures, and I didn't know how to respond to the many soldiers and sailors who saluted me en route. I suppose I managed, however awkwardly, to simulate their gestures, but I must have breached protocol several times by failing to salute officers to whom I owed this token of courtesy and respect.

As I was about to begin my military service, the war was nearly four years old, and I had reached the age of thirty-five. I didn't know what awaited me in my new calling and environment. What I did know from reading the daily papers was that Guadacanal was now in the hands of the United States Marines, and that the Allies in Africa had seized Tunis and Bezerte after having taken into custody thousands of German and Italian prisoners. The war, it appeared, was building up toward the eventual defeat of the Axis powers, and I had not yet played even the tiniest role in it.

11

IN MILITARY SERVICE
(1943-1946)

O n July 28, 1943, I reported for duty at the Naval Training School in Fort Schuyler, the Bronx, New York. My memory of what went on in the two months I was stationed there has grown dim, but I know that we were initiated into the ways of the navy. We studied military regulations, acquired a sailor's vocabulary, practiced signaling with flags, learned through screenings to identify the different ships and planes that formed the arsenal of the contending powers, read manuals on seamanship, and learned to march in cadence on the parade ground — to the drill master's shrill instructions. The names of those with whom I associated I have long since forgotten; where we slept and ate I do not recall; and what free time we were afforded now escapes me. I must have been able to get out at times, for I recall worshiping one Sunday at Manhattan's "Little Church Around the Corner," and I know that I spent an afternoon in town in search of an apartment. However, normally we were confined to barracks.

I knew from my orders that on my release from Fort Schuyler I was to report to the School of Military Government at Columbia University, and I was thus very happy that by September 20, I had found an apartment to my liking in the very shadow of its Teachers College. Our class graduated from the training school on September 24, 1943, and, having been detached and granted leave until October 1, I caught a train the moment I was released and arrived in Grand

The Recruit

Rapids early on September 25. Hilda and I spent the next four days visiting old friends and preparing for our joint return to New York. We entrained with considerable baggage on September 29, and on the 30th settled into our apartment on the corner of 118th Street and Amsterdam Avenue. Hilda was pleased with the apartment and found the landlady, Margaret Parks, affable and considerate. It was a large seven-story building that housed us; the uniformed elevator man conveyed us to our third-floor apartment; and Maude, the Harlem maid, came in weekly to dust and scour the two large rooms and small kitchen we occupied.

While we were performing our peaceful domestic duties, the war raged on and the Allied gains continued to mount. On July 25, 1943, before I had even reported for duty, the King of Italy had forced Mussolini to resign. While I was just learning to distinguish starboard from port in training school, Sicily was overrun by Patton's tanks. And before I had completed the course of instruction, General Clark had launched the Italian campaign by landing at Palermo.

At home, Clarence Bouma, Ralph Stob, and William Radius substituted for me in teaching selected courses in philosophy at the college.

$$* \quad * \quad * \quad * \quad *$$

On October 1, 1943, I began a nine-month naval course of instruction in military government and administration at Columbia University. There were forty officers in our class, and of this number only one was without an advanced academic degree; the exception, Lt. Cmdr. Guy J. Swope, had previously been governor of Puerto Rico. The regimen we were under was strict and demanding. We took twenty-three hours of course work every week. There were daily classes, and the assignments were extensive. Since we were being trained for work in Melanesia, Micronesia, Malaysia, Taiwan, Japan, and other eastern territories, we studied Japanese and Pidgin English, and followed courses in geography, economics, cultural anthropology, international law, the rules of warfare, and the history of military occupations. In the language courses we had to undergo testing and demonstrate our skills in understanding and communication. In the other courses we had to write numerous papers, a task that absorbed a good many of our evening hours. The faculty was largely recruited from the staff of the Columbia University and included, among others, Schuyler C. Wallace, Philip C. Jessup, Adriaan J. Barnouw, Grayson L. Kirk, Charles C. Hyde, and Ralph Linton. Mr. Bunji K. Omura taught us Japanese. Prof. Amry Vanden Bosch appeared on the list of faculty members attached to the naval school, but he was not involved in any of the courses I took, nor did I ever meet him on campus or elsewhere in New York.

Being run by the navy, the school combined academia with a modified form of military discipline. We were required to report for duty at eight o'clock every morning in order to answer a roll call and to attend to the day's announcements. Since I lived but a block

Hilda and Henry

from school, it was easy for me to be on time for these recurring exercises. Immediately after the morning's assembly we were sent off to our various classes and, except for an hour's reprieve at noon, we were kept busy with library and other assignments until five in the evening (the usual free weekend began at two o'clock on Saturday afternoon). Two periods a week were set aside for physical training: this normally consisted of military drills that took place on a barricaded street masquerading as a parade ground. Each of us took turns conducting the drills. Those of us who were slow in giving commands sometimes drove the marching column against a wall or scrambled it into shameful confusion, but eventually we all became tolerable drill masters. A pleasant feature of our work together was the biweekly dinner on Tuesday evenings in the prestigious faculty club: after cocktails and a good repast we would be addressed by some knowl-

Nick Van Til, Jerry Hertel, Henry, John Hekman, John Vanden Berg

edgeable person on a subject germane to our studies — and dismissed around ten o'clock.

Most of the students in our class lived off campus with their wives and went their own way. Consequently, I formed friendships with only a few of them; they included George Eddy, Roger Holmes, Eugene McColm, Raymond McLain, Gordon Prange, and Guy Swope. Closer to Hilda and me than any of these good men was Clarence Minnema. Clarence was a medical doctor and now a lieutenant commander in the navy. He was moreover a native of Grand Rapids who had been brought up in Hilda's north-side neighborhood. When he learned that I was married to one of the De Graaf girls, he was quick to come over to our house to meet his compatriot. Hilda remembered him and his family, and the two of them enjoyed reminiscing about the events and scenes of their earlier years. After his initial visit, Clarence came over often and we frequently studied Japanese together while Hilda looked on in amusement. There was some visiting back and forth with the others I have mentioned, but these goings in and out were casual and intermittent and have largely faded from memory. What I do recall, however, is our being invited one evening to Lt. Eddy's apartment for a meeting with Charles and Mary Beard, the distinguished historians, who were relatives of Eddy's wife.

The Beards were getting on in years, but their conversation was lively and perceptive, and we counted the evening well spent.

Our social life was enriched by others as well. The Hekman brothers took turns coming to New York in those days, and we were the dinner guests of Henry, John, or Jelle several times at the Hotel Commodore, where they regularly stayed when conducting business in town. Our good friends John and Helen Hamersma lived in nearby Paterson, and we exchanged visits with them on a number of occasions. New York was a port of embarkation for many servicemen, and this brought to our door for lunch — and sometimes for lodging — such friends as Leroy Vogel, Lester De Koster, Peter Katt, and Ira Slagter. And then there were the Calvin students, fresh from my classes, who had been called to the colors and who knew of our presence in the city. Many of these, including Nick Van Til, John Vanden Berg, Gerald Stob, John Hekman, Elmer Van Wieren, and Jerry Hertel, were visitors in our house and savored the products of Hilda's culinary skills. How Hilda managed I do not know, for rationing was in effect, and coffee, sugar, butter, and meats were always in short supply. But manage she did.

Since our evenings and weekends were generally unencumbered, Hilda and I were free to do as we pleased. When I was not working on some assignment, we read, listened to music, wrote letters, attended an occasional movie, explored the town, ate at a neighborhood restaurant, and kept up with world events through radio and press releases. We were regularly in church on Sunday mornings: sometimes we worshipped in the Riverside church, where we heard Harry Emerson Fosdick preach; sometimes we could be found in the Union Theological Seminary chapel, where we listened to sermons by Reinhold Niebuhr, John Bennett, Henry Sloan Coffin, and John Knox. A few times we attended the Cathedral of St. John the Divine, where Bishop William T. Manning presided; but the Broadway Presbyterian Church became our regular place of worship. John McComb was the senior minister there, and he preached the old-time gospel. But neither he nor his people invited us to participate in the life of the church, and we remained for the duration unattached to any particular body of believers.

Our brother-in-law, Dr. Thomas De Vries, joined us at Columbia in mid-December 1943. Left with two young children after the death of his wife, Hilda's sister Therese, Tom had remarried and was still a professor of chemistry at Purdue University. He came to New York to join the group of scientists who had been assembled at the university to work on what became known as the "Manhattan Project," work involving the development of the atom bomb. Tom settled in our neighborhood and, until he was joined by his family in late January, he took his evening meals with us and regularly spent Sundays in our company.

When the Christmas season came, we set up a tree in our living room and prepared to celebrate with joy and thankfulness the birth of our Savior. Tom was, of course, invited to join in the celebration we planned for the holiday, and we were pleased when we learned that Edward De Graaf, Hilda's brother, would be able to join in the festivities. Ed, an officer in the army's corps of engineers, was about to be sent overseas, and his two- or three-day stay with us was therefore especially gratifying. Joy turned into sorrow when we learned that John Zeilstra, my sister Gert's husband, had died on December 28, 1943, from the effects of diabetes and related complications. Unfortunately, we were not able to attend the funeral, but we deeply mourned the passing of a brother-in-law accredited by all who knew him, and we commiserated with a dear sister who was now left alone to care and provide for her three children. Our year's end celebration was muted in keeping with the events that had just transpired, but we did hazard a trip to Time's Square on New Year's eve and mingled cautiously with the crowd that hailed the birth of 1944 with boisterous acclaim.

Throughout the winter and spring I was kept busy at the school, where things proceeded quite as they had at the beginning. It was on May 15, 1944, that our studies came to an end and each of us was awarded a certificate attesting our completion of the long course of instruction. I had now been in New York for nearly ten months, had for most of this time led a life similar to the one I had long been accustomed to, and, in spite of the uniform I wore, had not made a single contribution to the war's advancement. It was to be expected, then, that with my training accomplished, I would be reassigned and made a working part of the established war machine. But this did not happen. I remained under the command of Captain John K. Richards and was ordered to join a small group of university-based military writers who were preparing handbooks on the far-eastern territories likely to be occupied and administered by the conquering Allied forces.

*   *   *   *   *

The four-month tour of duty I now began allowed Hilda and me to retain our residence at 430 W. 118th Street, and to continue the patterns of living we had adopted under even more favorable conditions. The work place to which I had been assigned, a large room in one of the university buildings, was only a block from our apartment, and I was able, as before, to come home for lunch on every working day. There were no more assemblies, no more drills, and no more ceremonies to attend. The five or six of us who had been recruited for research and writing arrived at our desks at eight in the morning, broke for lunch, left for home at five, and spent our evenings totally free of military discipline.

Yet the work was taxing. The navy had supplied us with worksheets indicating what sorts of information it desired, and it was our duty to consult every available source of knowledge pertaining to the area of our concern and set down in ordered fashion the result of our inquiries. The leader of our group was Lt. Kenneth Bunce, who in civilian life had been a professor of history at Otterbein College and had passed through the school of military government with the class that preceded mine. He was preparing a handbook on Japan, and I was asked to do one on Taiwan and on the adjoining Pescadores Islands. I found in Ken a kindred spirit, and we were soon collaborating on our respective assignments, with the result that during the long summer of 1944, I learned nearly as much about Japan as I did about Taiwan and its island satellites. As the weeks and months progressed, our association grew into companionship, and when we served together in other posts after that, a friendship grew up between us that outlasted the war. When September rolled around, each of us had completed our assignments and produced sizable manuscripts replete with information about the people and territories we had researched, and it was time to move on.

The distant war was meanwhile being carried on by those less favorably situated than ourselves, and at a tremendous cost in wounds, imprisonments, and deaths. Through these sacrifices, however, the Allied cause was being steadily advanced. General Clark's Fifth Army had moved from Palermo through Naples, Anzio, and Monte Cassino to Rome, which fell on June 4, 1944. On June 6 the Allies landed on the coasts of Normandy, and though meeting stiff resistance at every point, were able to liberate Paris on August 25 and allow De Gaulle to claim control of all of France. In the Far East the successful June battle of the Philippine Sea became a prelude to the equally successful Battle of Leyte Gulf, which enabled MacArthur to splash ashore on Leyte Island in October and proudly proclaim, "I have returned."

The academic year 1943-1944 at Calvin had by now run its course. The student enrollment, which had been at 385 in September, had declined to 345 by year's end. The faculty remained stable, except that Grace Pels resigned as dean of women in June in order to marry Chaplain Elton Holtrop. Enrollment in the three undergraduate classes at the seminary was 30, and at commencement eight graduates were ready to enter the active ministry. Prof. Berkhof, having reached retirement age, left his post in midsummer and was succeeded in the seminary presidency by Prof. Volbeda. That year the Board of Trustees expended the princely sum of $148,000 to run the two schools.

The Synod of the Christian Reformed Church met in June 1944 with representatives of nineteen classes in attendance. Asked to restudy the 1928 resolutions on worldly amusements, the Synod refused to do so on the grounds that the statement's principles were clear and its implications plain. Asked to support an incipient movement toward the establishment of a Calvinistic university, Synod judged that the proposal was premature and that what had to take priority was the enlargement and improvement of the college. Choirs were again in focus, but they were no longer banned; however, restraints were placed on them. Synod declared: "In cases where choirs exist or will be introduced, it is insisted that only those psalms or hymns shall be sung which are approved by Article 69 of the Church Order; or such anthems as contain only the exact words of portions of Scripture; or such anthems or hymns which have previous consistorial approval as to their Scriptural soundness." Synod also made the editorship of *The Banner* a full-time position and elected the incumbent part-time editor, Rev. H. J. Kuiper, to fill it.

With the arrival of September 1944, our stay in New York was about to end; but before we left the city, we were visited by Mother De Graaf and her young grandchild, Charles Ryskamp. Our guests stayed with us for two whole weeks and Hilda, besides caring for them at home, regularly accompanied them in their reconnoitering of the city.

*   *   *   *   *

I received orders on September 8, 1944, directing me to proceed to Princeton, New Jersey, and to report on the 16th to the commanding officer of the School of Military Government at Princeton University.

In the intervening week I wrapped up my work at the New York research center; and on an exploratory trip to Princeton, I was able, in spite of the housing shortage, to engage rooms minimally suited for residence. Early on the 15th Hilda and I entrained for Princeton and on arrival settled in the apartment I had rented. It was on the upper floor of a two-story house located at 12 Van Deventer Street. The landlords, Mr. and Mrs. Smith, occupied the apartment below, from which vantage point they could conveniently monitor our comings and goings. Our apartment was shabby and ill furnished, and Hilda was initially taken aback by its appearance. But purchasing curtains, lamps, and other accessories, and applying womanly ingenuity and resourcefulness, she was able to convert the erstwhile wasteland into a pleasant abode fitted for comfort and convenience.

I reported for duty on September 16 and was promptly made a member of the teaching staff. The School of Military Government at Princeton was unlike that at Columbia in that the courses there were taught not by professors at the university but by graduates of the Columbia school. Moreover, the courses at Princeton lacked the length and depth of those offered in New York. Army and navy officers up to the rank of colonel and captain were sent to the Princeton school for a period of six weeks to undergo instruction in the basics of administration and to gain some knowledge of the peoples and territories likely to be governed by the Allied forces. I was required to lecture on Japan, and this I continued to do as long as I remained with the school. Three different classes of "students" passed through the school during my time, and to each of them I discoursed on things Japanese, covering as well as I could a range of topics stretching from agriculture to Zen Buddhism. In order to do my work, I initially had to read extensively in the library; but my burden eased as time went on, and I eventually acquired sufficient leisure to enjoy the sights and sounds of the village with Hilda and to associate with friends new and old.

John Wevers and Henry Bajema, recent graduates of Calvin, were studying theology at Princeton Seminary at the time; our doors were always open to these former students of mine and we spent many a social hour with them. John and Helen Hamersma were fellow New Jerseyites, and we continued to visit each other as often as we could. Ken Bunce, Gordon Prange, and Guy Swope had also been transferred to Princeton, and we carried on with them as before. We formed new

friendships with other members of the staff, especially with Jim Roberton, George Warp, Dave Carpenter, and Stan Reese. In time Hilda
came to meet the wives of most of these men, and with them she
became a member of the Women's City Club, whose meetings she
attended once or twice.

Hilda had enjoyed relatively good health during most of the time
we had spent in the service, but in Princeton she had a severe attack
of kidney stones. She was relieved of the intense pain by shots of
morphine administered by a local doctor whom we had previously
engaged to monitor her new pregnancy. Free of the stones after days
of suffering, Hilda and the precious chid she was carrying remained
under the physician's care until we left Princeton in February 1945.
Her frequent visits to the doctor also brought her into steady contact
with Grace Wevers, who happened at the time to be serving as a nurse
in the doctor's office.

I don't remember how we celebrated Christmas 1944 or how we
ushered in the New Year, but I do remember that we spent Thanksgiving Day in Paterson with the Hamersmas, for we were driven back
to Princeton late that evening by Henry Bajema. The remembrance
of his heavy-footed driving down dark and narrow roads still scares
an apprehensive Hilda. That same November, I was elevated with
several others to the rank of lieutenant senior grade. The acquisition
of two full stripes and double bars entailed a raise in pay but hardly
any advance in dignity and status, for it was in unison that my friends
and I moved up the ladder of preferment; unlike some of them, I was
never thereafter allowed to increase my rank.

Near the end of our stay in Princeton, I was asked, along with other
Calvin Knights in armor, to submit a short piece for publication in
the Calvin College *Chimes*. I was reluctant to do so, since I resided
far from the scenes of battle and was totally unexposed to the war's
many hazards; I felt that I had nothing of significance to say to students
existing in circumstances similar to my own. I did, however, eventually
accede to the request, and this is part of what I said:

It is important that you remember it is from Princeton that I write.
Others will be writing from the Ardennes, or from Luzon, or from
the bitterly contested slopes of Italian mountains. Some may write
who fly in planes and sail in ships against the enemy. They will have
been in pain and peril, been lonely, perplexed, afraid. They will have

suffered, and what they say will require your first attention — and mine as well. They will tell us, I'm sure, that war is madness, and they will rightly bid us join them in every sound effort to banish it forever. They will do more. They will bid us develop, while pursuing the relatively undisturbed routine of our normal lives, the strong qualities of mind and heart that the best of them have acquired through the efficacious discipline of suffering. They will bid us do that lest they return to find us insensitive and irresolute, unchastened because untried. We may not refuse the challenge implicit in their sacrifice.

We had been in Princeton for about five months when on February 22, 1945, I was ordered to proceed to Monterey, California, there to prepare for duty outside the continental limits of the United States. I was detached on February 28 and was allowed to delay until March 24 my reporting to the commander of the Civil Affairs Staging Area (CASA) in The Presidio. Having packed our bags, and having had our possessions boxed and shipped by an accommodating navy, Hilda and I entrained for Grand Rapids on February 28, and on our arrival there we settled in with Mother De Graaf for the three weeks I was permitted to be on leave.

The 1944-1945 academic year at Calvin College was drawing towards its close, being run that year on a budget of $164,000. The shifting student enrollment stood at 420, but women outnumbered men, 295 to 125. Eighty of the resident women were now housed on campus, and the men were evicted from the dormitory, which had long been their exclusive domain. Mrs. Anna Dolfin served as dorm matron, and Mrs. Grace Hekman Bruinsma had come aboard as acting dean of women. Professors Johannes Broene and James Nieuwdorp were in their last years of teaching, and their going would impoverish the college, for they were estimable men with deep roots in the venerable past. Through the efforts of Mr. Nick Hendrikse, a sufficient amount of money had been collected to build a science building, but the actual construction would have to await the lifting of government restrictions. Twenty-six undergraduate students were enrolled in the seminary, eight of whom had completed the accelerated course in March 1945 and were now poised to enter the active ministry. Prof. Volbeda was completing his first year as president of the seminary, and Dr. Rutgers his first year as professor of systematic theology.

Meanwhile, things were happening in the outside world. In 1944, penicillin reached the civilian market, and Congress passed the GI bill. In November, Franklin Roosevelt, with Harry Truman as his running mate, defeated Thomas E. Dewey for the presidency and was inaugurated for a fourth term early in the new year. The war continued unabated throughout the winter. On December 16, 1944, Hitler hurled a powerful force against the thinly held American lines in the Ardennes Forest. The Battle of the Bulge ensued and it did not end until, on December 26, the German attack was halted at Bastogne. In February 1945, Roosevelt, Churchill, and Stalin met at Yalta and signed the ill-conceived Yalta Agreement. That month also saw the massive bombing of Dresden and the conquest of Iwo Jima. American troops reached the Rhine in March and, under General Patton, would soon penetrate deep into enemy territory. Tokyo, meanwhile, was reeling from the effects of the fire bombs being rained upon it by the U.S. eastern air force.

Hilda was by now quite visibly pregnant and was not feeling perfectly well; but it was not within my power to stay with her. I was under orders to proceed without her, which is what I did with great reluctance when my leave expired. Filled with concern for her, and uncertain about my own future, I left her in the care of God and the guardianship of her mother and sister, and flew to San Francisco on March 20, 1945. I reported for duty at The Presidio in Monterey on the 24th, was assigned a billet in one of the barracks there, and began a tour of duty that would last six months and carry me beyond the expiration of the war.

*   *   *   *   *

The Presidio of Monterey was an old army post. Covering four hundred acres, it had formerly been a garrison for cavalry and field artillery forces but had now been converted into a staging area for prospective military administrators. Situated on high ground, it overlooked Monterey Bay and afforded a glimpse of both Monterey and Pacific Grove. It was overshadowed by nearby Fort Ord, a much larger army base that was largely devoted to the training of recruits. Just inside its main gate stood a monument erected in honor of Fra Junipero Serra, the founder of the California Mission. The monument marks the spot at which he is presumed to have landed in the year 1770.

In 1945 the town of Monterey had a population of about eleven thousand. Located on the shores of the bay, it lay 125 miles south of San Francisco and within seventeen miles of the famous and picturesque village of Carmel, which one could easily reach by way of the rugged coast road that traversed the Del Monte Forest. To the east of Monterey lay the fertile San Joaquin Valley, in the midst of which was Salinas, the scene of one of our encampments. Said at the time to be the largest fishing port in the United States, Monterey was famous for its sardine industry and its celebrated "cannery row." The pride of the town was the old Custom House, erected by Spain and enlarged by Mexico, and now maintained by California's park commission as a historical museum.

The naval officers among whom I was numbered were now under army command, and we were inducted into a mode of life hitherto foreign to us. The apparent object of our training was to fit us physically for the occupancy of devastated lands deprived of requisite resources and facilities; to equip us for defense against a possibly hostile populace; and to provide us with the practical skills needed to perform relief and administrative tasks. To this end we were subjected to a regimen close to that imposed on raw recruits. We were supplied with army fatigues and combat boots, rooted out of bed at an early hour, made to stand in formation for roll call, and organized for a variety of schoolings and missions. We were taught how to fire, dismantle, and clean rifles and revolvers; how to crawl under low-strung barbed wire; how to set up tents large and small; how to build fires and cook meals in open spaces; and how to march long distances while carrying a backpack that grew heavier by the mile. We took target practice, constructed refugee kitchens, built camps on wet ground, and simulated managing a town deprived of water, electricity, and the ordinary means of communication. We bivouacked in desert places, slept in pup tents, and marched — the marches culminating in a twenty-mile hike undertaken while laden with full gear. Toward the end of our stay, a handful of us spent a week on a barge that plied the waters of San Francisco Bay off Tiburon. We learned how to handle the craft and also how to ascend from it to the deck of an anchored ship by means of a swaying rope ladder that threatened to throw us into the sea.

But it was not all work. There were times when we played softball — the officers pitted against the enlisted men — and there were the usual pauses in the day's activities. Moreover, except when we were absent on maneuvers, we were free to employ most evenings as we wished. There were weekend passes, too, but I don't recall ever making use of one. I used whatever freedom I had to visit Monterey a few times, and it was there that I had my first taste of abalone. I also drove to Carmel in a jeep that was at my disposal and was captivated by the charm of that quaint village. On a few occasions I went to the officers' club at Fort Ord, where Mr. Behrman tended bar; and I was once a dinner guest of Mr. and Mrs. Behrman, who often played hosts to the Christian Reformed servicemen stationed in Fort Ord. It was on that occasion that I met, among others, Rev. Harry Dykstra, who moved along the California coast as an itinerant chaplain. On the whole, however, I remained a home body. I normally spent Sunday at worship in the base chapel, and I spent my evenings writing letters, reading the books I borrowed from the library, or playing chess with Jim Roberton, who bunked beside me in the sparsely furnished barracks we called home.

Less than three weeks after I had arrived at The Presidio, the nation was cast into mourning by the death of President Roosevelt on April 12, 1945. The elevation to the Presidency of Vice President Harry Truman did little to allay the sorrow of the populace — and did nothing initially to bolster its hopes for the future. Truman was held in low esteem by most people and generally considered unfit to guide the nation in these troublesome times. As it turned out, the citizens need not have feared; for Truman proved to be a wise and prudent leader whose skill in management and whose folksy ways soon endeared him to the people.

The European war was now drawing to a close. During the month in which Roosevelt died, American troops reached the Elbe and the Russians entered the outskirts of Berlin. On April 28, Italian partisans effected the gruesome death of Mussolini, and on April 30, Adolf Hitler and a few of his close associates committed suicide in a Berlin bunker. After a short siege, Berlin fell to the Russians on May 2; the Netherlands was freed on May 5; and on May 7, General Jodl surrendered unconditionally at Rheims. May 8, 1945, was proclaimed Victory in Europe day, and it was marked by joyous celebrations throughout the western world. It was soon after this, however, that the world reacted with consternation and revulsion to the discovery of the German death camps at Buchenwald, Dachau, Belsen, Auschwitz, Linz, and Luben.

In June, July, and August 1945 the eyes of the Western world were turned toward the east. The forces of Japan were now in retreat on every front: Okinawa had already fallen into American hands in June, and Japanese cities continued to be heavily bombarded by the Pacific air fleet. Yet no one expected the Asian war to end very soon. The wisdom at the time held that, though the Japanese could be ousted from the territories they had seized, they could be subdued at home only at the cost of untold casualties. It was believed that, immured in their island fortress, the natives, inspired by their Shinto faith and their devotion to the emperor-god, would fight to the death — even with sticks, stones, and bamboo poles — rather than surrender. In such a scenario the Japanese casualties, plus those that would be incurred by the Allies in an amphibious assault, would be astronomical.

It was with this in mind that the Allied leaders met in Potsdam on July 17, 1945, and considered the adoption of a new and awesome tactic. In the aftermath of that meeting, Truman spoke out on July 26, issuing an ultimatum to the Japanese emperor: Surrender, he said, or else. Behind the ultimatum lay the unspoken threat of an attack the likes of which had never before been launched against an enemy. After years of scientific inquiry and the application of technological ingenuity, America had produced a batch of atomic bombs on its own soil, and one of these had been detonated successfully in the New Mexican desert. Receiving no response to his ultimatum, and sensing the presence of a fixed intransigence in the Japanese, Truman decided to reach into his secret arsenal and bring the Japanese to bay by deploying the world's newest weapon. On August 6, 1945, a B-29 bomber named *Enola Gay,* commanded by Colonel P. W. Tibbets, flew over Hiroshima and dropped the first atomic bomb ever employed in warfare; three days later, a plane piloted by Major Charles W. Sweeny dropped a similar bomb on Nagasaki. The unspeakable devastation and loss of life caused by these assaults moved Japan to sue for peace, and on August 14, 1945, Emperor Hirohito called off the war. The clash of arms had now ceased, and the whole world was provisionally at peace.

The events of those last several months, significant as they were, did not affect me as much as the one that was soon to transpire in Grand Rapids. I had been in almost daily touch with Hilda, and when the time of her delivery drew near, I secured a ten-day pass and flew home. I left the base on August 15, but because the military transport

I used was erratic, I did not arrive until the morning of the 18th. Although Hilda was due to be delivered about that time, no signs of labor were evident; and since Hilda, though encumbered, was in tolerably good health, we attended the wedding of her brother Andy to Barbara House on August 23 and happily joined in the festivities. My leave, however, expired on the 25th, and on the morning of that day there was still no movement. Hilda called her doctor and when she informed him of the situation, he ordered her into Butterworth Hospital and promised to induce labor. The procedure proved successful, and at 5:35 a.m. on Sunday, August 26, 1945, Hilda delivered into the world our darling daughter Ellen Margriet. She was a beautiful child, and about six o'clock I got to hold her in my arms while Dr. Leon Bosch, Intern Hubert Verwys, and several nurses stood by with tears in their smiles. I held Ellen for all of ten minutes, embraced my dear wife while smothering her with kisses, dashed down to the waiting taxi, and caught a 7 o'clock plane bound for California. It would be ten months before I would see my loved ones again, but I was happy as a lark and deeply grateful, for Hilda was doing well and God had blessed us with a well-born child.

On my return to The Presidio, things proceeded as before, but rumors were rife that some of us would soon be shipped out on assignment. We were still awaiting orders when, on September 2, 1945, the official Japanese surrender ceremonies were conducted by General MacArthur on the battleship *Missouri* in Tokyo Bay. It was shortly after this that MacArthur was designated Supreme Commander Allied Powers (SCAP) and elevated to the virtual premiership of the nation of Japan. I would later be attached to his command, but I had no inkling of that at the time.

With the coming of September 1945, the doors of Calvin College were being thrown open to admit a class of new students, some of them veterans; and to teach them a number of professors were being added to the staff. Henry Zylstra had returned in time to take up his duties at the school, and he was joined in the English department by John Timmerman, the recent recipient of a two-year appointment. John Bult had come aboard as instructor in physical education, and Helen Van Laar was brought in to teach art to prospective school teachers. My own classes continued to be taught by a set of my colleagues, but John Daling assisted them by teaching courses in logic and in the history of philosophy. Of course, I would not be available for teaching that year, but this not deter President Schultze from seeking my early release. On September 14 he wrote a letter to my superiors in which he said:

> Calvin College is seriously handicapped in its work without the services of Lt. Henry Stob in the department of philosophy. . . . The college is struggling along with inadequate assistant help, which affects the quality of work in that department quite seriously. . . . The release of the above named person for the purpose of resuming his position at Calvin College will enable the college to carry on its work acceptably and will be greatly appreciated by the authorities of the college.

This letter was dispatched without my knowledge, and, as was to be expected, no heed was given to it by either the army or the navy.

On September 28, 1945, I was ordered to proceed to the Fort Lawton staging area in Seattle, Washington, there to await passage to a duty station outside the continental limits. I was not alone. I had previously been incorporated into the Fortieth Military Government Headquarters Company, and this group was now to be shipped out as a unit: it consisted of ten army and navy officers and a company of enlisted men, and was headed by Lt. Col. J. E. Wilson. Only Lt. Vaughn Pierce and I were from the navy. When we arrived in Seattle, we were put up in barracks; as far as I recall, we did nothing there but wait until an appointed vessel carried us out to sea. It was on October 9 that we boarded a troop ship named the S.S. *Jean Lafitte,* and set out on a thirty-day journey to Korea. I had phoned Hilda the previous evening and was happy to learn that she and Ellen were well.

*   *   *   *   *

The *Jean Lafitte* was, I suspect, an ancient freighter that had been converted into a troop ship. In any case, it was an ugly duckling that waddled slowly across the vast expanse of the Pacific. It plied a zig-zag course, presumably to avoid floating mines, and seemed at times to be making no progress at all. There were troop contingents of various sorts aboard — some destined for Okinawa, some for Korea, and some for Japan. Those bound for Okinawa left the ship by rope ladders and were conveyed to land by LCM's on the day the ship anchored off that island. The remainder of us found the exercise diverting, for with little to do we were experiencing a general boredom. I did my share of lounging on the deck, and I engaged in small talk with the rest; but I also read what I could lay my hands on, and this did much both to preserve my equanimity and to improve my mind.

I shared a rather large cabin with Vaughn Pierce, and to it Jim Roberton often came for evening companionship. Conversation here tended frequently to turn toward religion, and on one occasion I ventured to lay out before my friends the lineaments of my Christian faith. This led to questions about the Bible, about disputed points of doctrine, about the validity of ethnic religions, about the nature and source of morality, and about other things besides. What surprised and pleased me was that word of our discussions soon spread among our fellow officers, and that several of them gradually began to join our company. What started out as unstructured palaver eventually turned into something like a seminar on religion, which, meeting nightly, sometimes drew as many as a dozen inquiring and disputatious savants into our cabin. I had never before — and I have seldom since — been as favorably situated to proclaim the gospel as I was then; and it is with tempered satisfaction and with gratitude to God that I now recall the animated discussions on religion that took place in our crowded quarters during an otherwise long and tedious journey.

I was still aboard ship when two events transpired back home that, when I heard of them, affected me deeply: one was the death of a beloved sister, and the other was the baptism of a precious child. In mid-October my sister Jen (Vander Molen) died at the age of 47 from the effects of rectal cancer, which had ravaged her frail body for some time. Of course, I could not attend the funeral nor communicate with the sorrowing husband and children; but I did correspond with the bereaved as soon as the sad news reached me, and I shared with them my own deep sorrow. This was the third time that the cold hand of death had reached into the immediate Stob family, but the pain it caused was assuaged in this case, as in the others, by the confidence we shared that the last enemy had been overcome by a blessed life that would never end.

On Sunday, October 28, 1945, Hilda, unattended by her husband, stood up in the presence of many worshipers and presented our baby

Ellen for baptism. The sacrament was administered in the East Leonard Church by Rev. John G. Van Dyk, and I am told that there were quite a few tearful eyes when the ceremony took place. This I can understand, for it was no small thing for Hilda, charged as she was with the physical care of the child, to also utter the vows committing her to the nurture of Ellen in Christian discipleship. Of course, I did not know of this event until I came ashore, but I have ever since been appreciative of Hilda's courage and resolution in this matter, and am deeply moved whenever I envision her standing in solitary devotion at that memorable baptismal font.

*   *   *   *   *

On November 8, 1945, after thirty days en route, our ship docked at the port of Inchon (Jinsen) on Korea's west coast. The members of our company disembarked dressed in field clothes and burdened with the gear we would need should no proper facilities be available ashore. As it turned out, we were bedded down in an abandoned warehouse, where I slept for a week without shedding my clothes, and where I shaved out of a helmet filled with cold water drawn from a source the nature and location of which I do not recall. We had, however, been assigned to the capital city, and we eventually proceeded to it. Our commander, Colonel Wilson, became the putative mayor of Seoul, and I was initially designated its civilian feeding officer.

The Koreans, I learned, subsisted on rice and kim-chi. Rice proved to be in fair supply, but the ingredients for making kim-chi were both scarce and expensive; in a city of a million inhabitants this became a matter of some concern. Kim-chi is a delectable food that I savored with pleasure on my first day in Seoul. Next to rice, it is the most important food Koreans eat. Made primarily of cabbage, turnips, salt, and pickled shrimps, its secondary ingredients are onion, garlic, ginger, red pepper, water cress, apple, and pear. The whole concoction is blended and allowed to mature in wooden casks, and then served with rice. It is normally prepared at home during the month of November in batches large enough to last the winter; but this year the going was rough. As someone said, "The only comfort the housewives have is that they are free from Japanese rule: this year they have to eat freedom with their rice."

The problem this posed did not long remain mine to solve. Having just begun to look into the matter of food, I was relieved of my responsibilities, transferred to an office in city hall, and put in charge of the city's educational affairs — an assignment more to my liking. I promptly called a meeting of the school authorities, inquired how we could help, and began an inspection of the schools. But while I was thus engaged, on November 27, barely twenty days after my arrival in Korea, I received orders freeing me from my duties with the 40th Military Government Group and assigning me to general headquarters in Japan.

Although I had enjoyed my association with the men of the 40th, and had formed a certain attachment to the few Koreans I had met, I relished the prospect of going to Japan. In reflecting on this turn of events, however, I sensed that I owed this change in fortune to a previously formed connection. I had earlier flown to Japan out of Kimpo Airport in order to report to the commander of the 7th fleet in Yokosuka; I surmised that word of my presence in the area had reached the ears of Ken Bunce, who was then working under General Douglas MacArthur in the government's Religious Affairs Department. As I later learned, he was indeed behind the move. The small staff he headed was knowledgeable about Shinto and Buddhist affairs, but he needed someone to head the Christian division, and his request for my transfer was met with a prompt and favorable response from his superiors.

The orders I received set no date for my reporting and, what is more, they allowed me to travel by air or sea, according to my preference. Not bound by time, I leisurely finished the work at hand, stayed to partake of a Thanksgiving Day dinner with my associates on the 29th, traveled in easy stages to Jinsen, and on December 3, 1945, boarded an American merchant ship bound for Japan.

The Grace Line steamer that was to be my home for the next six days bore the name *Cable Splice* and was captained by Edson Lee, a man of about my age who welcomed me aboard with naval courtesy and a friendly smile. I was the only passenger aboard and was promptly conducted to a spacious cabin, where I was waited on by a mess boy bearing a pot of coffee and some cake. The smallish vessel had a limited crew, and only three officers — the captain, a first mate, and a purser named John Titmas. Given the run of the ship, I dined with the officers on excellent fare, reclined in my cabin with books and magazines, strode the deck, engaged in target practice with a borrowed rifle, had my clothes laundered, relished the soft sea breezes, and enjoyed a vacation the likes of which I had never before experienced. A warm companionship — even friendship — grew up between Lee, Titmas, and myself during the course of that pleasant week, and on subsequent visits to Japan they visited me twice in my hotel. After traversing calm seas for six days, we reached Yokohama on December 8, 1945, where I reported to the base commander and was assigned a billet in Tokyo. Before disembarking, I was presented a bill by the purser. It read: "Subsistence for 6 days at $.70 per day — $4.20." I paid the bill with alacrity — and astonishment.

*　　　*　　　*　　　*　　　*

The Yokohama that I saw was a scene of desolation. Large areas of the city had been reduced to rubble by the fire and demolition bombs dropped on it by our air force, and when I reached Tokyo, a similar panorama spread before me: 60 percent of the city lay in ruins. The area around the palace had been preserved, and the several large hotels and commercial buildings near it stood erect; but the tinderbox houses in which most of the people lived had been consumed by flames, and vast sections of the city presented the appearance of a wasteland.

The people I saw on the street reflected in their posture and demeanor the aspect of the wasteland they were walking through. Saddened and humiliated, their broken spirit manifested no disposition to oppose the occupying forces or even to resent their presence. Their behavior toward the conquerors was a model of deportment. They showed an awesome regard for the magisterial MacArthur during my short stay, and they were submissive toward the rest of us and in most cases deferential. One could walk the streets at night in utter safety, and in a chance encounter one would experience nothing but Oriental courtesy.

Upon my arrival, I was billeted in the Shiba Park Hotel, where the accommodations were satisfactory though not elegant, but where the American food, served by Japanese waitresses, was tasteful and in good supply. I settled in on December 8 or 9 and on the 10th reported for work in the Radio Tokyo Building, located not far from the hotel. I was now under the indirect command of General MacArthur, the Supreme Commander Allied Powers (SCAP). Though Hirohito retained the title of emperor, it was the American generalissimo who

250

exercised sovereignty in the country. Calm, aloof, dignified, and impressive, the "Yankee Mikado," as someone dubbed him, sat in the driver's seat and both earned the respect of the common people and exacted the loyalty and cooperation of Japanese officialdom. He lived in the American embassy and had his office in the Dai Iche building, where he was surrounded by his immediate staff and deputies. The difficulty of his task was compounded by the fact that he not only governed Japan but also had jurisdiction over all the Allied forces deployed in the vast Pacific arena. It was under his supervision that four million Japanese soldiers and sailors were demobilized; and it was by his orders that more than five hundred minesweepers were engaged in cleaning the adjacent waters of well-laid mines. It was he, too, who moved the nation toward constitutional democracy, disestablished the state religion, initiated woman suffrage, and got the emperor to disavow his presumed divinity.

Under SCAP there were a number of administrative departments, one of which was the Civil Information and Education (CIE) Section, headed by Brigadier General Kenneth Dyke. Under his jurisdiction was the religious division of CIE, and this was headed by Lt. Cmdr. Kenneth Bunce. The work of this division consisted in monitoring the activities of the various Japanese religious communities and in enforcing the relevant directives emanating from SCAP, and it had for some time been performed by Bunce, Navy Lt. George Warp, and Army Cpt. Edward Kerr. But they had hitherto been absorbed in overseeing the operation of the Shinto shrines and Buddhist temples, and little or no attention had been paid to the Japanese Christian Church. I had been recruited to fill the gap, and I was made head of the Christianity unit on my arrival and put in charge of all matters relating to Christianity in Japan.

I selected an interpreter from the Presbyterian Reformed community by the name of Takeshi Matsuo, and with his assistance I carried on my work. Of my accomplishments there is not much to boast. This was partly due to the fact that my tenure was short-lived, and partly to the fact that I was increasingly drawn into the work of the other units in the division. But I did prepare a directive, endorsed by SCAP, facilitating and regulating the entrance of Christian missionaries into the country. I conferred frequently with the heads of the Kyodan, the United Church created during the war by imperial edict. I helped a small group of Reformed Christians break away from this forced union and establish the independent denomination with which the Christian

Reformed Church now has filial relations. And I was happy to support and attend a rendition of Handel's *Messiah* by a Japanese Christian chorus in the Tokyo Imperial University auditorium at Christmastime.

During the course of my work I was privileged to have an audience with Toyohiko Kagawa, the celebrated preacher, social activist, and author. Born in 1886 and converted to Christianity at the age of 15, he was nurtured in the faith by Southern Presbyterian missionaries. He had studied theology at the Meiji Gakuin and later at Princeton Seminary, lived an active life in the slums of Kobe and Tokyo, and became internationally known for his advocacy of a social gospel that envisioned the cessation of war and the reign of love and justice on earth. When I met him, he was fifty-eight years old, had been put upon by the Japanese authorities during the growth of military fascism in the thirties, had been largely silenced during the war, but was now active in Christian programs of relief and rehabilitation. I was with him in his humble dwelling no longer than two hours, but I was impressed by his frail presence and robust determination, and was glad to have made the acquaintance, however fleeting, of a distinguished Japanese Christian whose theory of the kingdom, though differing from my own, was reflected in a life of sacrificial service.

The members of the religious division operated as a team, and I was naturally drawn into engagements with representatives of the Buddhist and Shinto faiths. The typical Japanese is an adherent of several faiths: his daily life is shaped by Shinto naturalism, his death and burial falls under Buddhist auspices, and his group morality is rooted in Confucianism. Although there are no Confucian edifices, the land is filled with Buddhist temples and Shinto shrines, and our team inspected some of these several times. Shintoism was the native and — until the American occupation — the established Japanese religion. However, by an edict published before my arrival, that religion had been disestablished, and the maintenance of the priests and shrines was made dependent on private and voluntary contributions. To determine whether the enacted regulations were being observed, and to assess the reaction of the Shintoists to the military occupation, Bunce, Warp, and I were ordered by General MacArthur in mid-February to inspect the Grand Shrine of Ise, the seat of national Shintoism. We were accompanied on our five-day mission by Dr. Hideo Kishimoto, professor of religion at Tokyo University and our customary liaison with the native religious communities.

The events of those days remain vivid in my memory and now cause me some embarrassment. Various Japanese agencies had been informed of our projected trip, and on the day of our departure a special railroad car was reserved for the four of us on the Ise-bound train. We stopped en route at a station cleared for our arrival, and after traversing a red carpet, we were served tea and cakes by genuflecting attendants. At Ise we were received with supreme courtesy and deference by the chief priests and elders and, between stints of inspections and inquiries, we were feted, dined, and entertained like accredited ambassadors of a king. It was here that I first came into the company of geisha girls and imbibed my first drafts of sake. In subsequent weeks and months we made similar, though less triumphant, visits to Shinto shrines and Buddhist temples in Futami, Narita, Uji, Yamada, Nagoya, and Dyama, and were everywhere entertained like princes. At Dyama we were carried in sedan chairs to the top of a small mountain in order better to survey the landscape. I must remark that this land of trees, streams, mountains, rocks, and gardens appeared to me to be one of the most beautiful places on earth.

On January 1, 1946, I listened with interest to the radio broadcast in which Emperor Hirohito renounced his presumed divinity. On the first of February, I vacated my room in the Shiba Park Hotel and took up residence in the more prestigious Tokyo Kaikan in the center of the city. From my third floor window I looked out on the moat that sheltered the imperial palace lying beyond it. We ate here in a well-appointed dining room and were served by Japanese waitresses, who delivered to our cloth-bedecked tables the best food a generous military establishment could provide. Our lodgings were rent free, and for the three sumptuous meals we daily consumed we were charged the sum of seventy-five cents. The cartons of cigarettes we could buy at the PX were inexpensive, and we were allotted free rations of Japanese beer and American whiskeys; as a result, my expenses were reduced to a minimum. I was able in consequence to send Hilda the bulk of my salary, and this later stood both of us in good stead.

Except when we were off on out-of-town trips, I worked at my desk in the Radio Tokyo Building from eight to five each day and had the evenings to myself. Besides walking the streets on sight-seeing tours, engaging my associates in conversation and disputation, and reading the books and anthologies supplied by the Armed Forces Institute, I did little to celebrate my freedom and generally went to bed early. On one occasion, however, I was taken on a night tour of the Nagara River, where I witnessed a display of cormorant fishing. In a small boat propelled by an oarsman, a fisherman controlled a group of fishing cormorants with strings. Unable to swallow their prey because of the strings constricting their throats, the birds delivered their catch into the hands of their master. The performance of man and bird was impressive.

I had arrived in Japan on December 8, 1945, and was already eligible for discharge on January 1, 1946. But since I had just assumed new duties, I was indisposed to seek release and was in any case urged by my superiors to stay the course. I promised to stay on until the first of April, and even offered to remain until the first of July if I were to be promoted to lieutenant commander. A requisition for my promotion was sent in by Ken Bunce and endorsed by General Dyke; but the provision under which it could be granted was rescinded before the application reached the navy's bureau of personnel, and I continued to bear on my sleeve the double stripes I had obtained at Princeton.

As it turned out, I delayed my request for release to inactive duty until May 16, 1946; I was approved for discharge on the 21st and authorized to clear general headquarters on the 26th. I was formally detached on May 27, 1946, and on that day I sailed from Yokosuka on the *U.S.S. La Salle*.

*   *   *   *   *

I don't remember how I spent the fourteen days it took us to cross the ocean, but I know that I contemplated with joy the prospect of being with Hilda again, and of holding in my arms the baby girl I had left in the hospital a long ten months earlier. Two other things engaged my mind during the uneventful crossing. Hilda had sent a message that, in anticipation of my imminent return, she had bought a house on Sherman Street for twelve thousand dollars. We had indeed agreed that it would be pleasant to own a place of our own, and I was comforted to know that she had made the purchase in consultation with Henry Ryskamp and Mr. Denkema. But recalling that in 1942 we had decided that we could not afford to buy a well-constructed house on sale for six thousand dollars, I wondered faithlessly whether we could now afford a residence so costly and palatial.

254

Putting that aside, I reviewed the preceding three years and wondered why I had been led to take the several steps I took — while accomplishing so little. While men in battle bled and died, I was comfortably ensconced in New York, Princeton, and Monterey; and when the war was over, I was assigned to tasks in foreign lands that I could have performed without military training and presumably without any additional training whatsoever. Disquieted by thoughts like these, I nevertheless concluded that it is futile — and perhaps impious — to take issue with an overriding Providence. I was content to acknowledge that I had accumulated some experience and to believe that I had perhaps grown in maturity and wisdom in ways I had not yet come to understand. But of that I had then no fixed assurance.

Our transport docked at San Francisco on June 9, 1946. I secured from the ship's supply officer a receipt for the military gear left in his custody, and on disembarking reported to the officer in charge of the naval district's intake station. I was put up that night in the BOQ, and I entrained the next day for the separation center at Great Lakes, Illinois. Reporting there on the 12th, I was found physically qualified for release on the 13th, and on the evening of that same day — June 13, 1946 — I entered with exceeding joy the house at 762 East Leonard in Grand Rapids and embraced my dear wife and child.

Hilda had not had an easy time of it during my absence, but she was happily in good health and spirits, as was Ellen. The child I had last seen as a newborn baby was now ten months old, and, having been lovingly coached by her mother, could say with spirited distinctness both "daddy" and "patty cake."

With the years of military service behind me, I faced the time of adjustment and reorientation ahead of me with some trepidation, but also with a certain eagerness to get on with the job from which I had been wrenched by the exigencies of war.

*   *   *   *   *

The Calvin College academic year 1945-1946 had come to a close by the time I returned. In the course of that year — the third of my absence — the student enrollment had risen to 626, the increase due to the second semester enrollment of 165 discharged veterans, by whose accession the reign of the women on campus came to an end. To meet the teaching requirements, the retired Professors Johannes

Ellen

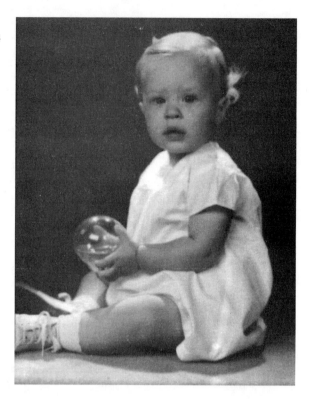

Broene and James Nieuwdorp had stayed aboard and were joined in the second semester by Harold Dekker and newcomers Gordon Buter and Henry Bruinsma. The Board of Trustees operated that year on a budget of $175,000. To meet the demands on the library, it appointed Miss Esther Vande Riet as a full-time assistant to Josephine Baker; it also made plans to enlarge the library. The board's appointment of Rev. J. J. Hiemenga as educational secretary was vetoed by the 1946 Synod, to the chagrin of many. The cost of living had apparently risen during the year, and the board increased staff salaries by ten percent to compensate. It also acquired two houses on Franklin Street and converted them into residences for women students.

The Synod of the Christian Reformed Church met in annual session in June 1946, and appointed Rev. Ralph Danhof to succeed the recently deceased John De Haan as stated clerk. It entertained a gravamen submitted by Prof. Kromminga and appointed a committee to investigate his millennial views. It also appointed a committee to assist Netherlanders planning to emigrate to Canada, and instructed the seminary faculty to consider the possibility of establishing a chair of missions.

In the world at large, the war crime trials at Nuremberg continued apace; and in Tokyo the trial of wartime Japanese leaders, charged with conspiracy to wage war, was just getting underway. Former Prime Minister Hideki Tojo headed the list of the people indicted, but Generals Itagaki, Doihara, Kinsura, and Muto were also on trial for failure to prevent the brutalization of prisoners and civilians. The Philippines were granted independence in July 1946, and at about that time the Bulgarian government fell into the hands of native communists. The United Nations Assembly, established earlier in San Francisco, held its first session in London in January, and in the spring the United States government observed the cessation of hostilities by lifting wage controls.

The house Hilda had bought was at 1334 East Sherman Street located in a fine residential neighborhood between Benjamin and Giddings; it was in the near vicinity of the Calvin campus. We moved into the three-bedroom stuccoed house on July 4, 1946. Hilda had made a down payment with the money she had saved from the military checks, and the remainder of the purchase price was covered by a mortgage supplied by the Old Kent Bank. After we had settled in, I addressed myself to my studies, but took time out to attend a session or two of the Reformed Ecumenical Synod, which came into being in August. This first meeting of delegates from South Africa, The Netherlands, and the United States was held on the Calvin campus and was chaired by Prof. Berkhof. The synod framed a constitution, established an agenda for the future, and pledged itself to a fruitful continuance.

After three long years in military service, I now looked forward to the opening of school. But before it opened, our little family joined in celebrating Ellen's first birthday. Hilda baked a cake and put a candle on it, and Ellen made a wish that she kept secret.

12

THE RETURN TO COLLEGE
(1946-1949)

The college to which I returned in September 1946 was quite unlike the one I had left in June 1943. The student body had grown in number from 385 to 1245, and the size of the faculty had increased from twenty-three to forty-five. Professors Rooks and Nieuwdorp were no longer teaching, but Professors Johannes Broene, A. E. Broene, and Jacob Vanden Bosch, although past or approaching the age of retirement, had been retained and continued to teach full time. At their side stood the remaining core of veteran teachers; but these were outnumbered by the newcomers who had been recruited to meet the demands of the burgeoning enrollment. A few of my friends from student days had come to join ranks with Henry Zylstra and myself — among them John Timmerman, Bill Spoelhof, and John Daling. In addition, the roster of new staff members exhibited such familiar faces as those of John Bratt, Harold Dekker, Bernard Fridsma, Martin Karsten, Gertrude Slingerland, Earl Strikwerda, John Tuls, Catherine Van Opynen, and Henry Van Til. These many accessions noticeably changed the shape and temper of the school. That the college to which I had come as a novice teacher in 1939 had entered a new era came forcibly to mind when I considered that I would now also be associated in teaching with men and women who had sat as students in my philosophy classes only a few years earlier. Among these were Donald Bouma, John Bult, Gordon Buter, Kay Hager, John

The Calvin College Faculty (1946-47)
Front row: Swets, A. Broene, Van Haitsma, J. Broene, Nieuwdorp,
Dekker, Pres. Schultze, Ryskamp, Rooks, Vanden Bosch, Hoekstra,
Meeter, Van Andel, Radius.
2nd row: H. Stob, Spoelhof, Strikwerda, Fridsma, Monsma,
Van Zyl, Baker, Slingerland, Vande Kieft, Van Opynen,
Flokstra, Bratt, Bouma, Van Til.
3rd row: Daling, Zylstra, Bult, De Vries, Smedes, Decker, R. Stob,
Drost, Wassink, Buter, Timmerman, Huizenga, Tuls, Karsten

Huizenga, and Lewis Smedes — all of whom were giving instruction
in one or another department of the college.

The male students outnumbered the women, 778 to 467. Many of
the men were veterans who, subsidized by the GI Bill, were either
making their first acquaintance with college life or returning to finish a
course of study that had been interrupted by the war. Although the
more gifted of these men were attracted to the liberal arts, a considerable number chose to enroll in professional courses, a tendency that was
said to prevail in schools throughout the land. In general, the level of
student talent, initiative, and industry rose appreciably with the accession of those who had grown to maturity in the service of their country;
the staff could not but be impressed with the many who addressed their
studies with disciplined attention, critical acumen, and sober judgment.

How to house the students adequately was among the many problems facing the administration. The women occupied the campus dormitory as well as the recently purchased residences on Franklin Street, but no college facilities were available for the men. Many of them eventually found lodgings in private homes, in the search for which they were ably assisted by the college office. To house the others, the administration leased eight rooms in the decaying Alexander Public School, furnished the rooms with army bunks and other service equipment, and sent the residents off to eat in the dormitory dining room, which, together with its kitchen, had been enlarged to accommodate the overflow. The seventy inhabitants of "Alexander Hall" were supervised by Prof. and Mrs. A. E. Broene, who graciously took up residence with the hapless male students lodged in that drab locale.

If housing was a problem, so was the issue of classroom space. In the days before the war, when rooms were plentiful, each department in the college tended to appropriate its own space. Since most departments were staffed by only one person, almost every professor met his students in a room that had become virtually his own by dint of regular and exclusive use. So it was when I first came aboard in 1939: the second floor room in which I habitually lectured was recognized as the place where students of philosophy gathered, and it was seldom, or never, used by anyone but myself. That had now changed. Not only were the various departmental classes scattered throughout the building, and not only were the available classrooms generally filled to capacity; there were simply not enough rooms to go around. Consequently, classes were held not only in the morning, as heretofore, but also in the afternoon and evening, and not only in the administration building but also in the library and in the seminary building.

The chapel also had become too small. Because it could not seat the entire student body, only half the number of those enrolled were required to attend chapel services on any given day. It was in this adventitious way that the age-old rule regarding chapel attendance began to be relaxed.

There was no way to increase the central office space, but the furniture was rearranged, and two new clerk-secretaries were employed to address the increased work. President Schultze was for the first time given a secretary of his own to help ease his burdens; and a newly appointed field representative, Mr. Samuel Van Til, was placed at his side and charged with securing funds for building expansion.

Because arrangements could not be made in time, the academic year 1946-1947 began a week later than usual. On September 12, 1946, President Schultze delivered the convocation address in the First Protestant Reformed Church, then located on the corner of Franklin Street and Fuller Avenue. I began my fifth year of teaching and entered on the eighth year of my tenure. Although most departments in the college now enjoyed the luxury of having multiple personnel, I was still the sole occupant of the chair of philosophy and responsible for all the offerings in my department. I did, however, receive some assistance: John Daling had been appointed to assist Johannes Broene in psychology, and he was also able to take over my classes in logic that year. But that left me with six different areas to cover, and with the usual fifteen hours of classwork to perform. In the fall semester I taught introduction to philosophy in three sections to 118 students; medieval philosophy to a class of 27 students; and ethics to a group of 8 seniors. With the opening of school, I also resumed sponsorship of the lapsed Plato Club, which that year was chaired by John Steensma and included in its membership John Medendorp, Ed Walhout, Clarence Flietstra, John De Kruyter, Z. Koster, and F. Blum. I also took a seat on the faculty's Educational Policy Committee, where I served with Radius, Monsma, Van Zyl, De Vries, and Zylstra, as well as with Dean Ryskamp and Registrar Dekker, who acted as advisors.

Hilda and I were still members of the Dennis Avenue Church in the fall of 1946; but we lived a considerable distance from the church and lacked the transportation needed to get to it. It was thus with some interest that we heard of a movement to establish a new Christian Reformed congregation on the southeast end of town. A group of people drawn largely from the Fuller Avenue, Neland Avenue, and Sherman Street congregations had secured classical approval for the founding of the proposed new church, and on October 18, 1946, a meeting to establish it was held in the college chapel. Hilda and I attended the organizational meeting and with Ellen became charter members of the new congregation, which upon its inception became known as the Calvin Christian Reformed Church. It held Sunday services in the college chapel and was served by guest preachers until Rev. Clarence Boomsma became its first pastor in January 1948. Its choice of name, its campus location, and its tendency to attract student worshipers, created resentment in some circles; so, to correct any misunderstanding, the trustees of the college found it necessary to declare in a public statement that the church had no official connection with the college.

The Board of Trustees met in February 1947 under the chairmanship of Rev. Gerrit Hoeksema. The Board revealed that it was operating the school that year on a budget of $248,000 and was charging non-Christian Reformed students $200 a year for tuition. The board also made several new appointments to the staff; but what was especially gratifying to me was its decisions to elevate me to the rank of full professor with life tenure. With this increase in status and security came a raise in salary: I was now to earn $3000 a year, this in addition to the medical and retirement benefits that had been put in place earlier.

The spring semester was now in progress, and during it I taught ancient philosophy in three sections to 127 students; modern philosophy to a class of 21 students; and metaphysics to a group of 7 in a senior seminar. During that semester President Schultze was often ill and on a few occasions hospitalized. Other things were happening as well. A sorrowing denomination mourned the death of Prof. Dietrich Kromminga; Harold Dekker announced that he was laying down his assistantship in speech to become pastor of a church in Englewood, New Jersey; Jim Bosscher and Jay Van Andel, owners of a local flight training school, petitioned the faculty to introduce a course in aeronautics but received a negative response; and the cornerstone of the old theological school, now dismantled to make room for an addition to the Christian high school, was offered to Calvin and accepted. The North Street Church of Zeeland at long last abandoned its remaining Dutch worship service just as Calvin's Board of Trustees decided that a reading knowledge of Dutch would be required for entrance into the seminary.

Before the school year ended, I engaged in a series of discussions and negotiations on an issue that impinged significantly on my department in the college. With the enrollment growing as it was, it seemed prudent to be on the lookout for an additional teacher in philosophy. It did not initially occur to me to look in the direction of Indiana University, but as the year progressed, there were several indications that Prof. Jellema would welcome an invitation to return to the college he had left in 1935. Several of his friends in and out of the faculty now began to plead his case; happy to join the chorus, I encouraged the administration to open a dialogue with the prospective candidate. Those of us in the know were aware, however, that Jellema did not enjoy the favor of every element in the community. There were those who retained a memory of his alleged humanistic tendencies and his supposed bent toward Anglo-Hegelianism. Although I shared with those people a concern for a philosophy consonant with biblical verities, and although I was aware of Jellema's earlier inclination toward a brand of Christian Idealism, I did not doubt that at bottom his views were shaped by Reformed principles and that his strong desire was to bring all thought in subjection to Christ. Therefore, I asked President Schultze to invite Jellema for an interview. Early in January 1947, Jellema appeared on campus and was engaged by the president and me in a long and satisfying conversation. The executive committee of the board met on January 24, and at one of its sessions Schultze announced that Jellema's name had been considered for a reappointment in philosophy, and informed the committee: "Dr. H. Stob and I have interviewed Jellema and found nothing objectionable."

A disposition on the part of the executive committee to submit Jellema's name to the board for consideration was strengthened on April 10, 1947, when board president Gerrit Hoeksema informed the committee that he had had a two-hour conference with Dr. Jellema and felt that "we should put forth efforts to bring him back to our college." The committee thereupon expressed itself as "favorably inclined to an appointment of Dr. Jellema" and recommended that the board "interview him with a possible appointment to the department of Philosophy in mind."

Meanwhile, I was in periodic touch with Jellema but also in almost daily contact with persons on and off the campus who were not happy with the ongoing course of events and who did not leave me in ignorance of their sentiments. With the imminent board meeting in view, I dispatched a long letter to Jellema on May 2, 1947. This, in part, is what I wrote:

Dear Harry:

You may recall our having inquired of each other the last time we met what kind of statement or pronouncement from yourself would be required to satisfy those who entertain doubts as to the wisdom of inviting you back to Calvin. . . . Word of your being considered for appointment is now going the rounds in Grand Rapids, and questions are being raised. I don't hear all of them, but many are

264

put directly to me. The most significant of these concern your philosophical position. I invariably answer these in the light of the eminently satisfactory interview President Schultze and I had with you some time ago, but to some specific questions I can give only a general answer and to others none at all. You would therefore help me (and all your friends who are ready to sponsor your appointment on a level above that of mere emotional partisanship) if you would set down on paper your views on the issues in dispute before you left Calvin for Indiana. . . . You can do this in a letter to me, or, if you prefer, to President Schultze. I can assure you that much will be gained by your so doing. . . . If the right words are spoken, they will pave a clear road to Calvin, enrich us immeasurably with your presence, reconcile all past differences, and close a thoroughly unpleasant and regrettable history.

Jellema did compose a statement of the kind I requested, and it was considered by the board when it met on May 7. It is a curious fact that the faculty as such had not been consulted in the matter of the proposed appointment up to that point. The issue was first aired at a faculty meeting on May 5, 1947; an item in the minutes of that meeting reads as follows: "The President informs the faculty that pressure brought to bear in and out of Calvin for the reappointment of Dr. H. Jellema in Philosophy has resulted in tentative plans and interviews by a faculty committee and by the chairman of the Executive Committee. He raises the question whether the faculty considers it wise to back the eventual appointment of Dr. Jellema. After a free exchange of opinion the following motion prevails: The faculty favors the appointment of Dr. Jellema for a position in philosophy — 20 yes's, 4 no's, 5 abstentions."

When the Board of Trustees met on May 7, 1947, a motion prevailed to interview Dr. Jellema and to invite Dr. Clarence Bouma and myself to sit in on the interview. Because Prof. Volbeda, the seminary president, had addressed to the board a faculty document bearing on the question of Dr. Jellema's appointment, the board decided that he and President Schultze should conduct the interview. The interview took place in my presence on May 8, and on the evening of that day, after considerable discussion, Dr. Jellema was appointed a full professor by a unanimous vote, and for an indefinite period. I believe that Jellema accepted the appointment soon after that, for on June 3 he met with the executive committee and asked, among other things, what his position would be in the philosophy department. When told by the committee that "he and Dr. H. Stob would be coordinate . . . he was well satisfied." It had been ten years since I had been appointed to replace Harry Jellema, and the eight-year period in which I had been the sole occupant of Calvin's philosophy chair had now come to an end. Jellema and I would henceforth man the department in tandem and share the teaching load in ways commensurate with our talents and predilections.

It was soon after the May board meetings had adjourned that Prof. Kromminga died. Thus the executive committee had to prepare a nomination from which a successor could be chosen. Among those nominated was my good friend, cousin, and classmate George Stob. George had served as chaplain during the war, was now pursuing graduate work at Princeton Theological Seminary, and possessed in ample measure the qualifications needed to fill the chair that was vacant. As it turned out, he was promptly elected at Synod as the seminary's new professor of church history and given a year to complete his studies at Princeton. His deserved election to this new office pleased me greatly, and I awaited his arrival on campus in the fall of 1948 with eager anticipation. Another of my friends was also honored by Synod: the denomination's radio ministry — the Back to God Hour — had for some years featured a variety of preachers, but it was now deemed expedient to have the broadcast speak with one voice, and Synod elected Peter Eldersveld as the church's official radio minister. Peter served the church with distinction until his voice was stilled by his untimely death.

The Synod of 1947 adopted a number of resolutions affecting the theological school. It endorsed a modified form of the summer field work program recently put in place by the seminary faculty; it authorized the establishment of a chair of missions, and encouraged the Board of Trustees to do whatever it could to qualify the seminary to grant a Th.D. degree; it also laid aside the gravamen submitted by Prof. Kromminga as no longer relevant, with the result that premillenialism became a matter of no existential concern. Congregational life received attention when a committee was appointed to address the issue of woman suffrage in congregational meetings; and family life was much affected when Synod decreed that an informed Christian who had remarried after an "unbiblical" divorce cannot be a member of the church unless he manifest repentance by returning to the former spouse or by ceasing to live with the present one. Life in society was eased when Synod refused to rule that membership in the AFL or the CIO is incompatible with membership in the church or with eligibility to church office.

During the course of that academic year a number of notable events took place on the world stage. In 1947, India achieved her independence; however, it came at no small cost: the split between Hindus and Muslims erupted into bloody conflict, and the uprising by the Sikhs in the Punjab resulted in the death of thousands. The Near East became the focus of attention when in 1947 the United Nations decided to subdivide British-mandated Palestine and provide a home for the Jewish diaspora. The cold war between the Soviet Union and the Western world was now in progress, and a wave of anti-communist sentiment swept through the American populace. On May 12, 1947, President Truman enunciated the Truman Doctrine, which committed the nation to the containment of Soviet aggression, and at home he launched a massive "loyalty" program, in accordance with which the Attorney General drew up a long list of supposedly "disloyal" organizations. Eager to join in the battle against the communist cells alleged to be nestled in the Washington establishment was a vociferous zealot from Wisconsin named Joseph McCarthy, a Republican who had won a seat in the United States Senate in the November 1946 election. In June 1947 the Taft-Hartley act placed controls on big labor, and in July details of the Marshall Plan to spur European postwar recovery were worked out at a conference in Paris.

Teaching six different courses in philosophy to 308 students immediately upon returning from three years of military service had exacted its toll, and I could have profited from a long summer's recess, but no respite was afforded. I was drawn into the college's summer school program, and for six weeks in June and early July I taught medieval philosophy to a class of eight students. I was called upon to preach as well, and on ten successive summer Sundays I conducted worship services in area churches. In August 1947 my review of E. E. Taylor's *Does God Exist?* appeared in the *Westminster Theological Journal*. It was a summer with little time for leisure and relaxation, and I provided

Hilda with no release from child care or from the performance of monotonous household chores.

*   *   *   *   *

The academic year 1947-1948 was ushered in with the usual convocation exercise. When the school doors opened in September 1947, there were 45 members on the faculty; eight additional staff members served as departmental assistants; and still engaged in teaching despite their advanced age and long tenure were the seasoned veterans Johannes Broene, A. E. Broene, and Jacob Vanden Bosch. New to the faculty were James De Jonge, Lester De Koster, Thedford Dirkse, Cornelius Jaarsma, and, in a sense, Harry Jellema. Among the newly appointed assistants were Henry Bengelink, Harold Geerdes, Helen Van Laar, Ann De Boer, Ruth Vande Kieft, and John Vanden Berg, the last three of whom had at one time or another been students in my classes. Assisting the president that year was Rev. Arnold Brink, who as educational secretary occupied himself with public relations.

The student enrollment in September stood at 1,394, an increase of 150 over the previous year. The Board of Trustees was operating both college and seminary on a budget of $308,000 and was charging non-Christian Reformed students $250 a year for tuition. Although the women still occupied the school's only dormitory, the men's "Alexander Hall" had been abandoned for want of applicants. The space crunch was slightly eased when 7,500 square feet of additional classroom and laboratory space became available through the acquisition of a portable building supplied by the War Assets Administration. The Osterink Construction Company had been engaged to begin building a three-story science building on campus in spring 1948 at a cost of $818,000; and to provide for future expansion, the college bought a seven-and-a-half acre tract of land from the nearby Clarke Home for $75,000. The money to defray these expenses was drawn from the $1.5 million expansion fund established through the efforts of the Messrs. Hendrikse and Van Til. During the course of that year, the college turned a portion of the Clarke acreage into a student parking lot, thus freeing the streets of the cars that had long been a source of annoyance to the neighbors.

Harry Jellema's presence in the department resulted in a reduction

268

*The Family,
July 1947*

of my teaching load from fifteen to twelve hours a week and enabled me to reduce the number of semester courses I would teach from four to three. Classes, however, remained large, and I was burdened with an inordinate number of exercises, tests, and papers to examine and appraise. In the fall semester of that academic year I taught introduction to philosophy in two sections to 67 students; medieval philosophy to 38 students; and logic to 34 students. I also published a review of Cornelius Van Til's *Common Grace* in the *Calvin Forum,* and on three occasions I preached in churches in Michigan and Illinois. I remained a member of the education policy committee until it was reconstituted on June 1, 1948, and also joined Hoekstra, Monsma, De Vries, Spoelhof, and Van Opynen on the discipline committee. Making up the Plato Club that year was a group of intelligent and congenial fellows with whom I found it a pleasure to work. Attending our monthly meetings in pursuit of philosophical learning were Ed Bierma, Calvin Bulthuis, Carl Danielson, George

Harper, Jake Hekman, Walter Lagerwey, John Malestein, Harvey Smit, Len Vander Linde, Jack Van Dyken, Bastiaan Van Elderen, Paul Van Lonkhuyzen, and Ed Walhout. With such students in attendance, there was no lack of cerebral activity.

Just after the school year began, Clarence Boomsma preached in Calvin Church on a classical assignment. He lodged with us that weekend, and, having heard the two good sermons that he delivered, I predicted not only that he would be put on nomination but also that he would be called to be our pastor. I wagered a chicken dinner on the soundness of my judgment and clairvoyance, and I put Clarence in my debt when in October 1947 the consistory issued him a call. I was very pleased when Clarence decided to leave Imlay City and come to Grand Rapids in January to take up his duties as the first minister of Calvin Church.

It was in that same month of October that one of the most distinguished members of the Christian Reformed Church passed from the scene. Rev. Henry Beets had been the first editor of *The Banner,* the church's director of missions and editor of *The Missionary Monthly,* the author of several books, and for forty years the stated clerk of the denomination. On October 29, 1947, he went to meet the Lord whom he had served with faithfulness and rare distinction.

A Sunday in October was set aside to commemorate the establishment of the Van Raalte colony in what is now Holland, Michigan. Not only did our churches celebrate the centennial, but the University of Michigan remembered the pioneer settlers by hosting an earlier convocation at which the Dutch ambassador and Senator Arthur Vanden Berg addressed the celebrative gathering. To further mark the centennial, Dr. Albert Hyma published his *Van Raalte* and Prof. Arnold Mulder his *Americans from Holland.*

Before the first semester ended and the calendar year 1947 came to a close, the faculty adopted a proposal to name department and division chairmen; the Back to God Hour began to use the school's facilities for its Sunday radio broadcasts; Prof. Swets conducted the college chorus and orchestra in the twenty-fifth annual rendition of Handel's *Messiah;* the issue of junior colleges began to be discussed within the faculty; the Calvin Church consistory sought to purchase a half acre of the land the college had acquired from the Clarke estate; the denomination returned some its missionaries to the recently reopened Chinese mainland; and Dr. John Van Bruggen was named general secretary of the National Union of Christian Schools, succeeding Mark Fakkema, who had become educational director of the schools connected with the National Association of Evangelicals. In England a young actor by the name of Alex Guinness was being hailed as a rising star; and in a royal wedding, Princess Elizabeth, the heir to the British throne, was married to Prince Philip Mountbatten.

When the second semester began in January of 1948, I went back to fifteen hours of teaching, the large enrollment requiring that I cover my three disciplines in multiple sections. I taught logic that spring in two sections to 90 students, ancient philosophy in two sections to 83 students, and metaphysics in a seminar to eleven students. Before the semester ended, I had also preached on eight different occasions in various local churches. On January 4, Clarence Boomsma was installed as the minister of Calvin Church. Sometime in March, Hilda announced, to our mutual gratification, that she was again pregnant.

What occupied a considerable amount of my time during that semester was the counseling I did with a number of gifted veterans who, imbued with the spirit of Calvinism, were concerned to have the church move out of its malaise and give vital and relevant expression to its genius and rich inheritance. The members of the "Youth and Calvinism Group" (as it was called) prepared papers on secularity, amusements, politics, science, literature, education, and preaching, and I was asked to examine and appraise them. The several papers produced by Lew Smedes, Dirk Jellema, Paul Van Lonkhuyzen, Clif Orlebeke, George Harper, Rod Jellema, and Len Vander Linde were published in the fall of 1948 by the group's secretary, Cal Bulthuis, and in the pamphlet that contained them I wrote a preface in which, among other things, I said:

> When young men still at school address themselves to so large an issue as Calvinism and The World, and point their remarks directly at their elders, they run the risk of receiving nothing but censure for their pains. A critical reader of the following essays will indeed find things to censure. The issue is not in every essay equally well-defined; the argumentation is not always faultless; and one could wish that the acerbity of certain passages was either tempered or removed. It would be a pity, however, if these and other faults should turn the reader away. This is a Report. It is a straightforward account of what Calvinism means actually and ideally, not only to the few

271

young men who here express themselves, but also the many more for whom they are the spokesmen. . . . But the book is not only a Report; it is also a Confession. The writers of these essays are committed to Calvinism. They may not completely understand it, but they apprehend that it possesses them in a way that leaves them with no alternative either within or without the Christian church. . . . The book, however, is not only a Report and a Confession. It is also a Criticism and a Plea. It calls for light. It wants Calvinists not only to define the elemental issues of life, but to disclose them as they lie in the folds of contemporary forms. It wants to see displayed what it believes to be Calvinism's relevancy to the existential situation. . . . It calls for a positive, vital, articulated Calvinism, and it challenges us to respond.

I don't recall what effect the pamphlet had on its readers, but the several authors were themselves enriched by the efforts they put forth, and all of them grew to be distinguished advocates of the cause they sponsored in their student years.

The Board of Trustees met in February 1948 and again in May, and would alter custom by meeting regularly thereafter during those two months of the year. The seminary had hitherto held joint commencement exercises with the college, but it was now authorized to hold separate exercises annually. To encourage scholarship and research, the board introduced a program of sabbatical leaves. It granted Clarence Bouma a year's leave, beginning in February 1949, to provide him an opportunity to write a book on ethics. The board also noted that in response to pressures from outside, the consistory of Calvin Church had withdrawn its bid to purchase a part of the newly acquired college lands; it adopted a plan to add laymen to its membership; it authorized the seminary faculty to grant the Th.D. degree to accredited theological candidates; and it reiterated its stand on disputed moral issues by ordering the inclusion in the college handbook of the following rule: "All cases of misdemeanor and offensive conduct in the matter of theater attendance, card playing, and dancing (which are regarded as forms of worldliness) will be disciplined to the extent of expulsion from Calvin College."

The Synod of the Christian Reformed Church met in June 1948 and from a slate of three candidates elected Harry Boer to the newly created chair of missions at the seminary. Harry was at the time a novice missionary in Nigeria, and to give him time to complete his initial assignment and afford him an opportunity for advanced study, Synod permitted him to postpone his appearance at the school until the fall of 1951. Synod endorsed the board's plan to introduce nine laymen into its membership, and among the persons appointed to fill the posts was my good friend John Hamersma, a distinguished lawyer with a large practice in New Jersey. I was delighted with the action, and Hilda and I would in subsequent years regularly play host to John and Helen when they came to Grand Rapids to attend board meetings. Synod also discouraged Mark Fakkema's school association from invading the territory of John Van Bruggen's National Union; appointed a committee to consider whether the church should continue membership in the National Association of Evangelicals; and appointed another committee to consider what attitude should be adopted toward those in the church who were advocating the establishment of junior colleges. To my regret, Synod refused to send a representative to the International Council of Christian Churches, which would convene in Amsterdam on August 12, 1948, and give birth there to a new World Council.

By the end of the school year 1947-1948, George Stob had returned to Grand Rapids from Princeton and had begun to prepare the lectures he would deliver at the seminary in the fall. Before settling down, he delivered the commencement address at the college, at which there was no academic procession because the requisite robes had not arrived in time. I myself was not set free by the closing exercises, for summer school would be again in session, and from June 17 to July 29 I was engaged in teaching. During that six-week period I taught a three-hour course in medieval philosophy to nine students and a three-hour course in logic to six students; for my efforts I was paid the sum of $390. I preached with a certain regularity and in the course of the summer conducted worship services on eleven successive Sundays. Meanwhile, Hilda was giving public evidence of her pregnancy and maintaining withal a large measure of good health. We looked forward with eager anticipation to the birth of another child before the calendar year should end.

During the first three quarters of 1948, a number of events occurred that significantly reshaped the face of the world. The state of Israel came into being on May 15, when the British mandate in Palestine expired, but its existence was threatened when five united Arab forces

The Plato Club, 1948-49
Standing: J. Morren, N. Vander Zee, G. Spykman, S. Vander Weele,
C. Orlebeke, H. Smit, R. Otten, W. Lagerwey, L. Vander Linde.
Seated: B. Van Elderen, H. Stob, C. Bulthuis, G. Harper, H. Stevens.

launched an attack on it. That it survived this attack and routed its enemies gave proof of its long-term viability. In Europe, communist forces went on the offensive: Czechoslovakia became a Soviet satellite when indigenous communists seized control of the government, and the Russians themselves menaced the West when they choked off land and water routes to internationalized Berlin. The Allies responded with the "Berlin Airlift," in which fliers — especially Americans — supplied the city with virtually all the provisions it needed. The world lost one of its most prominent figures when Mahatma Ghandi died in India at the hand of an assassin. At home, Congress authorized the "Voice of America" radio broadcast; the government took the lead in establishing the Organization of American States; and the House Committee on Un-American activities began its investigation into the affairs of Alger Hiss. The sports pages reported the death of Babe Ruth at age 53, the winning of the triple racing crown by Citation, and the winning of the decathlon by the seventeen-year-old Bob Mathias at the London Olympic games.

*   *   *   *   *

The academic year 1948-1949 was inaugurated in September 1948 with the usual convocation exercises. The teaching staff that year consisted of fifty-one full-time instructors and seven part-time assistants. New to the staff were Melvin Berghuis, Clarence Boersma, and John De Beer; pressed into service for yet another year were Prof. Vanden Bosch, the two Broenes, and even Prof. Nieuwdorp. Harry Jellema and I constituted the philosophy department, but Harry had been made divisional chairman, and this normally entailed a departmental chairmanship as well. In this instance, however, it did not: a supervisory chair made little sense in a two-man department, and it also would contravene the parity established by the board. Harry would later assume the chairmanship, and had that happened at this time, I would have gladly acquiesced in the appointment. He was, after all, my former teacher, my senior by fifteen years in age, and the possessor of a more than parochial reputation. But for the present we acted in tandem. Since neither of us was an administrator, we addressed our affairs on the run and settled them with a gesture.

The student body continued to grow, and course enrollments kept pace with the burgeoning population. The registered students now numbered 1,466, the men outnumbering the women, 973 to 493. Of the students enrolled, a disproportionate number crowded into my classrooms. In the fall semester I taught introduction to philosophy in two sections to 100 students, logic in two sections to 62 students, and medieval philosophy to a class of 51 students. I continued to serve, meanwhile, on the faculty's discipline committee. I again sponsored the Plato Club and was happy to see included in its membership such intelligent and inquiring young men as Clif Orlebeke, Steve Vander Weele, Robert Otten, George Harper, Walter Lagerwey, Bas Van Elderen, Gordon Spykman, Cal Bulthuis, Len Vander Linde, Henry Stevens, John Morren, Nelson Vander Zee, and Harvey Smit. That semester and subsequent ones were made more pleasant by the presence of George Stob, who had assumed the chair of church history in the seminary at the beginning of that academic year. George had settled with Joan in a house on Baldwin Street, and we frequently met

Son Dick

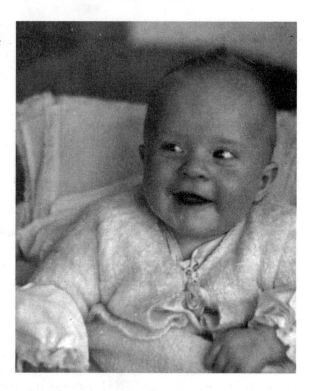

for sociability, informal chatter, and occasional theological discussions. We reinstated in this way the close fellowship we had once enjoyed, and which Henry Zylstra and I regularly exercised. Clarence Boomsma had now also been added to this pair of intimate friends. Clarence came to our house often, and our meetings were made no less prolonged and fruitful by the fact that Clarence was a bachelor and unencumbered by family.

Before the first semester ended and the year 1948 came to a close, a number of events transpired that affected our private and communal lives. The Calvin community was saddened in mid-term when Ted Dirkse, one of our colleagues, lost his wife in childbirth and also the twin infants that she bore. A sentiment of a different kind took hold when on December 2, 1948, the cornerstone of the new science building was laid in the presence of a festive crowd. That year's political campaigns attracted the attention of the citizenry: Thomas E. Dewey was running against the incumbent President Truman, and the pundits predicted a Republican victory; but Truman took to the rails during

the summer and fall and prevailed in the November election, much
to the embarrassment of the *Chicago Tribune,* which on election night
had bannered a Dewey victory. In other contests, Gerald R. Ford
succeeded Bartel Jonkman as the congressman from Michigan's fifth
district, and Lyndon B. Johnson was sent to the United States Senate
by his constituents in Texas. By the end of the year, about ten thousand
Dutch immigrants had arrived in Canada. Christian Reformed emissaries came to the assistance of these people with pastoral and financial
aid, and many of them were drawn into our ecclesiastical fellowship.
The war years were recalled when on December 23, 1948, General
Hideki Tojo, Japan's wartime prime minister, and six others, were
executed for war crimes.

In September 1948, I preached at Calvin Church and also in
Holland and in Byron Center. In October, I published in the *Calvin
Forum* a review of Herman Dooyeweerd's *Transcendental Problems of
Philosophical Thought.* And at a congregational meeting held on
November 29, I was, with others, elected to the office of elder in
Calvin Church. World events and routine personal engagements paled
into relative insignificance, however, when Hilda's pregnancy was
brought to term in early December with the birth of a bouncing baby
boy. On December 9, 1948, the Lord presented us with a dear son
whom we named Henry Richard; he was delivered in Butterworth
Hospital by Dr. Leon Bosch and weighed eight pounds and thirteen
ounces. Although labor was intensive, Hilda, at age 39, suffered no
complications, and when three-year-old Ellen and I came to bring our
precious pair home a few days later our thankfulness and joy knew no
bounds. "Dick," as we called our ruddy and cheerful little boy, was
gently treated by Ellen, and the sunshine he brought into our home
gave us ample cause to praise the covenant-keeping God who bestowed
this gift on us.

The Board of Trustees met in February 1949, and John Hamersma
came in to attend his first meeting. He and Helen spent a few days
with us, and John and I stayed up late in our nightly review of the
actions taken by the board. I learned that the plans for an enlarged
library had been approved; that the construction of a Calvin commons
was high on the board's agenda; that the board rejected a faculty
proposal to sell a parcel of college land to Calvin Church; and that it
elevated Henry Zylstra to the rank of full professor.

The second semester saw the number of faculty members increased by the addition in January of Enno Wolthuis, my college classmate. My philosophy classes were again overcrowded and, besides preparing lectures, I had to cope with masses of student papers, tests, and exercises. During the second semester I taught logic in two sections to 105 students, ancient philosophy in two sections to 86 students, and the philosophy of St. Thomas Aquinas to a class of 14 students.

I was installed as elder in Calvin Church on January 1, 1949, and was elected in February as an elder delegate to Synod by Classis Grand Rapids East. I addressed the seminary community at the March *Dies Natalis* banquet on the subject of a "Living Theology," was invited in April to become a member of the Board of Trustees of the Christian University Association of America, published in the May issue of the *Calvin Forum* a note on "John Calvin as Philosopher," and before the semester ended preached on six occasions in various churches. I had meanwhile become interested in local politics, had attended a May rally held in Fulton Park to protest against the perceived corruption that marred the administration of Grand Rapids Mayor Welsh, and assisted in the formation of a temporary organization called "Citizens Action." We persuaded Julius Amberg to assume the presidency of the organization, and I was appointed to the board and made one of its vice presidents. We circulated petitions and gathered the signatures of 27,000 citizens calling for the resignation of Welsh and the breakup of the Welsh-McKay machine. The mayor rejected the recall petition, challenged it in the courts, was finally rebuffed by the supreme court of Michigan, and in mid-July went into sullen retirement. I remained with Citizens Action for several more years, but abandoned it after the 1954 elections when I felt that it had outlived its usefulness.

Prof. William Hendriksen of the seminary was not happy with some of the things I said in my *Dies Natalis* speech. When he wrote me a letter expressing his concerns, I sent him a reply, the contents of which I here record because it expresses my thinking at the time, and because it marks the first of the several skirmishes I later had with various correspondents in the church. I said, in part:

> I wished to declare that, in orienting his theological reflections to life and practice, the student should make no concessions to the activistic, functional, pragmatic mind of the day. This one does, in my opinion, when one studies theology as a mere means to a specific practical end — with half an eye on next Sunday's sermon, or on

the imminent Board examination. One studies it best when one regards it as a system of truths that is valid independently of its functional efficacy, when one approaches it as a system of meanings that is worthy in its own right of being understood. . . . In theological studies 'useful' information should never be accepted as a substitute for disciplined judgment. The student should so conduct his studies that he is not only informed by a mass of data, but also formed and transformed by critical reflection and inner appropriation. A mind cannot be formed by consulting compendia, digests, and surveys, but only by wrestling in earnest with the classical literature, by being insinuated in and disciplined by an established tradition. . . . You did not like another reference I made. I had contended, and still maintain, that a living theology should address itself to the contemporary mind and respond to contemporary challenges. The theologian should take note of the present state of theological learning on the theory that the Spirit of God is still active in the church and that his presence is not limited to our segment of it. This means that we should ponder what others have to say, lest some part or aspect of the full truth be lost to us. . . . In saying these and other things I was concerned to warn the student against thinking himself educated when he had merely succeeded in fixing an outline or a scheme in his head, and had failed to attend to what was being thought and said in communities other than his own. I supposed that in so saying I was aiding and abetting the Seminary faculty in its educational efforts, and I should be extremely sorry to learn that my remarks were interpreted by anyone as reflecting unfavorably upon your self, your book, or your course.

The academic year 1948-1949 had now come to an end. The June commencement exercises were held in the Civic Auditorium, where diplomas were handed out to 254 college graduates. The faculty was dressed for the occasion in newly acquired caps and gowns that the board had purchased at a cost of $2,500.

The Synod of the Christian Reformed Church met in the college library from June 3 to June 17, 1949, and I attended as an elder delegate from Classis Grand Rapids East. Rev. Emo Van Halsema presided at our sessions, and I was assigned to the advisory committee on publications and appointed as its reporter. This was my first engagement in synodical proceedings, and I learned how taxing the work of synodical delegates is. A study report on the National Association of Evangelicals came into the hands of our committee, but we found it impossible to support either the majority, who wished to continue membership in the organization, or the minority, who wished to withdraw. We advised Synod to appoint a committee charged with preparing a proposal based on more substantial grounds. Our consideration of publication matters presented no problems, but we did process lists of nominees for eventual election to various posts. Rev. Van Halsema was appointed to succeed Rev. Keegstra as editor of *De Wachter*, and Clarence Boomsma was appointed as a member of the standing publications committee. In its address to college matters, Synod authorized the Board of Trustees to expand the library at a cost of $290,000; approved the building of a student commons as soon as possible; and required out-of-town college and seminary students to transfer their membership to a local church of their choosing. The Reformed Presbyterian Church wanted Synod to endorse its proposal to put into the Preamble of the United States Constitution the words "We the people of the United States, devoutly recognizing the authority and law of Jesus Christ, the Savior and King of nations. . . ." Although the delegates had little stomach for this, the matter was referred to a committee for study. Synod also appointed a committee to study the Boy Scout movement; and in another action it disapproved of ministers entering the industrial chaplaincy.

I made my first extended synodical speech when the issue of "worldly amusements" appeared once more on the floor of Synod. The pamphlet put out by the Youth and Calvinism group had not gone unnoticed: in an appendix to the published essays was an account of a poll taken among members of the Young Calvinist Federation showing that a considerable number of respondents had in good conscience attended movies and were of the opinion that the church's ban on such attendance was unwarranted. Alarmed by this disclosure, a number of consistories and one western classis overtured Synod not only to reaffirm its stand on worldly amusements but also to reemphasize its mandatory character.

When this matter came up for discussion, I arose to address it. I assured the delegates that as long as I had been teaching at the college, I had sedulously observed the rules governing student behavior; that I had, however, no disposition to censure students who played cards and went to movies under Christian restraints; that I myself had since

280

student days attended theatrical and cinematic performances with no observable adverse effects; that I deplored *The Banner* editor's reiterated insistence that selective movie attendance was not only hazardous but positively sinful; that I found it hard to believe that the Synod of 1928 intended to place an absolute ban on the cultural forms it characterized as amusements tending to cultivate worldliness; and that what was needed now was a re-examination and a reassessment of the position alleged to have been taken by the church.

The speech did not endear me to a number of my associates at Synod or enhance my reputation in the church; but I was not without supporters, and when the matter came to a vote, Synod decided to appoint a committee to re-examine the decisions of 1928. The committee was ordered to clarify the decisions and — considering that worldliness can take many forms — to amplify them where necessary and desirable. Restrictions were, however, to be observed; the decisions of 1928 were for the time being to remain in force, and their essence was to be preserved in any clarification attempted. The committee appointed to conduct this study consisted of seven ministers (L. Greenway, J. Vander Ploeg, J. Breuker, H. J. Kuiper, N. Monsma, W. Kok, and G. Hoeksema) and two laymen (E. R. Post and H. Stob). The assignment I inherited in the wake of my Synod speech would occupy a considerable portion of my free time in the next two years.

When Synod adjourned, I was not set at leisure: summer school awaited me, and in the course of the next six weeks I taught ancient philosophy to a class of 13 students and modern philosophy to a class of 14 students. Meanwhile, I continued to accept preaching engagements and during the summer conducted worship services in ten different churches.

Between January and September 1949, the world continued to turn on its axis. In our own country, Harry Truman began his second term as President; the United States Senate approved the formation of the North Atlantic Treaty Organization (NATO); Congress raised the minimum wage from 40 to 75 cents an hour; and book publishers advertised the appearance of Arthur Miller's *Death of a Salesman* and George Orwell's *Nineteen Eighty Four.* Europe and the Near East were in ferment. The Russians broke the United States nuclear monopoly by exploding an atomic bomb, but they also eased East-West tensions by terminating their blockade of surface shipments to Berlin. Germany itself was split in two. East Germany was established as an independent communist state, and a West German Republic was set up in Bonn with Konrad Adenauer as chancellor. In the Near East, Trans-Jordania annexed the West Bank, claimed sovereignty over the eastern half of Jerusalem, and took on the name Jordan. In China the revolutionary forces of Mao Tse-tung were poised to drive Chiang Kai-shek out of office and to set up a communist state on the vast mainland of Asia.

Thus ended my first three postwar years at Calvin college.

13

THE MIDDLE YEARS
(1949-1951)

When the academic year 1949-1950 began in September 1949, the number of students enrolled in the college stood at 1430. The faculty had grown with the addition of John Weidenaar in the department of biblical studies, but with only 46 people on the staff, the student-teacher ratio remained at the unacceptable level of 26 to 1; this was true even though Johannes Broene, A. E. Broene, and J. G. Vanden Bosch were retained to teach part-time. Harry Jellema and I still manned the philosophy department, and our classrooms were generally filled to capacity. Jellema taught modern philosophy, a course in philosophical perspectives, and another in ethics, while I pursued my studies in logic and in ancient and medieval philosophy. I functioned that year as a member of the faculty's discipline committee, but no longer served on the educational policy committee. The latter had been reconstituted to include the four divisional chairman (of which Jellema was one), the registrar, the secretary of the faculty and, of course, the academic dean, who presided at its meetings.

The Board of Trustees ran the college and seminary that year on a budget of $462,000 and paid full professors a salary of $4,500 to $5,500 a year, the variation depending on the recipient's length of service in that rank. Since the campaign to raise funds for building expansion had come to an end, Samuel Van Til resigned as field secretary in September 1949, and Mr. Voss was charged with collecting

The Plato Club, 1949-50
Standing: H. Stob, C. Terpstra, P. Lagerwey, C. Ryskamp, J. Stevens,
D. Oppewal. Seated: H. Stevens, N. Huizenga, J. Borst, R. Jellema

the pledges still outstanding. The science building was nearing completion, the student parking lot had been black-topped, and drapes had been hung in the chapel to improve acoustics.

In the fall semester of the 1949-50 academic year I taught introduction to philosophy in two sections to 81 students, medieval philosophy in two sections to 76 students, and logic to a class of 30 students. I again sponsored a Plato Club composed of excellent students who presented papers on a variety of philosophical topics. Constituting the membership that year were Dick Baay, John Borst, Nick Huizenga, Rod Jellema, Peter Lagerwey, Stuart Kingma, Don Oppewal, Charles Ryskamp, Henry Stevens, Joe Stevens, and Charles Terpstra. My extracurricular activities during that semester were not extensive: I preached at LaGrave Church in the month of September, and in October I addressed a civic audience on "The Dutch in Philosophy."

A citywide meeting was held in the Grand Rapids Public Museum, where a collection of Dutch art was on display; in my speech I traced the development of Dutch thought from Descartes and Spinoza to Vollenhoven and Dooyeweerd.

What engaged my attention throughout the year was the matter of enlarging the philosophy department. Harry Jellema and I had raised the issue as early as June 1948, but it was not until May 1949 that the educational policy committee acceded to our request and recommended the appointment of an additional staff member. Harry and I were agreed that Cecil De Boer was the man we would like to have as our associate; but when the committee began to consider candidates, the name of a certain Mr. Evan Runner kept coming up. Runner was interviewed by the committee on May 25 and put on their "long" list of candidates; but he fell out of contention when the committee effected the dual nomination of Cecil and Jesse De Boer. At its meeting held on May 31, 1949, the faculty endorsed the committee's nomination, but it added the name of Evan Runner as the third nominee by way of amendment. The Board of Trustees considered the three candidates on June 1, 1949, but deferred action on the nomination until it should meet again in semiannual session at the beginning of the next year.

On October 19, 1949, the educational policy committee again took up the matter of the philosophy appointment. This was somewhat odd, because the faculty had settled on a nomination in May, which now rested securely in the hands of the board. The fact was, however, that Jellema was opposed to Runner's nomination and had persuaded his fellow committee members to reopen the issue. His efforts were directed toward securing the nomination of the single candidate — Cecil De Boer — regarding whom he and I were in complete agreement. At that October meeting, Cecil De Boer was indeed renominated with my concurrence; but when it was decided to renominate Jesse De Boer as well, I argued that Runner's name should also stand. A motion by a committee member to restore his name, however, was not even seconded. To avoid further embarrassment the committee then decided to choose between Cecil and Jesse De Boer and present a single nomination; Cecil received the nod. But when this nomination reached the faculty on November 7, the faculty judged that the committee's proposal was out of order and that the multiple nomination agreed on earlier was still in force.

In a second effort to get Runner's name removed, the committee met on November 16, 1949, and decided to ask the faculty to rescind its decision of May 31 and make a new nomination. On December 5 the faculty did rescind its earlier action, and in accordance with the committee's recommendation named Cecil De Boer as its sole nominee. But when the executive committee of the board received the faculty's single nomination on December 8 and referred it to a subcommittee, the latter, on January 12, 1950, proposed that Runner's name be added to the nomination. The Board of Trustees met on February 8, 1950, and on the recommendation of its executive committee put both Runner and De Boer on nomination. The board did this despite the education policy committee's statement that argued strongly against Runner's nomination.

I had earlier refused to endorse the committee's statement because I considered its negative appraisal to be insufficiently grounded. Being aware of this, the board now asked Jellema and me to appear before it and give expression to our sentiments. I was not present when Harry gave his testimony, but when my turn came, I declared that I would be eminently satisfied with the appointment of Cecil De Boer, but I thought that Evan Runner was worthy of consideration and had no objection to his remaining in nomination. Noting a lack of unanimity in the department, the board decided to postpone action on its dual nomination until it met again in June of 1950.

At the board meeting held in June, Cecil De Boer was appointed to the staff at the rank of full professor and promised a salary of $4,900 a year. But that was not all: Evan Runner, a Harvard fellow who was now pursuing philosophy under Vollenhoven in Amsterdam, was also appointed to the staff "subject to the favorable outcome of a personal interview before the Board at its next meeting." Both appointments were ratified by the Synod of 1950. Thus, in the course of a single year, Calvin's philosophy department had doubled in size, though only DeBoer would be aboard when the school doors opened in September.

Feelings ran high both within and without the faculty regarding those appointments, and Jellema was not pleased with my refusal to oppose Runner's nomination. But I did not then share Jellema's dislike of the new Dutch philosophy nor his estimate of Runner's capabilities. Moreover, I thought that our homogeneous college staff would be enriched by the addition of an evangelical scholar who had not been bred in our circles and against whose academic credentials little could be alleged. I did not positively advocate Runner's nomination, much less his appointment; but neither could I, in fairness to an eligible candidate with wide support, join in the effort to put him out of contention. The course pursued by Runner after he joined the faculty in 1951 did not always generate sweetness and light, and I was led in subsequent years to wonder whether I should have acted differently during the nominating process; but what I did, I did in good conscience and am now satisfied to leave the entire matter to the judgment of history.

When the drama of the philosophy appointments was being enacted, there was action on the world stage as well. Before the first semester ended and the year 1949 drew to a close, the revolutionary forces of Mao Tse-tung had established a communist state on the mainland of China and had caused Chiang Kai-shek to flee with a remnant of his troops to the island of Formosa (Taiwan), where he was protected against further assault by the United States fleet. With the establishment of Mao's government, our missionary activity in China ceased, and by the end of 1949 all of the staff except Rev. A. H. Smit had been repatriated. China was evidently not regarded as a threat to Korea, because during that year the American troops that had been stationed in Korea since the end of World War II had been withdrawn and either sent home or transferred to Japan. Axis Sally and Tokyo Rose were convicted of treason that year; Cardinal Mindszenty went on trial in Hungary; the Dutch Calvinists kept coming to Canada and had by now established fourteen Christian Reformed churches in that country; and in the United States Dr. Edwin Land had introduced the polaroid camera.

When the second semester began in January 1950, my classes were again so large that I could not give the required attention to all the students enrolled. That semester I taught logic in two sections to 119 students, ancient philosophy in two sections to 102 students, and the philosophy of St. Thomas Aquinas to a class of 12.

In February, I appeared on radio to answer the charges made against Citizens Action by Mayor George Welsh. I also enlisted the populace in support of the candidates we had put forward to replace him and his cronies; in the election that followed, all five of our candidates were successful: Paul Goebel became mayor, and Doerr, Hoogerhyde, De Korne, and Gritter took seats on the city council. In March, Dr. Hideo Kishimoto, professor of religion at Tokyo University, paid a visit to Grand Rapids and was a guest in our house for two days. I had worked closely with him during my tour of duty in Japan, and I was delighted to see him again and review several of our joint ventures.

In April, I was made chairman of a committee charged with drawing up a set of resolutions on the race issue for the forthcoming Young Calvinist Convention. Serving with me were Garrett Heyns, Clarence Boomsma, Jack Stoepker, and Neal Rensenbrink. In May, I preached on three Sundays in local churches and addressed the seminary students on "honesty" at their annual Corps Fest. During the course of the year I met in several lively sessions with the other members of the synodical committee on worldly amusements.

Things were happening in and around school as well. Clarence Bouma resumed his post at the seminary in January 1950 after spending a sabbatical year in research and writing; at the same time, Case Plantinga joined the college faculty in the department of psychology. The completion of the new science building was celebrated at a dedicatory service held in the Civic Auditorium on February 6. In that same month the Board authorized the establishment of a series of annual college-seminary lectures featuring outside speakers. By March, work was in progress on the addition to the library. In April, Steve Vander Weele was offered an appointment as an assistant in English, and in May the Calvin Foundation was formally established as an agency for the support of Calvinistic studies and ventures. At the June 1950 commencement 307 graduates received their college diplomas.

The internal struggle that resulted in the appointment of two men to the college philosophy department, and which for a time put a strain on the relationship between Jellema and me, was minuscule compared to the struggle concurrently developing in the seminary. A sign of unrest first appeared at the February 1950 meeting of the board, when the student Corps voiced its dissatisfaction with the quality of teaching in the New Testament department. The students were only slightly appeased when in March the executive committee made a "friendly judgment," which the professor of New Testament, William Hendriksen, considered prejudicial. Within the faculty itself there was a split between the dominant four, who controlled the seminary offices, and the remaining two, whose sentiments on a variety of matters went unheeded and whose objections to certain tactics and procedures were dismissed as unfounded. A bone of contention was the proposed Th.D. program: supported by Volbeda, Wyngaarden, Hendriksen, and Rutgers, it was opposed by Bouma and Stob, who felt that neither the faculty nor the library met the standards requisite for its introduction. It appears that in the faculty discussions concerning this matter, it was particularly Prof. Bouma who roused the ire of the dominant four; for on May 23, 1950, it was only these five who, at a meeting of the executive committee, not only expressed their differences on the issue of the Th.D. but also aired complaints against each other's conduct in the management of affairs.

Tension was not eased when, by a vote of four to two, the faculty decided not to extend licensure to two students who were supposed to be "confused on some doctrinal points touching on Barthianism." Bouma and Stob supported the students at the executive committee meeting held on May 31; and at the June 1950 board meeting the students were vindicated and duly licensed.

On June 8, "the Four" presented to the executive committee a "peace proposal" affecting their dispute with Bouma; but reconciliation foundered on charges of collusion and pre–faculty meeting caucuses that allegedly created "deplorable conditions" in the seminary. At a meeting held on August 30, 1950, the executive committee heard evidence from George Stob in support of Bouma's complaint and advised the faculty both to appoint a different registrar and to dispense with the educational policy committee or reduce it to two members. The students entered the picture once again when the entire class of June graduates presented the committee with a document expressing its dissatisfaction with the quality of teaching in the departments of New Testament and Dogmatics.

The Synod of the Christian Reformed Church met in June 1950, and at its opening session was reminded that it had been now a century since our immigrant forefathers were received into the Reformed Dutch Church and were constituted as Classis Holland within the particular Synod of Albany. Synod ratified the appointments in the philosophy department but did not mention during its proceedings the trouble brewing in the seminary. The amusement committee reported that it had met four times during the year but had not completed its assignment and asked for another year of grace. The committee on woman suffrage was likewise unready with its report, but advised that, pending the outcome of its investigation, no church should undertake to introduce woman suffrage at its congregational meetings. Synod recognized the growth of the Canadian constituency when it authorized the formation of the Ontario churches into a separate classis.

The life of the college was affected when Gordon Buter was appointed as Calvin's business manager and Shirley Balk was appointed to teach piano and organ. The addition to Calvin's library had by now been put in place, and on a certain day the entire Synod recessed to attend a dedicatory service at which Henry Zylstra, chairman of the library committee, gave a stirring address. I was not a delegate to Synod but was given the privilege of the floor when a matter arose affecting Calvin Church. The Board of Trustees had recommended that Synod purchase an additional five acres of land from the Clark Memorial Home and lease one acre of this land to Calvin Church for a period of ninety-nine years at the price of $10,000. The leasing issue was opposed by seven local churches and, as it turned out, also by Synod's advisory committee. As an elder of that church, I argued as best I could for the leasing provision, but to no avail. Synod authorized the purchase of the property but made no concession to the church.

It was not uncommon, while Synod was in session, for friends to gather at our house for comment and appraisal. It chanced that near the close of Synod's 1950 session a number of those who had in one way or another been involved in Synod's proceedings were present in our living room. Jim Daane was there as a minister delegate from Classis California; so was Harry Boer, who had addressed Synod as a returning missionary from Nigeria and as the professor-elect of missions; George Stob, who had served as advisor to Synod, was present; as was Henry Zylstra, who had presided at the unveiling of the library cornerstone. After we had consumed the refreshments Hilda served, and when our survey of church affairs had reached a climax, the five of us arrived at a decision regarding a matter that some of us had contemplated on other occasions: we decided to launch a publication. Not satisfied with what we read in the pages of *The Banner*, and judging that the *Calvin Forum* was not an appropriate vehicle for the expression of our sentiments, we determined to put out a magazine that would articulate the vision that we shared. That evening we did not know how the venture would be financed, nor what the publication would be called, nor why it should be just this set of persons who should constitute its editorial board. But we said a prayer and decided to proceed. Following that meeting there was a nine-month period of gestation. With Daane back in California and Boer in Amsterdam for further study, the burden of launching the new venture fell largely on George Stob, Henry Zylstra, and me. In subsequent months we received the unstinting support of Mr. William Eerdmans, Sr., who offered to assume the expense of publication. After considering a host of fancy names to give to our projected creation, we hit upon a simple one, and in March 1951 the first edition of *The Reformed Journal* appeared in the mails. We hoped the periodical would exist for at least eighty years, but its demise came a few months short of its fortieth birthday.

The summer of 1950 was fortunately unencumbered by summer school, and I was able to devote a large part of it to my studies. Yet all was not peaceful in Zion. Toward the end of summer there erupted in *The Banner* a dispute in which some of us later became involved, and which caused some concern to the college authorities as well. The National Association of Evangelicals, of which the Christian Reformed Church was a member, had at its most recent convention endorsed a book by John T. Flynn entitled *The Road Ahead*. In *The Banner* of August 18, 1950, Lester De Koster bemoaned the endorsement: he denounced Flynn's opposition to the aspirations of black people, as well as Flynn's eagerness "to smear with the Red label all who differ with his own political and economic notions." H. J. Kuiper, editor of *The Banner*, replied in a lengthy editorial on August 25. Kuiper praised Flynn for his opposition to a "planned economy" and for his denunciation of the "socialistic virus" that was allegedly throttling the American spirit of free enterprise. He went on to say: "Frankly, we can't quite conceive of anyone reacting so vehemently to Flynn's book without wondering whether he is in sympathy with the socialistic trend in this country. . . . We should like to know where our Calvin teacher stands." This remark lit a fire that burned well into the new year, and which as early as August 30, 1950, was reflected in the minutes of the board's executive committee: attention was called to "the public criticisms directed toward members of our college staff for supposed leanings toward socialistic ideas," and the educational subcommittee was requested to give this matter its attention.

The twenty-seventh annual convention of the Young Calvinist Federation was held in Lynden, Washington, in late August 1950. With several other adults, I joined the assembled group. On Sunday, August 20, I preached in the Second Church of Lynden, and on the following day delivered the keynote address at the convention. The theme of the convention was "Kingdom Frontiers," and I spoke on "The Kingdom World Wide." The resolutions prepared by our committee on race relations were considered that same day and, after a lively discussion, adopted with élan. It was not until the mid-sixties that black people in America received widespread legislative protection against public apathy, abuse, and discrimination; but already in 1950 the young people of our church rose to the defense of their black brothers and sisters. In solemn assembly they declared, among other things, that

> the existing differences of race and color provide no warrant for the "indulgence of racial pride in and through discriminatory practices"; that "the Christian in his community should strive to honor the negro's intrinsic right to live, work, buy, and sell in free equality, and should do all within his power to initiate and support such legislative and educational programs as would secure for the negro rights and opportunities equal to those enjoyed by the other members of society"; that "the Christians should foster in every reasonable way the negro's integration into the community and the community's life"; and that "all measures which obstruct this end, such as forced segregation, should be condemned as a violation of Christian principle." With the South African situation in view, the delegates also declared that "although the Christian must always exercise concern and care for his fellowmen in keeping with the Gospel requirements, this demand is not to be taken as justifying the imposition of an unwelcome guardianship by one race upon another."

While these things were going on, other events at home and abroad were affecting our communal lives. During the first eight months of 1950, the communist scare in the United States grew unabated. Senator Joseph McCarthy charged that the state and defense departments were riddled with subversives; Congress passed the McCarron Internal Security bill; Julius and Ethel Rosenberg were put on trial for espionage; and Alger Hiss was convicted of perjury and sentenced to five years in prison. The economy held steady. The first of six hundred Volkswagens reached New York from a recovering German industry; ten thousand mass-manufactured houses transformed former New York potato fields into a bustling Levittown; a renewed Social Security act boosted benefits and enlarged the number of beneficiaries, and the New York telephone company was authorized to raise its basic coinbox charge from five to ten cents.

What dominated the news, however, was the outbreak of the Korean War. On June 25, 1950, a large contingent of troops from communist North Korea crossed the 38th parallel in Soviet-made tanks and moved toward Seoul, which they occupied three days later. The Security Council of the United Nations, whose permanent home had only that year been established on East 43rd Street in New York City, called on all members to provide assistance to South Korea. President Truman responded by activating Japan-based American air and naval units, and soon thereafter ordered MacArthur's ground troops into action. By the end of August, however, the North Koreans had advanced as far south as Pusan, and it was not until September that General MacArthur, previously appointed as the United Nations Commander of the entire operation, was able to outwit the invaders by making a daring amphibious landing behind enemy lines at Inchon.

*　　　*　　　*　　　*　　　*

Our daughter Ellen reached the age of five in August 1950, and when the academic year 1950-1951 began in September, both of us were in school. Ellen entered kindergarten at Baxter Christian School, and I began the twelfth year of my association with Calvin College. Cecil De Boer had come to join Harry Jellema and me in the department of philosophy, and his coming both enriched the department's offerings and afforded Jellema and me some relief from our teaching duties. At the beginning of that year the faculty had forty-fix full-time instructors; augmenting the established teaching staff were nine assistants.

In September 1950 the number of students enrolled in the college stood at 1,270; the Korean War had exacted its toll, and by the end of the first semester the enrollment had dropped to 1,169. In view of the war, the faculty considered for a time the introduction of accelerated courses, and even contemplated the introduction of an ROTC program; but nothing came of this and things proceeded at school in quite the normal way. The Board of Trustees ran the college and seminary on a budget of $517,000, and the tuition charged Christian Reformed students came to $115 a semester. That year

The Family

Gordon Buter assumed the newly created position of business manager, and when the venerable Mr. Voss died later in the year, Lester Ippel took on the duties of assistant treasurer. Jan Kingma assisted Van Andel in teaching Dutch; the women still occupied the campus dormitory; and plans were approved for the soon-to-be-erected student commons.

In the fall semester of the year 1950-1951 my teaching load was, because of DeBoer's presence, considerably reduced. I taught introduction to philosophy to 34 students, ancient philosophy to 16 students, and medieval philosophy in two sections to 50 students. I served again on the faculty's discipline committee with Hoekstra, Monsma, Spoelhof, De Beer, and Van Opynen, and sponsored as usual the ongoing Plato Club, where I met regularly with a group of budding philosophers that included Klaas De Ruiter, Sidney Newhouse, Jacob Oppewall, Gordon Oosterman, Joe Stevens, Frank Van Halsema, and John Vriend. In October 1950, I preached on one Sunday in an outlying church, delivered an address at the annual meeting of the board and staff of the Christian Hospital in Cutlerville, and, by way of an interview with a news reporter, commented in the *Grand Rapids Press* on "The Far East and its Prospects for Democratic Government." I met several times in the fall with the synodical committee on worldly amusements; and by the end of the calendar year we had our divergent reports ready for publication in the *Agenda*. I remained involved in the activities of Citizens Action, and also took a seat on the Grand Rapids Council on World Affairs, where I deepened my acquaintance with Duncan Littlefair, pastor of the liberal Fountain Street Church.

Some excitement was generated in the fall of 1950, when Prof. Cornelius Van Til of Westminster Seminary appeared on campus as the first lecturer in the college-seminary lecture series. His five addresses on Barthianism were well attended, but his characterization of Barth as a malevolent "neo-Modernist," while pleasing to some, struck a number of us as a representation suffering from misunderstanding and distortion. The socialist issue, which — like Barthianism — was being agitated in the church, was addressed by Harry Jellema when he joined Stanley High and Norman Thomas in a December symposium on "Christianity: Capitalism or Socialism" in Paterson, New Jersey.

In September, General Dwight Eisenhower, who was being courted by both national parties as a possible candidate for the Presidency, assumed his duties as president of Columbia University; and in November, Richard Nixon won a Senate seat in a California race against Helen Douglas. Before 1950 came to a close, the National Council of Christian Churches was launched in the United States; the 31-year-old Billy Graham began a revival campaign in California; and Pope Pius XII proclaimed the Virgin Mary's bodily assumption into heaven.

The Korean War, meanwhile, continued on its course. General MacArthur's September landing at Inchon resulted in the retreat of the North Koreans. On September 25, U.N. forces regained Seoul, and on October 19 they occupied Pyongyang, the capital of North Korea. In November, however, hordes of Chinese "volunteers" fell on MacArthur's extended lines and forced him to retreat. He there-

[Reformed Journal *Ad*]

upon appealed to Washington for permission to blockade China, bomb enemy bases in Manchuria, and utilize Chiang Kai-shek's Formosan troops. His request, however, was disallowed, and this enabled the North Koreans to reach the outskirts of Seoul by year's end. Washington's veto also created the rift between Truman and MacArthur that eventually led to the general's dismissal as field commander. MacArthur's general deportment, plus his determination to implement the battle plans he had himself conceived, did nothing to lessen the tension that steadily grew between himself and the President.

The second semester began in January 1951, and during its course I taught ancient philosophy in two sections to 81 students, medieval philosophy to 18 students, and a seminar on Aristotle to 6 students.

In February, I spoke on "Election and Missionary Activity" at the Mission Week Seminar held at the college; in the same month I was elected by Classis Grand Rapids East as an elder delegate to the Synod of 1951. A number of important matters came under consideration at the February meeting of the Board of Trustees, which I will report in due time; but here I will mention that the board assisted Calvin Church in its search for a suitable building site by agreeing to exchange a parcel of land held by the college for a similar one held by the church. The board also dealt lightly with Clarence Boersma, who refused to sign the Form of Subscription because, as he said, he did not "detest the Anabaptists" and did not regard the Catholic mass as "an accursed idolatry." Some of us who had signed the Form shared Boersma's sentiments but considered that we were not bound by expressions formulated in the heat of sixteenth-century battles, and we judged that the accepted creeds are best left unaltered and for historical reasons preserved in their integrity.

In late January the executive committee of the board had considered the appointment of two additional professors to the seminary faculty in order to further its development and to obviate the difficulties encountered in the effort to establish a Th.D. degree. They named C. Van Til, G. Berkouwer, H. Stob, and H. Ridderbos as possible candidates for these appointments; but in its February meeting the board decided to postpone action on that matter until the May meeting.

In March 1951, Calvin celebrated the 75th anniversary of its founding: the period from March 4 to March 11 was designated "Jubilee Week," and one of its highlights was an elaborate pageant presented before a full house in the Grand Rapids Civic Auditorium. Henry Zylstra wrote the text of the pageant: entitled "A Tree of Life," his moving production set forth the school's growth in terms of the vision that gave it birth, the beneficence of those who supported it, and the mercy of the Lord who blessed it. The whole was masterfully presented by a cast of actors recruited from the college community.

In that same month, *The Reformed Journal* made its debut. During the nine months of gestation preceding its publication we had been kept busy preparing for its delivery; but we had not bothered to inform others of its imminent birth until just before the first issue emerged from the press. We first supplied semi-public information about our project to our academic colleagues in a letter dated February 5, 1951, and signed by George Stob, Henry Zylstra, and me:

> We take this means to tell you about something we are going to do. We are starting another paper. It will be denominationally oriented, and will be devoted entirely to ideas, issues, and events which are important to our church in all matters of faith and life. We are prompted by our sense of the need for substantial and forthright discussion. We think this is the time to speak. The paper will come out monthly. We shall call it The Reformed Journal. It will be published by Eerdmans, and will differ in nature and purpose from The Banner and The Calvin Forum, with both of which we want to maintain active cooperation. . . . Our project has been a long while deliberated, antedates the recent tensions, and does not spring from polemics. Harry Boer and James Daane were with us from the beginning and are with us on the editorial staff. We know there is something bold about five men setting up this way. We talked about spreading the editorial base, wished sometimes that the thing could be done in full 'town meeting,' but in the end it seemed best to go on as we began. We hope and pray that we can manage a purposeful witness.

We advertised the *Journal* in the *Grand Rapids Press* on February 10, set the subscription rate at two dollars a year, and offered charter subscribers the ten monthly issues of 1951 for the price of one dollar. At a dinner hosted by Mr. Eerdmans, the editors — and Mr. Eerdmans as well — became charter subscribers by ceremoniously placing on the table the one-dollar bills they had extracted from their wallets. The twelve-page March 1 issue contained one editorial statement in which we commended the *Journal* to the attention of the Reformed community, another in which we celebrated the fraternity of the *Press,* and a third in which we sketched the genesis of our enterprise. To these were added seven articles by the individual editors: Harry Boer on "The New Orient and Missions" and on "Synodical Procedure"; James Daane on "Self-Examination Expanded"; George Stob on "The Diamond Jubilee"; Henry Stob on "The Call for Leadership"; and Henry Zylstra on "Interests and Education" and on "Liberalism and Dogma." The response to our offerings was gratifying and we were encouraged to proceed on our way.

A month after the *Journal's* arrival, another new magazine appeared on the scene: in April 1951 the *Torch and Trumpet* made its debut. The magazine was published by the Reformed Fellowship Incorporated, which in its turn was governed by a board of trustees consisting of Herman Baker, Arnold Brink, P. Y. De Jong, John De Vries, Leonard Greenway, Edward Heerema, Marvin Muller, John Piersma, John Van Bruggen, Fred Van Houten, Henry Van Til, and Henry Venema. *Banner* editor H. J. Kuiper commented on the appearance of the two new journals in a an editorial on April 20. He judged that

> the *Torch and Trumpet* is not the same kind of religious magazine as *The Reformed Journal.* Its purpose is not primarily to enter the arena of discussion and debate on issues that confront our church. Its principal aim is to present articles on important aspects of revealed truth. It intends to be polemic as well as constructive. Modernism, Barthianism, and other theological issues will be exposed in their anti-Scriptural teachings. The editors add, however, that 'when necessity presents itself' they 'will not hesitate to engage in controversy.' We were happy to read this.

It soon became evident that the *Torch and Trumpet* represented the ultra-conservative wing in the church and was out to cultivate a mind that valued safety above advancement and militancy above engagement. Consequently, the two magazines gradually grew apart, each occupying its own place in the life of the church.

In April 1951 the relationship between Truman and MacArthur reached the breaking point. In defiance of a restriction imposed upon him by Washington, MacArthur had on March 24 released to the press a fresh plan for ending the Korean War. Truman was furious, and at a meeting held in Hawaii shortly after this, the general compounded the mischief by arriving late for a scheduled interview. MacArthur's tenure ended when, on April 11, Truman stripped him of his field command and replaced him with General Matthew Ridgeway.

Within the Calvin community, on May 24, 1951, the executive committee of the Board of Trustees received from seven advanced preseminary students a complaint against six of their college professors. The complainants — Dick Bouma, John Byker, Cecil Tuininga, Harry Van Dyken, Gerard Van Groningen, Alvin Venema, and Richard Venema — alleged that the instruction they had received in certain classes was lacking in Christian orientation and emphasis, and was hardly distinguishable from what could be obtained at a secular university. The charges were brought without consulting or informing the President, the faculty, or even the professors involved; and when the faculty considered this breach of protocol, it referred the matter to the discipline committee, of which I was a member. Our committee, in turn, sent to the board a protest against the students' procedure, together with a defense of our colleagues, whom we knew as estimable professionals, apt at integrating faith and learning and strongly disposed to make a Christian witness on any fitting occasion.

The Board of Trustees took the students' complaints seriously enough to interview the professors and to rediscover that they were worthy of the trust and esteem they had long enjoyed. The complaining student group came to be known in time as the "Sacred Seven," and it is not surprising that, after serving for several decades as Christian Reformed ministers, three of them finally left the church in protest to what they regarded as its slide into laxness and deformity.

The controversy that had earlier erupted in *The Banner* about the relevance of John Flynn's book to the social and economic thought of Reformed thinkers carried over into 1951. A number of us did not like the tone in which the editor of *The Banner* conducted the discussion, and we resented his suggestion that the Calvin faculty was riddled with crypto-socialists. The 1950-51 school year had barely begun when Henry Zylstra and I composed a letter for *The Banner* column "Voices," to which we secured the signatures of an additional sixteen colleagues. Our brief statement appeared in *The Banner* of September 15, 1950: it simply voiced our shared conviction that the context in which Flynn set the principle of individual freedom was not one to which a Reformed Christian is necessarily committed.

H. J. Kuiper did not, of course, look upon our letter with favor. In his editorial comments about it, he declared, among other things, that he knew that "some of these eighteen brethren believe in a large measure of control of industry, but we did not know that so many of them refuse to feel alarmed at the constantly increasing power of civil government in our country." Kuiper was also dissatisfied with the brevity of our report and with its lack of argumentation. This led him to ask, "Who is ready to agree with the utterance of these men merely because they are professors at our school and in number eighteen?" To this he added: "The Bible is contrary to the present drift toward more and more state control of our economic life. If that is wrong, as these eighteen professors seem to believe, we should like to be convinced from Scripture."

At this point Lester De Koster again entered the fray, as did those who endorsed the editor's position and joined in his lament about conditions at the college. We, "the eighteen," decided meanwhile to withdraw from a controversy that was going nowhere. In a statement published in *The Banner* of September 29, 1950, we said in effect: Mr. Flynn is indeed a champion of freedom. So were Voltaire and Rousseau. Flynn favors the unbridled economic liberalism of the 19th century. We do not. Being neither socialists nor socialist sympathizers, we embrace the historic Reformed economic and socio-political principles expressed in the writings and labors of Calvin, Kuyper, Talma, Colyn, and others in our tradition. To this we added words that now appear to be somewhat lacking in patience and forbearance; we concluded by saying to the editor: "We are of the considered opinion that, in view of your kind of editorial writing and comment, no further statement in *The Banner* can be fruitful."

This did not end the turmoil. Already on September 14, 1950, the day before "the Eighteen" appeared in "Voices," the executive committee of the board had addressed a communication to the Christian Reformed Publishing House expressing its regrets that *The Banner* had editorially cast unwarranted suspicion on the college faculty. In subsequent days and weeks the committee interviewed Lester De Koster, Don Bouma, and myself, and received assurance from us that we and our colleagues held none of the sentiments that the *Banner* editor had ascribed to us. However, complaints continued to pour in from those the editor had aroused. Gilbert Den Dulk, for instance — plus twenty of his medical associates — complained to the board about the "socialist leanings" of Calvin faculty members. H. J. Kuiper himself accused the board of tolerating unsound teaching, of being lax in making appointments, and of being reluctant to exercise effective discipline. The executive committee responded in *The Banner* of October 20, 1950: it expressed its disapproval of the editor's conduct in the controversy with De Koster and "the Eighteen," and it emphatically disavowed the editorial allegations made against them.

In the end, Lester De Koster, whose noncompliant letter to the editor had started the whole thing, was not only reappointed as associate professor of speech but also nominated as the first director of the library. As late as June 1951, however, the president of the college reported that he was still being told by various persons that the faculty was sheltering Bolshevists. Indeed, it was rumored that when the Russians finally landed on our shores, De Koster and I would be proudly seated on the Soviet tank that rumbled at the head of the invading forces. What started innocently enough with a letter to the editor developed for a while into a storm; but after a year the storm subsided, and the whole thing proved to be no more than a tempest in a teapot.

Of more lasting significance was the situation that was developing in the seminary. The internal strife that had begun during the previous year continued unabated in the course of 1951, and the executive committee and board were kept busy processing the various documents and presentations emanating from the contending parties. On one side were Clarence Bouma and George Stob, and on the other were the dominant four: President Volbeda, Registrar Wyngaarden, Secretary Rutgers, and Prof. Hendriksen. The first issue to arise that year concerned the position of registrar: to prevent the recurrence of an earlier dispute about grading practices, the executive committee had instructed the faculty not to re-elect Wyngaarden to the post. Volbeda, however, regarded that instruction as "gratuitous advice," and the faculty renewed Wyngaarden's appointment in September of 1950 despite objections raised by Bouma and Stob. But there was more. In the interval before the re-election of the registrar, Volbeda had declared that the executive committee had exceeded its authority regarding this matter. Bouma vehemently protested that remark; but when the minutes of that meeting were read at a subsequent faculty meeting, though they reported Bouma's protest, they failed to report the remark to which he had objected; the minutes in fact recorded a revised and milder version of it. When George Stob brought these things to the attention of the executive committee in October and November, the committee reiterated its demand that the registrar be replaced and rebuked the secretary for his failure to keep accurate minutes.

Prof. Hendriksen now became registrar, but reports of executive committee members who visited his classes were often unfavorable, and student complaints concerning the quality of his teaching continued. What lent significance to these complaints was the fact that Hendriksen's term of appointment would expire at the end of that academic year, and the issue of his reappointment would soon have to be faced. When the Board of Trustees met in February 1951, it received a request from the student Corps, and another from Prof. Bouma, to make a thorough investigation of the seminary situation before considering a reappointment. When the "Four" endorsed this proposal, presumably because they considered Dr. Bouma to be at the root of the trouble, the board appointed a five-member committee to undertake the investigation. John Hamersma, a lay board member who was a guest in our home at the time, was named as a member of the committee.

The investigating committee submitted two reports to the board when it met again in June 1951: the minority report was signed by Hamersma and the majority report by N. J. Monsma *cum suis*. The board undertook a line-by-line consideration of these reports, but soon abandoned that as unexpeditious and took up only selected matters for consideration and resolution. One of these concerned a disagreement between William Hendriksen and George Stob, which was resolved in Stob's favor. The board thereupon considered Hamersma's recommendation that Hendriksen not be reappointed; after much discussion, the board decided to concur in Hamersma's recommendation. The decision not to reappoint Prof. Hendriksen was based on a negative assessment of his methodology, on his perceived failure to disclose the broad revelational lines of the New Testament, and on his reluctance to relate the gospel message to the critical issues of the day. This action did not meet with the approval of every board member; several of them had their negative votes recorded.

The prospects for academic stability and growth in the seminary were not bright at that point. The tenure of Hendriksen was uncertain; the performance of Rutgers was being judged unsatisfactory by most students; the mandatory retirement of Volbeda loomed on the horizon; and now a distinguished member of the faculty fell seriously ill. Clarence Bouma had returned from a sabbatical in January 1950, but he had come back without the manuscript that he had hoped to write, and this, I had noticed, preyed on his mind. It was also reported that he was sometimes chided by his colleagues for his failure to produce the promised text. In the year that followed his return, he also became deeply involved in the disputes, large and small, that broke the peace in the seminary. To what extent these things played a role in bringing on his collapse no one can say for sure; the fact is that in late February

1951 he was laid low by a psycho-physical disorder from which he never fully recovered. On March 17 he was put under the care of Dr. Mulder at Pine Rest Psychiatric Hospital in Cutlerville; but he underwent no marked improvement there, and on the advice of his physician, the executive committee decided in early May to grant him "at least one year of sick leave." The tragic decline of my good friend and colleague meant that he would not be available to teach in the academic year 1951-1952; it also meant that the students in his current classes were left in mid-semester without a mentor and without the benefit of final grades. It is ironic that, under these circumstances, the seminary faculty could not even agree on what to do about the student grades. George Stob favored waiving some of the requirements for graduation, but the majority argued for giving the students a passing grade; the executive committee resolved the issue by agreeing with the majority.

On May 10, 1951, the executive committee considered how it might fill Dr. Bouma's position during his long absence. C. Van Til, H. Stob, H. Schultze, and G. C. Berkouwer were mentioned as possible candidates for the job; but before proceeding to place some or all of these men in nomination, the committee decided to ask the seminary faculty for its recommendation. The faculty recommended Prof. Cornelius Van Til of Westminster, and in late May the Board of Trustees decided to appoint him as professor in the department of systematic theology for an indefinite term. The board judged that Van Til was not only qualified to teach the courses in ethics and apologetics during Dr. Bouma's absence but was also equipped to supplement the work of Dr. Rutgers by giving special attention to significant trends in contemporary theology, especially to the Barthian "theology of crisis."

During that year there was an important development in the college as well. Prof. Schultze was now in his eleventh year as president of the college. He had during most of his tenure performed his work with unostentatious efficiency and with evident ardor, but he had been ill frequently in recent years, and it appeared that his health was in decline. This affected his performance, and toward the beginning of the 1950-1951 school year the executive committee wondered whether the college was suffering from a lack of vigorous leadership. In February 1951 the committee informed the president that it was troubled about the state of his health and discussed with him the possibility and utility of his early retirement. Schultze's response was prompt and decisive: having been advised by his physician several times earlier to engage in less strenuous activities, he submitted his resignation to the committee on March 8. He cited health reasons for his action and indicated that he wished the resignation to go into effect no later than September 1951. The committee accepted the resignation with regret, and it asked the faculty to submit a slate of candidates fit to replace a president who, in the judgment of all, had written a commendable record as administrator.

The faculty assigned the nominating task to its educational policy committee, which for this purpose was enlarged by the addition of five professors who were elected in plenary session. After due deliberations — and against the background of a lengthy report it had prepared on the qualifications an ideal candidate should possess — the committee presented to the faculty its slate of candidates. Recommended for appointment as president, and named in the order of preference, were Henry Stob, George Goris, and George Stob. Adopted by the faculty on April 10, this officially sanctioned nomination was received by the board's executive committee on April 18. At a meeting held on May 10, the executive committee added to the faculty's submitted list the names of William Spoelhof and John De Vries. However, those two asked that they be eliminated from consideration since they fully supported the faculty nomination. The committee thereupon did scratch the name of John De Vries, but referred the question of whether Spoelhof's name should stand to the judgment of the full board.

At a meeting held on June 3, 1951; the Board of Trustees added to the faculty's nomination the names of several other candidates, including that of William Spoelhof. There followed a process of elimination. Finally, being disposed to present to Synod the dual nomination of Henry Stob and William Spoelhof, the board asked the faculty to react to this proposal. The full faculty convened on June 5 and adopted the following resolution: "The faculty wishes to reiterate to the Board that our original nomination is still our preference, and that it was arrived at after careful and lengthy deliberation." With reference to Dr. Spoelhof, the faculty declared that, though it did not find him unacceptable as a candidate, it felt that there were on the faculty several persons who were at least as qualified as he, and that if his name were to be retained, the faculty would like to add to its nomination the names of Harry Jellema, Henry Ryskamp, and Henry Zylstra. On receiving that communication, the board deliberated for some time, retained the name of Spoelhof, asked Spoelhof and me to appear for an interview, and finally decided "to submit the names of Dr. H. Stob and Dr. W. Spoelhof to Synod as its nomination for President of Calvin College."

The matter of the presidency would be settled at Synod, but so would the issue of worldly amusements, with which my mind had been engaged off and on during the past two years. The study committee to which I had been appointed had received from the 1949 Synod a mandate that was simple and direct: it was not to change or refine the position the church had adopted in 1928; it was to make no evaluation of it; it was to pass no judgment on its soundness or unsoundness; it was simply to "clarify" and, if necessary, to "amplify" it. The committee had to answer only one question: What in fact is the stand of the church on worldliness, more particularly on worldly amusements, more particularly still on movie attendance, dancing, and card playing? What precisely do the resolutions of 1928 say?

The committee had not been able to produce a unanimous report: it had submitted to Synod a majority report signed by Henry J. Kuiper, William Kok, Nicholas J. Monsma, John Breuker, and Leonard Greenway, and a minority report signed by Gerrit Hoeksema, John Vander Ploeg, Egbert R. Post, and me. The two reports manifested a wide area of agreement, but they differed on one point: the moral status assigned by Synod to the three practices specifically mentioned in the resolutions. The question that divided the committee was this: Did the Synod of 1928 say that movie attendance, card playing, and dancing are essentially and invariably sinful, or did it not? The majority maintained that Synod did say that, and the minority maintained that it did not. That was the only point in dispute between the two parties.

The majority represented Synod as saying: You may not under any circumstances dance, go to the movies, or play cards; to do so is incompatible with a Christian profession. Commitment to Christ requires total abstinence from these activities. They are simply, pervasively, and unqualifiedly evil. Engagement in them, however infrequent and selective, is sin. The minority denied that Synod said this, or that it made a catalogue of sins. Did Synod then, it might be asked, approve a limited and judicious participation in the three amusements? To that question the minority answered, No! It said: There exists no synodical rule prohibiting all participation in the three amusements. But it also said: there exists no declaration permitting such participation. Synod made no pronouncement either way: it did not ban participation, but neither did it justify participation. It was now up to the Synod of 1951 to determine whether the majority or minority had read the 1928 resolutions correctly.

The Synod of the Christian Reformed Church met in the Calvin College auditorium from June 13 to June 26, 1951. Rev. Henry Baker served as president of the Synod; associated with him on the podium were Martin Monsma (vice president), William Haverkamp (first clerk), and John Gritter (second clerk). I was present as an elder delegate from Classis Grand Rapids East and was appointed reporter for the advisory committee on protests and appeals, of which committee George Stob happened to be the faculty advisor. Confirmed at this Synod was the appointment of Evan Runner as assistant professor of philosophy at the college, of Henry Ippel as instructor in political science, of Lester Ippel as assistant treasurer of Calvin College and Seminary, and of Lester De Koster as director of the library and as ecclesiastical archivist.

There have always been those in the church who maintain that Reformed Christians should not hold membership in non-Christian organizations. This sentiment came to expression when Synod discouraged membership in the Boy Scouts of America on the ground that its program was "based upon a philosophy evidently that of the Modernist." The church's ecumenical outreach was somewhat shortened when Synod decided to withdraw from the National Association of Evangelicals; but that withdrawal appeared to me as a justifiable retreat from an organization whose eccentric and truncated Christian witness was quite inconsistent with our own. Gratifying was Synod's decision to engage a black person for "Negro evangelism," as was its decision to appoint a committee to study the issues relating to creation and evolution. I was happy to learn that this committee would be working with a statement framed by the Reformed Ecumenical Synod of 1949, which read, in part: "The human form of the biblical revelation should prompt the church to proceed with caution and modesty, and to refrain from making various kinds of pronouncements in the field of natural science." In response to persistent calls from various sections of the church, Synod appointed a committee "to keep Synod informed with respect to the feasibility and need of Junior Colleges among our people."

When the time came to consider seminary matters, Synod took a number of significant steps. Aware of the fact that Prof. Volbeda would reach retirement age in 1952, and not being prepared at that juncture to name a successor, Synod asked him to stay on for an additional year, which he promptly agreed to do. President Schultze was about to leave his post at the college, and not wanting him to be without significant employment, Synod tendered him an indefinite appointment as Professor Extraordinary in the seminary. Schultze accepted the appointment and resumed his seminary teaching career in September 1951. The board's appointment of Dr. Cornelius Van Til as professor of systematic theology was confirmed by Synod, but Van Til was given a year's time to respond to the appointment. Upon the recommendation of the seminary faculty, however, he was asked to teach at the seminary during the second semester of the academic year 1951-1952. Because he was to be on sabbatical leave during that term, he readily consented to that.

Synod did not adopt the board's recommendation to terminate Prof. Hendriksen's association with the seminary; nor did it accord to him the indefinite appointment he would normally have received. In the light of all that was happening in the seminary, it reappointed him "for the next school year." Fraught with a significance not sensed at the time was Synod's appointment of a committee to inquire into the "seminary situation." The "seven" appointed to the committee — H. Baker, P. Van Tuinen, H. Kuiper, W. Vander Haak, D. Walters, J. Vander Ploeg, and G. Gritter — were instructed to make a thorough study of prevailing conditions, to consider in particular the issue of reappointments, and to report to and advise the Synod of 1952. Prof. Berkhof was appointed as advisor to the committee.

The whole of Friday, June 22, 1951, was taken up with a discussion of the two reports on worldly amusements. Later that evening, when the final vote was taken, it became apparent that the authors of the minority report had prevailed. What the Synod of 1928 had said or had not said was, of course, the issue. In its address to that issue, the Synod of 1951 declared that the 1928 resolutions (1) condemned worldliness; (2) laid down the principles that are to guide the Christian in his relation to the world; (3) did not pass judgment as to whether or not theater-attendance, card playing, and dancing are sinful in themselves; (4) did urgently warn against these activities, and did not condone participation in them; (5) left to the judgment of the consistory the determination of just what constitutes such "offensive conduct" as calls for admonitions and discipline; (6) required consistories to receive from those who wish to make profession of their faith "satisfaction as to their stand and conduct in the matter of worldly amusements"; and (7) did not prescribe a hard-and-fast rule as to how this inquiry is to be made.

There is a mixture of ingredients in these declarations, as in all declarations born out of compromise; but what finally emerged did reflect what the minority had been concerned to say, and when the debate finally ended, I took satisfaction in the conclusion we had reached. There were others, however — and these our friends and supporters — who were troubled by what was said in statement four: that the Synod of 1928 "did not condone" participation in the three so-called "worldly amusements." To them this seemed to say that 1928 did not "allow" such participation. In fact, the word "condone" was lifted out of the minority report, where it was employed to declare that Synod did not "sanction" or promote such participation. Synod, we had declared, did not forbid participation, but neither did it "license" it; it had made no pronouncement either way. Although one could wish that the word "condone" had not been used, it is in this context and with this meaning that the word must be understood by all who would make a fair and accurate assessment of Synod's action.

The Synod went into executive session on June 20 and again in the morning of June 21 to consider the appointment of a college president. It was toward noon on the second day that the vote was announced to the people waiting in the halls: William Spoelhof had been elected. The friends who were gathered around me expressed their disappointment with the outcome. Since losing is not what one exults in, I too was somewhat taken aback by the news that reached me. However, I did not become disconsolate. I received Synod's judgment with the respect that was its due and bore it, I dare say, with matching equanimity.

I sought Bill out and congratulated him, and he came to our house later that day, in part to express his own mixed feelings and in part to commiserate with a cheerful Hilda, who had hoped all along that her husband would not be drawn into this new venture. By the time we retired for the night, Hilda and I had not only completely acquiesced

309

in the verdict of an overruling Providence, but we were also buoyed up by a quieting sense of relief. We would not be in the spotlight, and I could stay in the classroom and be free of administrative duties bound to be onerous and taxing.

I was tempted later to inquire why things turned out as they did, but I soon recognized that every effort to do so would turn out to be an exercise in futility. There is no way to account for a public vote. In the last analysis, one can only register the fact that one candidate is preferred over another. And I should say here that Synod made an excellent choice: Bill Spoelhof was an excellent teacher, a respected scholar, and a sensitive and ingratiating person. He did not aspire to high office, shunned rivalry, and was a faithful friend who in his acceptance speech at Synod paid me compliments that went far beyond my deservings. It became abundantly clear as the years went by that the Synod of 1951 had not erred in its judgment. For twenty-five years President Spoelhof guided the college through fair weather and foul to heights of attainment and stature never before reached. I doubt that I could have matched his achievement.

In an earlier session of Synod three delegates were chosen to attend the Reformed Ecumenical Synod, which was scheduled to convene in Edinburgh, Scotland, in 1953. Our church was permitted to send one theological professor, one ordained clergyman, and one consistorial elder, and I was chosen as the elder delegate. There appeared in the June 1951 issue of *The Reformed Journal* my article on "The Majority Report Examined," and in the July issue I published a piece called "Synod on Worldly Amusements." It was also in July that I was interviewed on the radio by a Mr. Dunbar concerning the goals and strategies of Citizens Action, with which organization I continued to be associated. At about this same time the executive committee of the board felt that Prof. Volbeda needed help in conducting his seminary classes in practice preaching, and I was asked whether I would be willing to provide such help during next year. I respectfully declined, and learned later that Carl Kromminga would come to Volbeda's assistance.

Truce talks began in Korea on July 10 of that year, but fighting did not stop and the war proceeded on its course. After Synod adjourned there were not many weeks left in the summer recess period, but during this time I preached on eight successive Sundays in various local churches, and I also managed to deepen my understanding of the subjects I would again be teaching in the fall.

14

A YEAR OF TRANSITION
(1951-1952)

When the 1951-1952 academic year began in September 1951, our daughter Ellen had reached the age of six and was enrolled as a first grader in Baxter Christian School. Dick was not yet three, but he was a robust and active boy who liked to wrestle me to the ground when we played on the living room floor. Hilda ran the ship we sailed in, and clothed, fed, and educated the children and me. She also played hostess to numerous guests and visitors, participated in the life of the school, and continued to draw and adorn our walls with artistic productions done in oils and water colors.

The college opened its doors on September 11, 1951. On that day Bill Spoelhof was installed as Calvin's president at a convocation held in the nearby Protestant Reformed Church, and here he delivered his first formal address to the assembled college community. The faculty was augmented that year by the addition of Henry Ippel and Evan Runner, and now boasted 51 members. Along with that number were four full-time and nine part-time assistants, among them the venerable A. E. Broene, as well as the much younger seminarians John Stek and Bastiaan Van Elderen. There were 1,170 students enrolled in the various classes, and of these 466 were women, a number of whom were lodged in the three guild houses established on Franklin Street. The Board of Trustees ran the college and seminary on a budget of $557,000, and charged Christian Reformed students $115 a semester for tuition. The campus dormitory was now back in the hands of the men; the chapel exercises continued to be broadcast over WFUR radio; John Tuls came to the assistance of coach Chuck Bult by becoming coach of the freshmen basketball squad; and, in an accommodation to reality, the president was authorized to permit "controlled smoking" in the classroom building.

The seminary had enrolled 31 new students in September, and this brought the total of those registered to 116. The number of faculty members had increased to seven with the addition of Henry Schultze and Harry Boer. Harry, the incumbent of the seminary's new chair of missions, had been installed in office on August 23, 1951, in his home church in Holland, Michigan, and was now beginning his first year of teaching. In response to a request by the board, he was also coaching students in the use of conversational Dutch. Prof. Volbeda was in the last year of his incumbency and was being assisted part-time by Carl Kromminga, who came to the seminary twice a week from his church in Harderwyk, Michigan, in order to conduct a class in practice preaching. Professor Schultze had been at the Mayo Clinic for consultation and therapy during the summer and, though not robust, was now in fair health. He enjoyed full faculty status and shared with Dr. Hendriksen the responsibility of giving instruction in New Testament subjects. The condition of Dr. Bouma had not improved; he remained hospitalized in Pine Rest, and his classes in ethics and apologetics went untaught until the second semester, when Cornelius Van Til arrived to fill the gap.

The philosophy department in the college was now manned by four instructors, and was amply staffed, if not perhaps overstaffed. No one of us now taught more than twelve hours a semester, and our classes were no longer overcrowded. One of Evan Runner's offerings attracted no students, and to fulfill the 12-hour requirement he undertook to teach a course in Latin. My first impression of Runner was not as favorable as I had hoped it would be. To welcome him to the college, and to lay out to him what courses we would like him to teach, I visited him at his home in midsummer and was treated to a lengthy discourse on what constitutes a truly Calvinistic philosophy and how he, a junior associate fresh out of graduate school, was disposed to articulate it. I left wondering what sort of person this might be who at a first meeting would undertake with such freedom and animation to instruct me in philosophy, while

The Plato Club, 1951-52
Standing: John Rupke, Alvin Plantinga, Joel Nederhood,
Calvin Seerveld, Dewey Hoitenga, Wilbert Van Dyk, Johan Westra.
Seated: Jack Bolt, Lloyd Kamps, H. Stob, Frank Van Halsema,
Nicholas Wolterstorff

attending only minimally to the proposals I had made for his insinuation into our fellowship.

Having surrendered ancient philosophy to Runner, I was able that year to concentrate on the other subjects that had hitherto resided within my province. In the first semester I taught introduction to philosophy in two sections to 45 students and medieval philosophy in two sections to 39 students. I again took my place on the discipline committee and continued my association with the Plato Club. Constituting the membership of the club that year was a set of excellent students, many of whom later distinguished themselves in academia. The roster of truth seekers included Jack Bolt, Dewey Hoitenga, Lloyd Kamps, Joel Nederhood, Alvin Plantinga, John Rupke, Calvin Seerveld, Wilbert Van Dyk, Frank Van Halsema, Johan Westra, and Nick Wolterstorff. School activities were just getting underway in September when I preached in Lamont, in Cutlerville, and at Seymour and

Brother Tom

LaGrave churches in Grand Rapids. In that same month H. R. Niebuhr published his book *Christ and Culture,* and the United States concluded a treaty with Japan which formally ended both the state of war and the long-lasting occupation.

In October 1951, I addressed the Michigan Christian Fellowship in Ann Arbor on "Faith and Reason" and published an article in the *Reformed Journal* on "Principle and Practice." The college benefited in October from two generous bequests: the Calvin Foundation set aside $5,000 to finance the production of a "Calvin Report"; and Mr. L. L. Cayvan bequeathed to the school a precious set of 8,000 musical recordings. The faculty promised to cooperate fully in the preparation of the "Report," and the executive committee of the board allocated

314

$4,000 to house and service the Cayvan collection. It was also in October that the executive committee accepted an offer from Owen-Ames-Kimball to construct the long-projected student commons at a cost of $397,000.

H. J. Kuiper published in the October 19 *Banner* an editorial entitled "Some Ideas on the Race Question." In it he suggested that there might be the same inequality of gifts and talents between races that exists between individuals, and he argued that black converts are better assembled in a racially segregated chapel than in an integrated church. This evoked a critical response from Harry Boer, and I also wrote a piece in which I rejected the thesis of indigenous racial inequality and hailed the day in which the church would embrace into its ranks, and on every level, people of every tribe and color. In subsequent issues of *The Banner*, Kuiper also took issue with some statements in the race resolutions adopted by the Young Calvinist Federation at its 1950 convention. Satisfied that we had spoken appropriately and well in these resolutions, I made no response to the editor's comments.

October also brought tragedy and sorrow into our lives. My brother Tom had been recovering in the hospital from a major operation when a vagrant blood clot arrested the flow of his life and caused his death. He was only 59 years old when he died on October 14, 1951, and we all felt that he was too young and too indispensable to be so suddenly taken from us. Tom was the third oldest child of our parents, but in all our affairs he enjoyed the primacy. It was to him that the family looked for help and counsel whenever the need arose, and it was from his resourcefulness and willingness to serve that the broader community regularly profited. Tom had earlier been president of the highly influential South Water Market Credit Association, and was at the time of his death the license officer for the town of Cicero and president of the Berwyn-Cicero Real Estate Board. But most of his energy throughout his life had been spent in kingdom causes. A sometime elder in the church, he was an avid supporter of Christian missions; he was for many years a director of Chicago's Helping Hand Mission and a board member of the Chicago Tract Society. His heart, however, was in Christian education. He served on the board of the Chicago Christian High School and on the executive committee of the National Association of Christian Schools. The local Timothy school was the focus of his interest: for 25 years he was treasurer and was twice the president of its board. To all of these institutions and agencies he not only gave unstintingly of his time but also of his goods. Tom was withal a devoted husband, father, son, and brother whose wisdom, love, and charity we cherished and now sorely missed. The funeral service was held in the First Christian Reformed Church of Cicero on October 17; the burial took place in Mount Auburn cemetery, where a stone slab marks his grave.

In November 1951, I spoke on "Christian Ethics and Political Action" at the college during Education Week. In December the college mourned the death of John Hekman and gratefully acknowledged in a public statement his life-long efforts in behalf of Calvin. Hilda and I were also saddened by John Hekman's death: it was he who often entertained us at his hotel when he came to New York on business during the war years; and during the last three years of his life I had the privilege of serving with him on the consistory of Calvin Church. John and Cora were considerably older than we, but in the course of the years we came to be good friends, and we frequently assembled in each other's houses for food and fellowship. The death of this good man created a vacuum in the life of the Christian community and also in that of the entire city.

On January 1, 1952, my term of office as elder expired and I was released from my consistorial duties. Although I was never again to serve the church as an elder, I was happy to have had that one opportunity to do so, and I dare think that the experience I acquired in office was constructive. On January 11 there took place on campus what was, I believe, the first "homecoming" reception for the alumni; the day of celebration featured a basketball game between the varsity squads of Calvin and Hope colleges.

The Board of Trustees met in semiannual session in February 1952 and made a number of decisions affecting the seminary, the nature and bearing of which I shall presently indicate. Affecting the college was the board's decision to appoint Calvin Andre as instructor in physics, Arthur Otten as instructor in French, and John De Beer, the incumbent associate professor of education, as dean of students. The complaint of the "sacred seven" about the lack of Christian emphasis in the teaching of some professors was again before the board, as were complaints about the board's decision to award the student commons contract to a builder who conducted a closed shop with AFL labor. The college was at that time hurting for lack of adequate facilities, but there was as yet no thought of moving to a larger campus; there was only a concern to enlarge and supplement what the existing grounds contained. At this meeting the board had before it a plan developed by the long-range planning committee to erect one or two new dormitories on the recently acquired college land and to add two wings to the standing Administration Building. No action was taken on the committee's proposal, but the board did declare that it deserved earnest consideration.

In February 1952 the second semester was already underway, and I was teaching introduction to philosophy to 18 students, medieval philosophy to 25 students, and a seminar on Thomas Aquinas to 11 students. I preached in February at Fuller, at LaGrave, and in Kelloggsville, and published in the *Journal* an article on "Movies, Television, and the Christian." It was also in February that I appeared on radio for the third time as the spokesman for Citizens Action. In a half-hour broadcast I took issue with former Mayor George Welsh, who in the February primary was running for office in opposition to the incumbents we supported. My task was made more difficult by the fact that Welsh had appeared on radio a few days earlier to proclaim his conversion to a new way of life. He had passed, he said, through the open door of John 10:9 into the fold of Christ, where peace is found, and comfort, and eternal life. In my speech I had to accommodate myself to this most laudable development, but I had also to consider what Welsh had said in the *Shopping News,* which he edited. In an article he wrote within days of his conversion speech, he made statements that were without parallel for error, misrepresentation, and truculence. He said that the incumbent commissioners were puppets, the willing, effective, and therefore dangerous instruments of outside influence; that they had given the city the most incompetent and extravagant administration in the history of Grand Rapids; and that Citizens Action, which sponsored their candidacy, was a ruthless machine conceived in hysteria and born in frenzy. To these and other charges I responded with facts and figures, and in the election that followed, Mayor Goebel and Commissioners Gritter and De Korne were enthusiastically returned to office.

In March the executive committee gave renewed attention to the complaint of the "Sacred Seven," but was unable to give them satisfaction. It was also in March that Cal Bulthuis assumed the part-time position of instructor in English at the college. On April 16, 1952,

Her Majesty Queen Juliana of The Netherlands and His Royal Highness Prince Bernhard paid a visit to the Calvin campus. As I recall, a tree was planted in honor of the royal couple, and with the queen's consent an existing college chair was renamed the Queen Juliana Chair of Dutch Language and Literature. At a gala reception held in the Pantlind Hotel that evening Hilda and I were among the many invited guests.

On April 21 the college faculty had an informal discussion with Prof. G. C. Berkouwer, who had been brought to this country from The Netherlands by the Calvin Foundation for the purpose of presenting a series of lectures in the city and across the nation. I would see Dr. Berkouwer often during his stay, and he was a guest in our house on more than one occasion. It was in April, too, that General Mark Clark replaced Ridgway as Commander of the U.N. forces in Korea; and that Chuck Bult, Calvin's basketball coach, declared his intention to leave the college and accept a position with the Hekman Biscuit Company.

Prof. Cornelius Van Til had taught courses in ethics and apologetics at the seminary during the second semester of that year, and in the month of May he engaged Dr. William Masselink in a debate about "Common Grace." The debate was held in the seminary chapel before a full house. I judged that Masselink ably defended the view advanced by Kuyper, Bavinck, and Hepp; but Van Til found the position of these stalwarts untenable and averred that, if it prevailed, one might as well blow up the science building with an atom bomb. This injudicious and provocative remark did not sit well with many of us, but one could hear it echoed in following days by certain partisans who tended to think that truth was held in custody by the orthodox at Westminster Seminary. Dr. Van Til had been tendered an appointment to the chair of systematic theology at Calvin Seminary by the Synod of 1951, but was given a year to ponder the appointment and render a decision. For reasons best known to himself, he now declined the appointment and returned to his post in Philadelphia.

The college, meanwhile, continued to have its detractors. Although a full year had gone by since they had made their initial move, the "Sacred Seven" were still in the lists with their complaints. The executive committee had several times sought to reassure them, but they remained unwilling to withdraw their charges, and the committee finally decided to drop the matter and take no action regarding either the complainants or the accused professors. It was at this juncture that H. J. Kuiper joined in the chorus. In late May 1952 he drew up a petition to Synod and sent copies of it to friends around the country who were asked both to sign it and to secure additional signatures; the petition was eventually signed by 147 concerned citizens.

"It is no longer a secret," the petition said, "that some of the former pre-seminary students, now in the seminary, have expressed their grievances about the instruction in the college in documented form." The petition went on to say, "It is an open secret that some of the college professors themselves are convinced that there is a marked difference of approach and emphasis between them and the other professors. . . . There is an emphasis in the English department which is unwholesome and deleterious. It seems that form is stressed rather than content. The reading and study of salacious novels is condoned. . . . Professors give instruction which is more or less color-less and neutral. . . . They stress common grace far more than the antithesis. . . . There is no pronounced spiritual atmosphere in our college." On the basis of these and similar observations, the petitioners asked Synod to "purify our college, improve its spiritual tone, remove teachers who are confused as to our Reformed faith, and make sure that in the future no teachers are appointed unless they are enthusiastic for our Reformed outlook on life."

Although not all members of the faculty were equally adept at integrating faith and learning, all were committed to the task, and none were chargeable with the faults Kuiper attributed to the group. Indeed, at the very time the petition was in circulation, the faculty presented to the Board of Trustees a statement assuring it that all members of the college staff embraced the aims set forth in the college catalogue and were then, as in the past, determined to be guided in their teaching by the presuppositions of the Christian faith. Signed by every member of the faculty, the statement fulfilled the board's desire and served to allay the suspicions generated among the people by the ill-informed and prejudicial attack launched by Kuiper and his associates.

When the Board of Trustees met in May 1952, it added a number of persons to the college teaching staff. Appointed for varying terms and at various levels were George Harper in English, Ann Janssen in speech, Robert Otten in Latin and Greek, and David Tuuk in physical education. Appointed to begin service in September 1953 were Walter

Lagerwey in Dutch and Barney Steen in physical education (Steen would assume the coaching position vacated by Bult). A letter from Gerald Nyenhuis severely criticizing the instruction he received at the college was read at the board meeting, and also the document of the "Seven"; but in view of the faculty's statement and in the light of its own investigation, the Board dismissed the complaints as unfounded and moved on to more important business. Recognition was given at this meeting to the fact that Harry Dekker had completed thirty years of distinguished service in the college and that Lambert Flokstra and Edwin Monsma had served with comparable distinction for twenty-five years. The college announced that it would grant diplomas to 214 graduates that year and that 26 of these would enter the seminary in September 1952.

*   *   *   *   *

The Board of Trustees is the agency authorized to exercise jurisdiction over the college *and* the seminary, but during 1952 its governance of the latter was curtailed by the presence on campus of a synodically appointed "investigating committee" charged with inquiring into the "seminary situation." The findings of this committee and the recommendations it would make to Synod were to be reported to the board, but the findings were not subject to the board's review, nor the recommendations to its endorsement. Consequently, it was the committee rather than the board that tended to move toward center stage. The board did receive some correspondence and some oral testimony bearing on the "situation" from members of the seminary faculty, but the intelligence thus gathered was commonly left unappraised and referred for judgment to the committee. Meanwhile, the board was not deprived of all its competencies. It remained free to supervise the normal activities of the staff; it was free to license students, declare vacancies, make nominations, and the like. But under the circumstances, it could hardly play its usual commanding role in regard to the tenure of professors. This had its consequences, for the solution proposed and finally adopted for the release of tension within the seminary impinged directly on tenure: it consisted in effecting nothing less than the dismissal of four professors and the virtual dissolution of the faculty.

What had originally created a worrisome "situation" in the seminary was a series of intrafaculty disputes about policies, procedures, and

320

management. Disputes of this sort continued to occur, but they took place during the course of that year against the backdrop of a larger issue — the issue of fidelity to Scripture and the creeds. It was suggested that there were in the student body those who were connected but loosely to the Reformed tradition, that these erring students enjoyed the favor and support of a minority in the faculty, and that this was the true cause of dissension within the seminary. Prof. Hendriksen sought to give some credence to this view of things in June 1951, when he was up for reappointment. The students had complained about the quality of his teaching, and the board had recommended that on account of incompetence he not be reappointed; but he rose to his own defense by declaring at Synod that "there are questions of a more fundamental character involved in the matter of my reappointment: for example . . . shall the aggressive presentation of the infallible Word prevail at our Seminary or shall we begin to yield little by little to those who oppose this doctrine?" In a petition submitted in support of Hendriksen, Rev. A. A. Koning echoed this sentiment when he declared that "the question at stake is essentially the question of accepting revelation as revelation." Then Prof. Wyngaarden arose at Synod to say that at the bottom of the whole protest against Dr. Hendriksen was the spirit of students who knew a good deal more about modern theology than about Reformed theology and who were more interested in liberal and Barthian writings than in those of the Reformers.

Against this backdrop occurred an incident that became the centerpiece of that year's controversy. In October 1951, senior seminarian Raymond Opperwall preached a sermon in Eastern Avenue Christian Reformed Church in which he considered the fact that God had answered Hezekiah's prayer for the extension of a life destined for imminent extinction. To Opperwall this seemed to indicate quite clearly that God could change his mind and revoke a plan of action he had previously adopted. The Eastern Avenue consistory took exception to this thesis: it judged that Opperwall had lost sight of God's immutability, and it lodged a complaint against him with the seminary faculty. The faculty had now to adjudicate the case and determine whether Opperwall was guilty of doctrinal defection or had done no more than replace the staticism of Greek ontology with a slice of biblical historicism.

The heresy charges against Opperwall were received by the faculty on October 11, 1951, and in considering them, the faculty split in two: on the one side were the dominant "Four" — Volbeda, Wyngaarden, Hendriksen, and Rutgers — and on the other were Stob, Boer, and, to an extent, the reserved and detached Henry Schultze. Although the two sides were differently disposed toward Opperwall, the disputes that ensued were less about doctrine than about procedure. Having as early as May 1950 expressed misgivings about the "soundness" of Opperwall, the "Four" were disposed to lend credence to the charges filed by the Eastern Avenue consistory and indisposed to examine those charges in the light of Opperwall's rejoinder and in the face of relevant evidence. Stob and Boer had in many meetings urged the faculty to adjudicate the case in hand; but to the growing chagrin of those two men, the "Four" dallied and repeatedly declined to make an explicit pronouncement. By a majority vote, afterward rescinded, the faculty once decided to refer the whole matter back to the consistory for "action." At another time it sent a batch of undigested materials to the board for possible assessment. For this action the faculty was rebuked by the investigating committee, which in February of 1952 declared that "the faculty should adjudicate the Eastern Avenue complaint and not attempt to divest itself of this obligation by turning over the accumulated data to the Board of Trustees."

Having as yet formed no judgment concerning Opperwall's guilt or innocence in the Eastern Avenue case, the faculty met again on November 30, 1951, and witnessed an explosion. At that meeting the chair entertained a motion made by Wyngaarden and seconded by Hendriksen: that "the faculty recommend to the Board that Mr. Opperwall's license be taken away and that his status as a regular student at Calvin Seminary cease." The boldness and insensitivity of this move astounded Stob and Boer, but the grounds adduced in support of it evoked their greater consternation. Offered in support of the motion was the fact that at the end of Mr. Opperwall's junior year the faculty had not recommended him for licensure; that the Eastern Avenue consistory had voted unanimously to file charges against him; and that a certain Rev. Venema experienced "uneasiness" upon hearing an earlier sermon by Opperwall. The opposition pointed out that the faculty's action in May 1950 had not been endorsed by Professors Bouma and Stob nor heeded by the board which, upon examination, had promptly licensed the harried junior student. They further pointed out that charges are not grounds for punitive action but occasions for judicial assessment, and that in this instance no assessment had been made. The opposition finally pointed out that a young man's status and prospects are not to be jeopardized by the "impressions" received by a casual listener and reported after the lapse of several months. With these objections to the motion brought forward, the motion still hung in the air and was about to be voted on when Boer moved that the meeting be adjourned — and that without prayer. When this seconded motion was not entertained by the chair, a vexed and angry Harry Boer left the meeting and was followed by George Stob. The outrageous motion which precipitated their exit was withdrawn after Boer and Stob departed, but their unlicensed departure, though apologized for, counted heavily against them in the investigating committee's final evaluation of the role they had played in the creation of a "seminary situation."

With the advent of 1952, the procedural issues that had hitherto occupied the faculty's attention receded into the background and the doctrinal issue came to the fore. On January 18, 1952, after several months of indecisive maneuvering, without regard to the evidence and against the protest of the minority, the majority of the faculty proclaimed that "there is reasonable doubt as to Mr. Opperwall's soundness in the Reformed faith," and so it informed the board. The investigating committee was even more outspoken: it judged that statements in Mr. Opperwall's sermon were "in conflict with the Reformed faith" and asserted that "the position of Mr. Opperwall violates the express revelation of God which declares that God is immutable." George Stob and Harry Boer did not agree with this verdict; they defended Opperwall to the end and were vindicated in their judgment when the Synod of 1952 admitted Opperwall to candidacy by a vote of 74 to 2. Synod did this after examining him in a special session on the exact point in question. A few months later, Opperwall was unanimously admitted to the "ministry of the word and sacraments" by the Classis of Wisconsin.

However, George Stob and Harry Boer, whose competence in teaching was never called into question and whose conduct throughout was governed by a desire to see justice done, did not escape unscathed from the proceedings recorded here. They were accused of failure to honor the established canons of faith and of tolerating doctrinal divergences. Boer was censured by the investigat-

ing committee for his "failure to acknowledge the errors in the Opperwall sermon" and for his "refusal to uphold the teaching of Scripture." Stob was also censured by the committee: he was charged with
"failure to champion the cause of the Reformed faith in conjunction
with other faculty members when the situation demanded precisely
that."

Similar judgments about these two professors were made by others
after H. J. Kuiper circulated his slanderous petition to Synod. Kuiper
professed to be alarmed about "the doctrinal uncertainty and confusion of some of our Seminary students" and said that "his concern
was intensified by the fact that two of the Seminary professors, instead
of recognizing the seriousness of the complaint (against Opperwall),
have done all in their power to discredit and suppress it." He thereupon begged Synod "to investigate why two of the Seminary professors have minimized the doctrinal confession in the minds of some of
the Seminary students and why they have sought to suppress the
charges by a Grand Rapids consistory against one of them; also to
inquire carefully concerning their attitude toward the deviating views
of some of the students." Kuiper expressed those sentiments in late
May 1952, just when the investigating committee was declaring that
it "had failed, after rather thorough investigation, to discover any
evidences that there are Barthian leanings or sympathies among the
students," and just before the 1952 Synod met. That Synod declared
Opperwall a candidate, approved of two other unrecommended
seniors, and laid Kuiper's petition aside for being out of order — and
fractious as well.

The executive committee of the board had been kept up to date of
most of the things happening in the seminary. On December 13, 1951,
it received letters from George Stob and Harry Boer and also a statement
from the investigating committee concerning the controversy that
erupted on November 30. On January 10, 1952, it was informed that
in the estimation of the investigating committee the seminary faculty was
stalling on the Opperwall case; on that same day, Stob and Boer appeared
in person before the executive committee and indicated that the situation
in the seminary was becoming increasingly intolerable. They even suggested that, since there were two parties in the seminary, representatives
of both parties — and not Volbeda alone — should sit in on the meetings of the board and its executive committee. The committee, quite
wisely, did not follow that suggestion. As for Opperwall, the committee

advised Prof. Volbeda not to book any preaching engagements for him while the charges against him were under consideration. Meanwhile, support for Opperwall was growing in the student body: a letter expressing confidence in him was signed by 33 of his fellow classmates and would presently be submitted to the board.

* * * * *

The Board of Trustees met in mid-February 1952 and received from the investigating committee a report the contents of which formed a considerable part of its agenda. The intrafaculty debate about the wisdom of implementing a Th.D. program had by this time retreated behind other more pressing concerns, and the investigating committee now recommended that, owing to a deficiency in faculty personnel, the whole matter be held in abeyance. The board concurred.

A report about Prof. Rutgers was filed: though it did not have the concurrence of Prof. Berkhof, advisor to the investigating committee, it was signed by all the members of that committee, and it declared that Rutgers "does not evidence the quality and degree of scholarship and pedagogical competence for the training and guidance of seminary students." The committee recommended that he not be reappointed. A motion to adopt the committee's recommendation failed, and the board finally agreed to say no more than that "it does not feel free to recommend Professor Rutgers for an indefinite appointment."

The investigating committee could not at first reach an agreement about Prof. Hendriksen, who had been accorded a one year's extension on his lapsed tenure at the 1951 Synod. A majority wished to have him reappointed for a two-year period, and a minority held that he should not be reappointed at all. The committee finally settled on a compromise, recommending that because Hendriksen "has not given sufficient evidence that he possesses the scholarly spirit requisite for work of seminary caliber" and because "he has given evidence of personality weaknesses which create doubt as to whether his personality is such as to exert the proper influence in the Seminary," he not receive an indefinite appointment. The board thereupon decided to inform Synod that it was withdrawing its 1951 recommendation that Hendriksen not be reappointed, and that it was now prepared to say only that "it does not feel free to recommend Professor Hendriksen for an indefinite appointment."

The investigating committee had not come to a final judgment about Professors Stob and Boer at that point. However, it was prepared to say that it had "come to hold certain serious misgivings with respect to them." It felt that "Professors Stob and Boer have, by reason of certain readily observable weaknesses, contributed appreciably to the aggravation of faculty tensions," and declared that "unless through frank consultation with them, and through diligent efforts on their part, definite improvement becomes evident, their tenure must be considered insecure." The board received this as information and took no further action.

In commenting on intrafaculty relations, the investigating committee referred to the faculty altercation that took place on November 30, 1951. It judged that Professors Boer and Stob had not been justified in leaving the meeting, but it also acknowledged that an ill-considered proposal had aroused their ire. The committee exempted no one from blame when it characterized faculty meetings as beset by "barriers which obstruct the free flow of discussion" and declared that "serious tensions and frequent clashes hinder the efficient execution of faculty business." "Faculty deliberations," it said, "are not always characterized by mutual confidence"; there is not that "frank interchange which is required for arriving at a corporate judgment." On the basis of these observations, the committee made a radical proposal to the board. It recommended that, "in view of the faculty's inability to administer its affairs properly," a committee be appointed to "function in cooperation with the President of the Seminary in the administration of faculty affairs." Heeding that advice, the board decided: "(1) that, during the emergency, the administration of faculty affairs shall be taken out of the hands of the faculty; (2) that the President, Secretary, and Vice President of the Board shall act as a committee for the administration of faculty affairs, in consultation with the Seminary President; (3) that during this time no faculty meetings shall be held except with the consent of, in the presence of, and under the direction of said committee; and (4) that during this emergency arrangement all faculty decisions shall be advisory in character."

The adoption of these revolutionary measures did not please President Volbeda, nor the three others who stood at his side. On March 26, 1952, the "Four" addressed to the investigating committee and the board a letter in which they objected not so much to the new arrangement as to the reason given for its adoption. They asked, "Why do you speak of 'the faculty's inability'?" "You have," they said, "leveled a charge against the entire faculty, particularly the officers. It is our conviction that the blame should have been placed where it properly belongs; namely, with two of the faculty members, Professors Stob and Boer. . . . Why should all be penalized when two members make themselves guilty of reprehensible conduct? . . . These two professors have consistently and most vigorously defended the students [whose licenses were suspended]. In the process of this defense they have made themselves guilty again and again of unparliamentary and rude behavior." This bold charge, reminiscent of a similar charge made earlier against Prof. Bouma, was without foundation in fact and can only be interpreted as slanderous. Incredibly, the "Four" went on to suggest that "the entire matter could have been settled by the withdrawal of their [Boer's and Stob's] right to attend faculty meetings." But this was not all. The "Four" sent copies of this letter to the stated clerks of every classis in the church.

For this propagandistic ploy and breach of good order they were promptly reprimanded by both board and committee. In a letter dated April 14, 1952, the Investigating Committee told the "Four" that it considered this action both out of order and prejudicial. "Your letter," it said, "jeopardizes a fair and just appraisal of the Seminary Situation on the part of the church. . . . It is not correct to assume that the recommendation of the Investigating Committee re the suspension of preaching license of some of the Senior students constitutes a vindication of the action of the majority of the faculty. . . . Nor is it correct to anticipate the judgment of the committee with respect to the distribution of responsibility for 'the faculty's inability to administer its affairs properly. . . .' Hence our urgent request that you recall your communication from the Stated Clerks."

The investigating committee also dispatched letters to the stated clerks: the secretary who signed the letters declared, "I have been instructed to advise you that consideration of this material by the Classis would be highly improper, since the investigation has not been completed. The communication of these four professors is not a full presentation of the facts, and a consideration of the matter contained therein by the Classes would jeopardize a fair and just appraisal of the Seminary Situation."

The midyear sessions of the Board of Trustees ended on February

20, 1952. Before it adjourned, the board suspended the licenses of three senior seminarians whose doctrinal soundness was called into question by the investigating committee; it began and then abandoned an effort to prepare a nomination for the chair of practical theology; and it instructed the executive committee to inquire once again into the condition of Prof. Bouma. In the interim between February and May, the executive committee learned that Dr. Volbeda had fallen ill, had not been able to meet his classes since April, and had decided not to stay on for another year, as he had planned, but to go into immediate retirement. The committee also consulted Dr. Mulder and his associates at Pine Rest and learned to its regret that Prof. Bouma's condition had not improved, and that in the opinion of his physicians he would not be able to assume his teaching duties at any time soon.

The investigating committee continued to inquire into the "seminary situation," fixing its attention on some actions of the "Four" to which Stob and Boer had raised objections. Prof. Wyngaarden was found to have erred on at least six counts: among other things, he had, as registrar, considered the grades Stob gave to his students in church history to be below the norm, and, before the grades were processed or officially reported, he leaked them to selected students and encouraged them to complain. For this he was severely reprimanded by the committee. But particularly offensive was Wyngaarden's reaction to a speech George Stob had given. The following is Harry Boer's account of what took place: "In September of 1951 Stob delivered a welcoming speech to the entering Juniors in which he urged the importance of a community of thought among those preparing for ministry in the church. On February 8, 1952 — five months later — Dr. Wyngaarden made a motion in the faculty charging that in that speech Professor Stob proposed that we fellowship with liberals. The motion was supported by Dr. Rutgers and was entertained by the President. I remonstrated, but to no avail. The motion was passed and was placed on the books. I was amazed that Dr. Volbeda entertained this slanderous motion. In the whole period of five months between the time of Professor Stob's speech and this faculty action, not one faculty member had talked to Professor Stob about his speech, much less raised questions or expressed criticism concerning it. Dr. Wyngaarden was later forced by the investigating committee to repudiate this motion in the severest of the committee's denunciations of Dr. Wyngaarden's actions." The truth of this account is reflected in the committee's report, which says, among other things, that "Dr. Wyngaarden's charge is not sustained by the manuscript of the address."

Professors Wyngaarden, Hendriksen, and Rutgers were also interviewed as a group. The three acknowledged that, as Stob and Boer had contended, "student visiting might have been more thorough"; that "the Minutes were not written as carefully as they might have been"; and that "with respect to the awarding of a prize, greater discretion should have been exercised by one of us." Beyond this they made no concessions, which led the committee to declare: "The three failed to explain satisfactorily a number of other matters which in the Committee's view placed them in an unfavorable light." The three nevertheless had the temerity to offer counsel. Confident that, in contrast to a number of erring students and to two compromising members of the faculty, they stood firmly with the president for orthodoxy, truth, and righteousness, they said to the committee: "It is our conviction that the fundamental doctrinal issue should be thoroughly examined, with respect to both college and seminary."

* * * * *

The Board of Trustees met again in May 1952, and the Investigating Committee submitted to it a final, but divided, report on Professors Stob and Boer. The majority of the committee members had come to believe that George Stob was to a considerable extent responsible for the creation of a "seminary situation." They declared that "Professor G. Stob has been a great contributing factor in bringing about a condition which is most deplorable." They admitted that "Professor Stob has certain excellent qualities which could make him a real asset in our Seminary." They acknowledged that "he has pedagogical ability, an alert mind, and a facile pen"; but — in contrast to what I knew of him — they judged that "Professor G. Stob's personality is such that it generates an atmosphere of tension and creates a definite barrier to the efficient operation of the faculty in the administration of its affairs." They held that Stob was impulsive, arrogant, prejudiced, and judgmental; that he was overly concerned about technicalities; and, above all, that he "failed (in the Opperwall case) to champion the cause of the Reformed faith when he really had no alternative." Having made this assessment and having come to believe

329

that "drastic action is imperative," the majority recommended that "Professor G. Stob's tenure of office be terminated at the close of this school year."

A minority of two dissented. "It is our conviction," they said, "that the recommendation of the majority is premature and that the grounds adduced do not sustain the drastic action proposed." Their defense of Stob was, however, weak and vacillating and hardly calculated to persuade a person otherwise disposed. Nevertheless, it was strong enough to give the board pause. Having received the two reports, the board decided "to receive as information the judgments and advice of the Investigating Committee re tenure of Prof. G. Stob, and to take no further action at this time."

The majority in the investigating committee judged that Harry Boer, too, was in great part responsible for creating unrest and dissension in the seminary. "The talents which Prof. Boer has revealed have not gone unappreciated," they said, but they found his "personality" offensive. They held him to be opinionated, rash, impetuous, accusatory, and lacking in self-control — a judgment that misinterpreted and masked his unrelenting "zeal" for justice and good order. What really did Boer in, however, was his steadfast defense of Opperwall. "We are alarmed," said the committee, "by a development of recent date which confirms our opinion that Professor Boer's nature is such that he will adamantly retain a position which he has previously taken even when that position places him in a poor light as a theological professor who is called upon to champion the Reformed faith and to enlighten students who are theologically confused. Ever since the Eastern Avenue protest was brought to the attention of the faculty, Prof. Boer has consistently championed the cause of Mr. Opperwall and . . . in his document of April 19, 1952 . . . he has again without qualification defended Mr. Opperwall."

I hazard the opinion that what was really alarming in this situation was not Boer's steadfast defense of an accused student but the committee's failure to recognize that God's immutability is not to be construed in static terms but in terms of an accommodating mobility that is a feature of all God's engagements with a world in process. However that may be, the majority recommended, on the basis of Boer's "personality" and on his "failure to acknowledge Opperwall's error," that "Professor H. Boer's tenure of office be terminated at the close of the school year." As in the case of George Stob, two members of the committee registered their dissent from this recommendation. The Board of Trustees received the two reports as information and took no further action.

Having been informed that the investigating committee was recommending to Synod the untimely dismissal of Professors Stob and Boer, the Board of Trustees reconsidered its previous decisions regarding Professors Hendriksen and Rutgers. It had earlier dared to say only that those professors should not receive an indefinite appointment; it now decided to recommend to Synod that the tenure of both be terminated. Approved in the face of slight opposition was the resolution: "It is the judgment of the Board that Dr. W. Rutgers . . . and Dr. W. Hendriksen . . . should not be reappointed." It was not known how Synod would respond to these multiple recommendations, but should all of them be adopted, the faculty of the seminary would be depleted, and professors would have to be chosen to fill the vacancies created.

Being charged with presenting slates of candidates for existing vacancies, the board did not know quite how to proceed with respect to the chairs that were under siege but still occupied by Hendriksen, Rutgers, Stob, and Boer. Because it had taken no action respecting the tenure of Stob and Boer, the board made no suggestion regarding their replacement. It felt obliged, however, to prepare nominations for the tenuous positions still occupied by Hendriksen and Rutgers. For the chair of New Testament the Board nominated Herman Ridderbos, Ned Stonehouse, and John Weidenaar; for the chair of systematic theology it nominated G. C. Berkouwer, Herman Kuiper, and Alexander De Jong. By the nature of the case, these nominations, prepared for a contingency, were held in reserve: the names of the nominees were not published in the papers, and they would be presented to Synod only if the situation warranted it.

Things proceeded differently when it came to the consideration of possible replacements for Professors Volbeda and Bouma. The chair of practical theology was declared vacant in view of Dr. Volbeda's impending retirement, and the chair of ethics and apologetics became vacant when, "in view of the medical opinion expressed, the board decided to recommend to Synod that Professor Bouma be emeritated." The board now took steps to fill these officially established vacancies: it nominated Carl Kromminga for the chair of practical theology, and nominated Fred Klooster and me for the chair of ethics

331

and apologetics. These nominations *were* published in the church papers before Synod met, and Synod's consideration of them was unrelated to the actions it took relative to the incumbent professors under indictment.

*   *   *   *   *

The Synod of the Christian Reformed Church met in the Calvin College auditorium from June 11 to June 25, 1952, and was chaired by Rev. Herman Bel, who was assisted on the podium by William Kok, Peter Holwerda, and Peter Van Tuinen. It was ironic that the four professors whose fate hung in the balance sat as advisors to Synod and helped shape the reports of the many committees that served the assembly with advice. Synod examined the seminary graduates who were standing for candidacy and found them qualified. Among them were Raymond Opperwall and Ralph Baker, who had failed to obtain the recommendation of the faculty; Ed Walhout was another student whose orthodoxy had been called into question, but he had elected to go into high school teaching and thus was not required to undergo examination. Others — not of that graduating class — were also declared ministerial candidates: among them were Robert Sutton and Eugene Callender, both of whom had studied at Westminster; Marten Woudstra, a member of the Free Reformed Church, was granted a preaching license for one year, a license that would be renewed only if he became a member of the Christian Reformed Church.

As usual, Synod made several appointments. Those nominated for positions in the college were approved. John Hamersma was re-elected to membership on the Board of Trustees, and Henry Evenhouse was made director of missions. In matters of substance, Synod declared that an unbiblically divorced person who remarries is guilty of engaging in continual adultery. But apparently unsure of itself, Synod at the same time appointed a committee to inquire into the soundness of that position. Respecting education, Synod judged that the establishment of a Reformed University in America was at this stage not feasible, but it heartily endorsed a financial campaign to raise $2 million for college expansion.

It was, of course, the "seminary situation" on which the attention of Synod was chiefly focussed. Before it got into the center of that sad business, Synod granted honorable emeritation to Professors

Volbeda and Bouma; disapproved of the action of the "Four" in sending copies of their protest to the stated clerks of the classis; rebuked H. J. Kuiper and his associates for circulating petitions in violation of good order; and decided that "the taking of steps toward the awarding of the Th.D. degree shall be held in abeyance for the present." In order to consider the reports presented by the investigating committee and the Board of Trustees, Synod appointed a special advisory committee that operated without the assistance of a faculty advisor. On the advice of this committee, Synod adopted a set of rules in accordance with which "the trial" would be conducted. "All professors," it said, "shall be permitted to remain during consideration of all matters in order that they may (1) state their case, (2) raise questions as to fact, (3) criticize reports and recommendations, and (4) answer all questions put to them; but final discussion and decision shall take place in their absence."

I do not know — or do not recall — whether or to what extent the professors seized the opportunity to testify in their own defense; but it is a matter of record that Synod discussed the reports bearing on the case for the better part of three whole days. From its advisory committee the Synod received the following recommendations: "That Dr. Rutgers and Dr. Hendriksen be not reappointed; that Professor Stob's and Professor Boer's tenure of office be terminated; and that Professor Wyngaarden be dismissed." On the afternoon of Wednesday, June 25, 1952, Synod went into executive session and, after some discussion, proceeded to vote. The result of the balloting was devastating: Hendriksen, Rutgers, Stob, and Boer were cast out, and Wyngaarden was retained in office by a small margin.

George Stob and Harry Boer were most gracious in defeat: a few hours after they were ousted, they sent letters to Synod submitting to its verdict and wishing it Godspeed in its efforts to restore the seminary to health and fruitfulness. Professors Schultze and Wyngaarden were, at this juncture, the only professors left in a shattered faculty, and Wyngaarden went home burdened with a synodical admonition.

Synod had before it nominations for the positions vacated by Volbeda and Bouma, and it had during the course of its meetings given some attention to possible replacements for the men just released. It now proceeded to form a new faculty. Exercising extreme caution, it decided to make — with one exception — only one-year interim appointments. The one exception was Dr. G. C. Berkouwer, who was given an indefinite appointment as professor of systematic theology. Ned Stonehouse was appointed to the chair of New Testament; the recently retired R. B. Kuiper to the chair of practical theology; John Kromminga to the chair of church history; and myself to the chair of ethics and apologetics. The chair of missions was left vacant. With this accomplished, the executive committee of the Board of Trustees was instructed to name from among those chosen a seminary president for the coming year; and it was also asked to inquire whether Cornelius Van Til would be willing to teach parttime during the coming year in the area of ethics and apologetics, the department assigned to me.

The Synod was now finished with its work, but before it adjourned, it prepared an "announcement" for publication in the church papers: in it Synod told the people that there had existed in the seminary "a situation so serious that it damaged the prestige of our Seminary, created an atmosphere which was detrimental to the training of our prospective ministers, and threatened the peace and welfare of our churches." It declared that it was in response to this situation that it had dismissed, without prejudice, the four professors who were most closely involved in the situation. The announcement went on to say that Synod did not establish or deny the guilt or innocence of any member of the faculty; that it made no judgment concerning any real or alleged defection in conduct or belief on the part of any member of the faculty; that it did not depose from (ministerial) office or otherwise discipline any member of the faculty; and that its action was taken simply out of consideration for "the peace and welfare of our churches."

*　　*　　*　　*　　*

I had not been called upon to make many career choices in the course of my life. At the age of seventeen I had chosen to study for the gospel ministry; when I was nearing my twenty-ninth birthday, I was led to accept an appointment to teach philosophy at Calvin College; and now at age forty-four, in the midterm of my life, I was placed before another choice. As is often the case in similar situations, I was pulled in two directions. I was reluctant on the one hand to leave my present post: the lure of philosophy remained fastened on me; I was *en rapport* with my peers at the college; and the students were generous in their assessment of my offerings while I found pleasure in their company. I thought, on the other hand, that if I should ever make a change, now would not be an inappropriate time to do so. And, of course, the appointment I had been tendered had its own attraction: I would be teaching students who had already earned a college degree; since ministers still played a leading role in community life, I would have a hand in shaping the mind of the church; and in the process I would not stray far from the center of my academic interests, for what I was being called upon to teach could fairly be called philosophical theology.

Tilting me toward the seminary were also some recent happenings. Cornelius Van Til, whose presence in my department — even on a part-time basis — I would not have relished, indicated that he would not be coming to Calvin in any capacity. In addition, both Berkouwer and Stonehouse sent letters regretfully declining the appointments they were given. In this situation with Synod in recess, the seminary would obviously be hurting if I should also withdraw.

But there was more. There had been in the seminary — and there was present in the church — a state of mind that, inclined toward safety on the one hand and toward militancy on the other, impeded the progress of thought and growth and encouraged the development of a narrow and stultifying conservatism. *The Reformed Journal* articulated a different "mind," and those who shared it not only supported my candidacy for the seminary position, but urged me to accept the appointment without qualms or reservations. "Your voice," they said, "should be heard in the sanctuary." I was not a "liberal," for the Christian verities were dear to me; but I disliked "stand-pattism" and did not think that we held the truth in pawn and could learn nothing from those who differed with us. Falsehood and error, I thought, were parasitic and therefore existed through the sufferance of a residual truth that sustained them and was worth retrieving. In my teaching at the college I was concerned to arrive at a Christian judgment concerning the world's philosophers, but I didn't think that they were to be attacked frontally and from the outside. One should, I thought, enter with empathy into the structure of a philosopher's thinking, discover what aspect of reality induced him to think as he did, and only then undertake to find fault with his possible misplacement or misinterpretation of it. I had learned that the philosopher in question could meanwhile disclose to me a side of the many-faceted truth that had previously been hidden from me. I believed that ministers and theologians should be aware of this, and I thought that I could perhaps be serviceable in the seminary to this as well as to other ends.

In accordance with these reflections, after much prayer, and with Hilda's concurrence, I decided to accept the appointment tendered me. On July 10, 1952, I dispatched a letter to the stated clerk of synod, in which I wrote: "I accept in the confidence that the call is from the Lord, upon whose qualifying grace I utterly rely." Without my asking, but with notice conveyed, the executive committee of the board had made my move easier by deciding "to grant Dr. H. Stob a year's leave of absence from the college in the event he accepts the appointment to the Seminary offered him by Synod."

At about the time I made the decision to transfer to the other end of campus, the executive committee was informed by Kuiper and Kromminga that they too were accepting their appointments. The three of us would now join Schultze and Wyngaarden and together form a faculty of five that would be hard pressed to live up to the standards a good seminary should maintain. With Stonehouse unavailable, Prof. Schultze would single-handedly man the New Testament department; and in the absence of Berkouwer, the work in systematics would be done by a trio of part-time lecturers operating outside of, but under the supervision of, the faculty. Appointed to give instruction in the various loci of dogmatics were J. T. Hoogstra, W. Masselink, and J. Bratt. R. B. Kuiper, who like the rest of us had received no more than a one-year interim appointment, was named temporary president of the seminary by the executive committee, and the president, vice president, and secretary of the Board of Trustees were charged with making the necessary arrangements for the opening of school in September.

*   *   *   *   *

During six weeks in June and July of 1952, I was occupied at summer school, where I taught a course in introduction to philosophy to fourteen students, most of whom were public school teachers in quest of additional college credits. I preached in June on four successive Sundays, and I also published in the *Journal* an article entitled "Shall We Expand Catechesis?" In that same month I was invited by the American Committee to deliver a major address at the International

Calvinistic Congress to be held in Montpellier, France, in July 1953. I readily accepted that invitation, partly because the congress would be held just prior to the meeting of the Edinburgh Synod, to which I had been delegated, and partly because I would have a whole year in which to prepare the promised lecture. I preached in local churches on three Sundays in July, and I published in the *Journal* a meditation on "What Think Ye of the Christ?" In August I published an article on "Academic Freedom at Calvin" in the *Reformed Journal*. These activities left me relatively little time to prepare for the new tasks I would face in September, but by seizing every moment, I sought earnestly to acquire at least some of the competency required.

The article I wrote on academic freedom did not sit well with certain persons, and in the course of the ensuing school year it was cited more than once to prove my unacceptable libertarianism. There was, I thought, no grounds for such an assessment, for early in the article I had rejected the thesis that scholarship is incompatible with faith and commitment and had advocated a freedom rooted in obedience and regulated by the Truth authoritatively disclosed in the sacred Scriptures. I had, however, declared that Christian scholars are sometimes put under arbitrary restraints and subjected to spurious heteronomies. From these, I said, they must be freed. I suggested, among other things, that those appointed to teach at Calvin

> . . . should not be compelled to establish anyone in his private conceits, nor to further the ambitions of any party. They must be free, within the framework of a shared commitment, to come to a conclusion that contravenes the majority opinion, or perchance the opinion of an articulate and militant minority. They must be at liberty to explore new areas of truth, and to do so in their own responsible way. And they must have the same liberty to hold at arm's length new ways of thought, however impatiently presented for adoption. They should, moreover, not have men breathing down their necks and constantly peering over their shoulders. They can't work that way. What they need is trust. They must be free to attack knotty and complex problems in the knowledge that they have the confidence of the church, and they must have the freedom to express and expose to public criticism tentative ideas that may require revision or abandonment. They also need freedom from the weight of custom and from the tyranny of venerable names. What they need,

too, is freedom from fear and reprisals. And what they need most of all is freedom from the sting of uninformed prejudice, freedom from name-calling, and freedom from silent but enervating suspicion.

These were the sentiments I expressed, but there were those who took no pleasure in them and entered them into their file.

During that summer I was in touch with my friends and fellow editors George Stob and Harry Boer, and I observed with great satisfaction their determination to carry on despite their recent setback. George returned to Princeton in September to complete his dissertation, and would obtain a doctorate in church history within a year. Harry left at about the same time for Amsterdam, where, upon completing his graduate work, he was granted a Th.D. in missions by the Free University. Meanwhile, I was forced to sever, for a year at least, the strong ties that bound me to the college and to take up residence in the seminary. I would there occupy the chair vacated by Clarence Bouma, and I hoped that during my brief tenure I would not tarnish the luster with which my predecessor had endowed it. As it turned out I remained in the seminary for the next thirty years, twenty-three of them as professor of moral and philosophical theology, and seven of them as an auxiliary lecturer during the years immediately following my formal retirement. Of this long period in my life I hope someday to give a detailed account. Here I can only say that, although the wind was not always at my back, I was at all times upheld by a gracious God and supported by caring colleagues, charitable students, kind friends, and an indulgent public — to all of whom I remain deeply indebted.

Index of Names

Hughes, Charles E., 20
Huiner, Red, 90, 97
Huizenga, Bart, 221
Huizenga, John, 259-60
Huizenga, Nick, 284
Huizengas (Chicago neighbors), 21
Huizers (Chicago neighbors), 22
Hyde, Charles C., 231
Hyma, Albert, 270

Imanse, Ruth, 213
Ippel, Henry, 307, 311
Ippel, Lester, 294, 307
Itagaki, Gen., 257
Iwemas (Chicago neighbors), 22

Jaarsma, Cornelius, 268
Jacobsma, Mr. (grammar school
   teacher), 34
Jacobsmas (Chicago neighbors), 21
James, Henry, 76
James, William, 173, 213
Jansma, Ted, 90, 100
Janssen, Ann, 319
Janssen, Prof. (Calvin Seminary),
   54, 132
Jaspers, K., 170
Jellema, Dirk, 271
Jellema, Harry: as HS's colleague,
   275, 283, 285-86, 288, 293;
   and controversy, 131, 135, 142,
   165, 166, 201; reappointment
   of, 263-66, 268; as HS's
   teacher, 83, 85, 94, 99, 104,
   112, 115-16
Jellema, Joe, 67
Jellema, Rod, 271, 284
Jellema, William H. See Jellema,
   Harry
Jeremias, Joachim, 158, 162, 163,
   177
Jessup, Philip C., 231
Jodl, Gen., 243
Johanson, Prof. (Hartford
   Seminary), 137-39
Johnson, E. E. S., 140, 147, 163

Johnson, Lyndon B., 277
Jonker, Doctor (Nathaniel Insti-
   tute), 118
Jonkman, Bartel, 277
Juliana, Queen of the Netherlands,
   318

Kagawa, Toyohiko, 252
Kaltenbach, Fred, 154
Kamp, Mr. (butcher), 72
Kamps, Lloyd, 313
Kapteyn, Arthur, 88, 90, 96
Karsten, Martin, 259, 260
Kass, Carl, 111
Katt, Peter, 234
Keegstra, Rev. Henry, 71, 280
Kerensky, Alexander, 45
Kerr, Capt. Edward, 251
Kett, Mr. and Mrs. (dormitory
   "parents"), 118
Kiemels (Chicago neighbors), 21
Kierkegaard, S., 177-78
Kingma, Jan, 294
Kingma, Stuart, 284
Kinsura, Gen., 257
Kirk, Grayson L., 231
Kishimoto, Hideo, 252, 287-88
Klempt, Frau (landlady in Göttin-
   gen), 154, 168
Klempt, Herbert, 154
Klempt, Ilsa, 154
Kloet, Cornelia, 101
Klooster, Fred, 221, 331
Knox, Frank, 225
Knox, John, 234
Koch, Theodore F., 7
Koelikamp, Mr. (high school jani-
   tor), 73
Kok, Rev. William, 209, 281, 306,
   332
König, Prof. (University of Göttin-
   gen), 173, 179
Koning, Rev. A. A., 321
Konings (Chicago neighbors), 21, 23
Kooistra, Mr. (grammar school
   teacher), 34

345

Kooistra, William, 40, 73
Kostelyk, Cornelius, 75
Koster, Z., 262
Kreyenbroek, Mr. (elder in Amsterdam), 192
Krombeen, Nell, 143
Kromminga, Carl, 310, 312, 331
Kromminga, John, 334, 336
Kromminga, Rev. Dietrich H.:
   death of, 263, 266; as pastor,
   85; on seminary faculty, 121,
   125, 129, 131, 133, 256
Kroon, Philip, 213
Kropatchek, Hans, 164, 168, 181
Kruger, Paul, 16
Kuiper, B. K., 79, 85
Kuiper, Henry (grammar school
   principal), 34, 40
Kuiper, Herman, 308, 331
Kuiper, Mr. (conference speaker),
   104
Kuiper, Mrs. R. B., 129
Kuiper, Rev. Henry J., 71, 333;
   criticism by, 300-301, 315, 319,
   324; as editor, 85, 237, 291,
   299; and synod committee, 281,
   306
Kuiper, Rev. R. B., 95, 98, 111,
   123, 129, 334, 336
Kuyper, Abraham, 59, 130, 190,
   318

La Botz brothers (bakers), 13, 23
Lagerwey, Peter, 284
Lagerwey, Walter, 269-70, 274,
   275, 319-20
Lamberts, Jack, 101, 102, 106
Lamberts, Peter, 90
Lamberts, Rev. L. J., 165-68, 202
Land, Edwin, 287
Landon, Alf, 154
Lanengas (Chicago neighbors), 7,
   22
Lanning, Arthur, 73
Lautenbach, Herr (orientation
   leader), 162

Laval, P., 211
Lee, Edson, 249-50
Leenhouts, Mr. (embalmer), 23
Leitch, John, 213
Lenin, Nicolay, 45, 59
Lenton, Mr. (conference speaker),
   104
Levov, Prince, 4
Lewis, John L., 135
Lewis, Sinclair, 72
Lindbergh, Charles, 72-73, 118,
   211
Linton, Ralph, 231
Lippmann, Walter, 94
Littlefair, Duncan, 295
Lobbes, Mr. (grammar school
   teacher), 34
Locke, J., 163
Long, Huey ("Kingfish"), 135
Louis, Joe, 176
Louis Napoleon, King of the
   Netherlands, 4
Luther, M., 130

MacArthur, Douglas, 98, 216, 220,
   237, 245-52 passim, 293, 295-
   96, 299
Macartney, Clarence E., 54
McCarthy, Joseph, 267, 292
McColm, Eugene, 233
McComb, John, 234
McCormick, C., 42
McCosh, James, 213
Machen, J. Gresham, 56, 94, 104
McKay, Mr. (Grand Rapids politician), 278
Mackenzie, Prof. (Hartford Seminary), 134, 139
McLain, Raymond, 233
Malestein, John, 270
Manfred, Frederick. See Feikema,
   Feike
Manning, Bishop William T., 234
Mao Tse-tung, 282, 287
Marshall, George, 211
Masaryk, Thomas, 142

346

Masselink, William, 318, 336
Mathias, Bob, 275
Matsuo, Takeshi, 251
Maude (Harlem maid), 230
Medendorp, John, 262
Meeter, Henry, 83, 94, 99, 201, 206, 221, 260
Mencken, H. L., 59, 124
Mensingas (Chicago neighbors), 21
Miller, Arthur, 281
Milstein, Nathan, 193
Mindszenty, Cardinal, 287
Minnema, Clarence, 233
Misch (author), 170
Monsma, Edwin, 83, 201, 206, 214, 260, 262, 269, 294, 320
Monsma, Martin, 210, 307
Monsma, Nicholas J., 281, 303, 306
Montgomery, Gen., 221
Morren, John, 274, 275
Morse, S., 42
Mountbatten, Philip, 271
Mouw, Harry, 64, 73, 76
Mulder, Arnold, 270
Mulder, Dr. (physician), 304, 328
Mulder, Ella, 40
Mulders (Chicago neighbors), 22
Muller, Marvin, 299
Murray, John, 98, 104
Mussolini, Benito, 48, 54, 135, 154, 193-94, 231, 243
Muto, Gen., 257
Muyskens, Albert, 135, 202, 206, 213, 215

Nederhood, Joel, 313
Neurath, O., 170
Newhouse, Sidney, 295
Nicolas II, Emperor of Russia, 45
Niebuhr, H. R., 314
Niebuhr, Reinhold, 138, 234
Niemöller, Martin, 172
Nietzsche, F., 170, 174
Nieuwdorp, James: as faculty member, 83, 201, 240, 275; retirement of, 256, 259, 260

Nieuwdorp, John, 103-7
Nixon, Richard, 295
Nohl, Prof. (University of Göttingen), 158
Norden, Mr. (Calvin custodian), 90
Norlag, William, 40
Norlags (Chicago neighbors), 21
Nydam, Angeline, 65
Nyenhuis, Gerald, 320

O'Banion, Dion, 61
Omura, Bunji K., 231
Oostendorp, Elco, 133, 134
Oostendorp, Evelyn, 191, 193
Oostendorp, Lubbertus, 191, 193
Oosterman, Gordon, 295
Opperwall, Raymond, 321-25, 329, 330, 332
Oppewal, Don, 284
Oppewall, Jacob, 295
Orland, Vitorio, 47-48
Orlebeke, Clif, 271, 274, 275
Orwell, George, 281
Otten, Arthur, 316
Otten, Robert, 274, 275, 319
Ottenhoff, Cecilia, 67
Ottenhoff, Conrad, 22, 23
Ottenhoff, Elizabeth, 75
Ottenhoff, George, 22, 23
Ottenhoff, Walter, 22, 23
Otto, Rudolph, 138
Ouwinga, Menko, 112
Ouwinga, Paul, 204, 205, 213
Owens, Jesse, 154

Paauw, Doug, 221
Paget, Rev. John, 192
Parks, Margaret, 230
Pastoor, Bill, 84
Pastoor, Don, 84
Pastoor, Edith, 84
Pastoor, Harm, 84, 85, 88
Pastoor, Hildred, 84
Patton, Gen., 231, 241
Pauck, William, 138
Peary, Admiral, 10

347

Van't Hof, Jack, 221
Van Til, Cornelius, 95, 269, 295, 318; appointed to college faculty, 135, 142, 166; appointed to seminary faculty, 225, 297, 304, 308, 312, 334, 335
Van Til, Henry, 191, 193, 259, 260, 299
Van Til, Nick, 213, 218, 233, 234
Van Til, Samuel, 261, 268, 283
Van Til, Sis, 191, 193
Van Tuinen, Peter, 112, 308, 332
Van Wieren, Elmer, 214, 215, 234
Van Wyk, Rev. W. P., 202
Vanzetti, B., 49, 73
Van Zyl, Henry, 83, 201, 260, 262
Vauth, Enna, 151, 153, 164, 169
Vauth, Heine, 151, 152
Vauth, Hilda, 151, 152
Vauth, Mr. (father of Wilhelm), 150, 151, 152
Vauth, Mrs. (mother of Wilhelm), 151
Vauth, Sophie, 151
Vauth, Wilhelm, 180-81, 193; at Hartford Seminary, 138, 139, 140; in Rusbend, 149, 150-53; in Vehlen, 162, 164, 165, 169, 170
Veen, Caroline, 203, 213
Veenema, Ralph, 214, 215
Veldmans (Chicago neighbors), 21, 23, 38
Veldsma, Grietje, 171, 185
Veldsma, Harry, 150, 171, 175, 185, 186
Veldsma, Thomas, 196
Velzen, Bernard, 213
Venema, Alvin, 299
Venema, Henry, 299
Venema, Rev. (controversialist), 322
Venema, Richard, 299
Venhuizen, Aldert, 102
Venhuizens (Chicago neighbors), 22
Verbrugge, John, 102
Vertregt, Elizabeth, 83, 98, 106

Vertregt, Marcellus, 103
Verwys, Hubert, 245
Villa, Pancho, 21
Vincent, Jo, 194
Visscher, Bernard, 133, 134
Visser, Edward: as high school student, 75; as seminary student, 133, 134
Visser, John, 205
Vogel, Leroy ("Bird"), 90, 113, 234; in Germany, 159, 160, 169; as HS's roommate, 108-10, 119, 121, 122, 124; at seminary, 133, 134, 142
Volbeda, Samuel, 265, 308, 310, 312; and controversy, 289, 302, 303, 322, 324-29; as faculty member, 119-20, 133; as HS's teacher, 121, 125, 129-31; as president, 237, 240; retirement of, 328, 331, 332-33
Vollenhoven, Prof. (Free University of Amsterdam), 167, 172, 186, 191, 194, 208, 214, 285-86
Voltaire, 301
Von Hinderburg, P., 123
Von Münchhausen, Gerlach Adolph, 157
Vos, Mr. (Calvin College bookkeeper), 202, 283, 294
Vriend, John, 295

Wainwright, Gen., 220
Walhout, Ed, 262, 270, 332
Wallace, Henry, 216
Wallace, Lew, 38
Wallace, Schuyler C., 231
Wallace, W., 104, 116
Walters, D., 308
Warfield, B. B., 130
Warp, Lt. George, 239, 251, 252
Washington, George, 41
Wassenaar, Nicholas, 133, 134
Wassink, Harry, 106, 202, 206, 260
Weber, Max, 170, 173-75, 179